THE **BEST** GUITAR METHOD

by Brian K. Rivers

THE BEST GUITAR METHOD

by Brian K. Rivers

Includes 118 Videos and 355 Audio Tracks

VOLUME 1

Copyright © 2019 Brian K. Rivers

First Edition

Published by Best Music Publications
471 Wood Avenue
Cincinnati, Ohio 45220
www.bestmusicpublications.com

Editing: Ronny Schiff, Julie Ann Baur and Laurie Rivers
Design and Layout: Charylu Roberts, O.Ruby Productions
Cover Design: Hans Schellhas
Photography: Brian K. Rivers
Lead Videography and Video Editing: Nicole Wood
Video Production and Editing: Maddie Amend and Grace Yearout
Additional Video Editing: Oscar Stec

TAYLOR GUITARS® and certain of its distinctive detailing are registered trademarks of Taylor-Listug, Inc.
All Rights Reserved.

REVEREND GUITARS® and certain of its distinctive detailing are registered trademarks of Reverend Guitars, Inc.
All Rights Reserved.

Published in the U.S.A.

ISBN 978-1-7338231-0-4

All Rights Reserved. Used by Permission.

No portion of this book or the associated electronic media may be copied, reproduced or transmitted in any form or manner without written permission from the publisher.

Dedication

The Best Guitar Method is dedicated to guitar teachers and their students, especially…

…the traditional classroom music educator who is teaching guitar. Despite guitar being the most popular instrument in America, guitar instruction is missing from most school music programs. You are the trailblazer—thank you for mainstreaming guitar education.

…the private guitar teacher, who often toils in a closet-size room in the back of the music store. You have been the backbone of guitar instruction for decades. You have inspired countless students, some of whom have become our true guitar heroes. Without your efforts, the guitar would not be the most popular instrument in America.

…and the guitar student, beginning through advanced. The desire to play music comes from a place deep within the human spirit. When we celebrate, mourn, worship, protest, hunt, or even battle, music is the accompaniment that gives inspiration. The power of music is undeniable. By making and sharing music, you are participating in life at its deepest levels. If you are rising to the challenge and practicing, you have earned this dedication.

Table of Contents

Foreword xi
Introduction for Teachers. xiii
Introduction for Students. xv

UNIT 1 • About the Guitar — The Types of Guitars, Holding, Playing, Practicing and Notation 1
- **Lesson 1:** The Most Important Lesson in the Book 1
- **Lesson 2:** Getting Ready to Play the Guitar 2
- **Lesson 3:** Right-Hand — Plucking Individual Strings Using the Fingers and Thumb 6
- **Lesson 4:** Picking Individual Strings Using a Pick 8
- **Lesson 5:** The Three P's of Tone Production 9
- **Lesson 6:** Tuning 11
- **Lesson 7:** Guitar Chord Notation and Notes on the Guitar 12
- *Review and Summary* 14

UNIT 2 • Chords in the Key of G Major — "G" Is for Guitar! 15
- **Lesson 1:** Primary Chords in the Key of G — G, C, D, and D7 (I, IV, V, V7) 16
- **Lesson 2:** Strumming the Strings Using the Fingers and Thumb 19
- **Lesson 3:** Strumming the Strings Using a Pick 20
- **Lesson 4:** Strumming the Strings with a Steady Beat 21
- **Lesson 5:** Playing Songs — "Hot Cross Buns" and "Merrily We Roll Along" (Songs) 23
- **Lesson 6:** Standard Strum Patterns in 4/4 time 25
- **Lesson 7:** "Down by the Riverside" (Song) 28
- **Lesson 8:** Other Strum Patterns in 4/4 time 29
- **Lesson 9:** 3/4 Time 32
- **Lesson 10:** Pickup Measures, Changing Chords, and Repeats Signs 34
- **Lesson 11:** "The Streets of Laredo" (Song) 35
- **Lesson 12:** 12-Bar Blues (Chord Progression) 36
- **Lesson 13:** Adding Root Notes to any Song 39
- **Lesson 14:** Finding the Root Note of a Chord 41
- **Lesson 15:** "Oh My Darling, Clementine" (Song) 42
- *Review and Summary* 43

UNIT 3 • Notes in the Key of G on the Highest Three Strings 44
- **Lesson 1:** Notes — B, A, and G 45
- **Lesson 2:** How to Practice Song Melodies and Chords from Written Music 47
- **Lesson 3:** "G to B — Changing Strings" (Song) 48
- **Lesson 4:** "G to A — Keeping Your Left-Hand Fingers Ready" (Song) 49
- **Lesson 5:** "Hot Cross Buns" with Melody (Song) 50
- **Lesson 6:** More Notes — C and D 51
- **Lesson 7:** "Aura Lee" (Song) 52
- **Lesson 8:** "German Waltz" (Song) 54
- **Lesson 9:** More Notes — E, F♯, and G 55
- **Lesson 10:** G Major Scale and Key Signatures 56
- **Lesson 11:** Dotted Quarter Note Rhythm 57
- **Lesson 12:** "Merrily We Roll Along" (Song) 58
- **Lesson 13:** Dynamics and Dynamic Markings 59
- **Lesson 14:** "Ode to Joy" (Song) 60
- *Review and Summary* 62

UNIT 4 • Secondary Chords in the Key of G — Am, Bm, and Em (ii–iii–vi) 63
- **Lesson 1:** Secondary Chords in the Key of G — Am, Bm, and Em (ii, iii, vi) 64
- **Lesson 2:** "On Second Thought" (Song) 66
- **Lesson 3:** "Minor Inconvenience" (Song) 68
- *Review and Summary* 70

UNIT 5 • Notes in the Key of G on the Lowest Three Strings 71
- **Lesson 1:** More Notes — D, E, and F♯ (Fourth String) 72
- **Lesson 2:** First and Second Endings 73
- **Lesson 3:** "Old MacDonald" (Song) 74
- **Lesson 4:** The Pickup Measure 75
- **Lesson 5:** "The Streets of Laredo" (Song) 76
- **Lesson 6:** "Brother John" (Song) 77
- **Lesson 7:** Syncopation 78
- **Lesson 8:** "This Little Light of Mine" (Song) 80
- **Lesson 9:** "Amazing Grace" (Song) 81
- **Lesson 10:** "Oh My Darling, Clementine" (Song) 82
- **Lesson 11:** More Notes — A, B, and C (Fifth String) 83
- **Lesson 12:** "Yankee Doodle" (Song) 84
- **Lesson 13:** Accidentals and Fermatas 85
- **Lesson 14:** "Santa Lucia" (Song) 86
- **Lesson 15:** More Notes — G (Sixth String) 88
- **Lesson 16:** G Major Scale — Two Octave 89
- **Lesson 17:** G Major — No Training Wheels 90
- **Lesson 18:** "On Second Thought" (Song) 92
- *Review and Summary* 94

UNIT 6 • The Key of E Minor 95
- **Lesson 1:** Relative Minor Keys 96
- **Lesson 2:** Primary Chords in the Key of E Minor — Em, Am, Bm and B7 (i, iv, v, V7) 97
- **Lesson 3:** Resolution 99
- **Lesson 4:** "Minor Problem" (Song) 100
- **Lesson 5:** Secondary Chords in the Key of E Minor — G, C, and D (III, VI, VII) 102
- **Lesson 6:** "St. James Infirmary" (Song) 103
- **Lesson 7:** New Notes — D♯ and C♯ 105
- **Lesson 8:** Minor Scales — Natural, Pentatonic, Harmonic, Dorian and Melodic 106
- **Lesson 9:** Other Chord Variations that are Common in the Key of E Minor 108
- **Lesson 10:** Single Note Slur Techniques — Hammer-On, Pull-Off, and Slide 109
- **Lesson 11:** Hammer-On (Slur) and Pull-Off (Slur) Chord Technique 111
- **Lesson 12:** "Western Slurry" (Song) 112
- *Review and Summary* 114

UNIT 7 • The Key of D Major 115
- **Lesson 1:** Primary Chords in the Key of D — D, G, A, and A7 (I, IV, V, V7) 116
- **Lesson 2:** Transposing to a Different Key — The Same Only Different! 118
- **Lesson 3:** "Amazing Grace" (Song) 120
- **Lesson 4:** Secondary Chords in the Key of D — Em, F♯m, and Bm (ii, iii, vi) 122

Lesson 5:	Notes — High A and Review of C♯	124
Lesson 6:	Sixteenth Note Rhythms	125
Lesson 7:	Arpeggio Style Finger Picking	128
Lesson 8:	"Canon in D" (Song)	130
Lesson 9:	D Major Scale	133
Lesson 10:	The Key of D Major — No Training Wheels	134
Lesson 11:	Alternate Bass	136
Lesson 12:	"Yankee Doodle" (Song)	138
	Review and Summary	140

UNIT 8 • The Key of A Major ... 141

Lesson 1:	Primary Chords in the Key of A — A, D, E and E7 (I, IV, V, V7)	142
Lesson 2:	Transposing "Hot Cross Buns" to the Key of A	144
Lesson 3:	"Janice and Bobby" (Chord Progression)	145
Lesson 4:	Triplets and "Swing" Feel	147
Lesson 5:	2/4 Time — "Itsy Bitsy Spider" (Song)	150
Lesson 6:	"12-Bar Blues Shuffle in the Key of A" (Chord Progression)	151
Lesson 7:	Secondary Chords in the Key of A — Bm, C♯m, and F♯m (ii, iii, vi)	154
Lesson 8:	Power Chords — or, We Interrupt this Unit to Learn a Cool Trick!	156
Lesson 9:	Common Variations of the 12-Bar Blues Form	158
Lesson 10:	"12-Bar Blues Variation with Secondary Minor Chords" (Chord Progression)	160
Lesson 11:	G♯ Notes	161
Lesson 12:	A Major Scale	162
Lesson 13:	The Key of A Major — No Training Wheels	163
Lesson 14:	"This Beautiful Day" (Song)	165
	Review and Summary	166

UNIT 9 • The Key of C Major ... 167

Lesson 1:	Primary Chords in the Key of C — C, F, G, G7 (I, IV, V, V7)	168
Lesson 2:	F Notes and the C Major Scale	170
Lesson 3:	The Key of C — No Training Wheels	171
Lesson 4:	"Will the Circle Be Unbroken?" (Song)	173
Lesson 5:	Grace Notes	176
Lesson 6:	"Wildwood Flower" (Song)	177
Lesson 7:	Secondary Chords in the Key of C — Dm, Em, and Am (ii, iii, vi)	180
Lesson 8:	"Aura Lee" (Song)	181
	Review and Summary	182

UNIT 10 • The Key of A Minor ... 183

Lesson 1:	Primary Chords in the Key of A Minor — Am, Dm, Em, and E7 (i, iv, v, V7)	184
Lesson 2:	Secondary Chords in the Key of A Minor — C, F, and G (III, VI, VII)	185
Lesson 3:	Alternate Chord Voicing for E7 — "St. James Infirmary" (Song)	186
Lesson 4:	Relative Minor Key and Minor Scales — Natural, Pentatonic, Harmonic, Dorian and Melodic	188
Lesson 5:	New Chord — Fmaj7	190
Lesson 6:	6/8 Time Signature — "House of the Rising Sun" (Song)	191
	Review and Summary	195

UNIT 11 • **The Key of E Major — "E" is for the End!** 196

    Lesson 1:   Primary Chords in the Key of E — E, A, B and B7 (I, IV, V, V7) 197
    Lesson 2:   "Turn Myself Around" with Lifted Chord (Chord Progression) 198
    Lesson 3:   Secondary Chords in the Key of E — F♯m, G♯m, and C♯m (ii, iii, vi) 200
    Lesson 4:   D♯ Note Review and the E Major Scale 201
    Lesson 5:   Key of E — No Training Wheels 202
    Lesson 6:   Palm Mute — "12-Bar Blues Shuffle in the Key of E" (Chord Progression) 204
    Lesson 7:   Accented Syncopated Eighth Note Rhythms 206
    Lesson 8:   "Bo's Blues" (Song) 208
    Lesson 9:   "Grand Final-E" (Song) 210
    Review and Summary 218

Foreword

I am delighted to introduce you to *The Best Guitar Method*, a unique and innovative new guitar method book. Author Brian K. Rivers has relied on his background of over 30 years of guitar instruction and his expertise as a music educator to create an innovative approach for group guitar instruction. Unlike other group guitar method books, Rivers has constructed this method to smoothly dovetail from previous school music learning (recorder instruction, general music study, or piano knowledge) into new understandings for guitar-specific skills. This method starts where many students with recorder experience feel comfortable: with the commonly known notes B–A–G and the tune "Hot Cross Buns" (a regular part of recorder instruction and often featured in instrumental band/orchestra beginning books). This ensures school musicians will have immediate success in their learning when starting from their previous musical knowledge base. The method begins with the key of G—the pedagogically-favored key of guitar players which promotes excellent left-hand technique. Rivers also helps students develop rhythmic awareness and build skills with right hand techniques early on—the guitar is after all, a rhythm instrument! Another novel aspect of this series is the ability of all students to play both the accompaniments and the melodies providing more time on task for student musicians and preventing classroom discipline issues before they arise. Each exercise has been designed to provide differentiated learning opportunities for all students (especially if there are students in the class with previous guitar experience); there are challenge chord fingerings in addition to the more simplified ones appropriate for true beginners. Theory concepts are nested within the skill-building exercises and tunes. With his original "Play & Do" activities, Rivers has provided sound instructional practice and has created effective sequential pacing in which students rely on skills and knowledge developed from previous lessons. Students will be able to pursue study in a variety of styles and genres after using this method for beginning instruction because of their strong foundational skills. Online video tutorials are included which can help all students learn more rapidly. Lesson planning is facilitated with the online resources and reference materials provided. In short, I know you will find this method book to be pedagogically sound, musically diverse, but most importantly, enriching and engaging for students and teachers alike. Congratulations on making an excellent selection for use in your group guitar classroom.

~Ann Porter, PhD
Professor of Music Education, College-Conservatory of Music
University of Cincinnati

Acknowledgments

No book is created by one person. Without the support and encouragement of my family, the publishing team, former teachers, industry sponsors, and students, this book would not exist.

First and foremost, I want to thank my amazing family for their love and encouragement as I encountered the inevitable roadblocks of writing a book—I love you so much. Laurie, you bring out the very best in me, and I am forever grateful to share my life and work with you. TJ and Janeen, guiding you from childhood to adulthood taught me so many valuable lessons. These lessons have found their way into this book. I also thank you for serving as models in the book! To my late brother Bill, thank you for exposing me to a wide range of music as a child.

Thank you to everyone who helped me with the production of this book. Special thanks go to Charylu Roberts of O.Ruby Productions for expert graphic design and music engraving, Ronny Schift for proof-reading of the musical notation and editing of instructional content, Hans Schellhas for cover design, Julie Ann Baur for general text proof-reading, Nicole Wood for lead videography and video and audio editing, Maddie Amend for videography and video and audio editing, Grace Yearout for videography, and Oscar Stec for additional video editing.

Thank you to my former professors at the University of Cincinnati College-Conservatory of Music. I give special thanks to Dr. Ann Porter for providing me with key insights into how students learn music, Dr. James Smith for setting the bar high in my guitar performance skills, and the countless clinicians and colleagues who generously shared their knowledge and inspiration over the years. Taken together, all of you have enabled me to bridge the worlds of professional guitarist and music educator in writing this book.

Thank you to Tim Godwin and the staff at Taylor Guitars, Ken and Penny Hass and the staff at Reverend Guitars, and the staff at DR Strings for supplying me with the very best in musical equipment.

Thank you to my students for providing me with valuable on-the-job "ah-ha moments" that have enabled me to continually grow and evolve as a music educator. Also, thank you to my students who served as guitar performance models in the book: Maddie Amend, Caroline Gavin, Lara Geiger, Evan Griswold, Kaitlyn Griswold, Lee Jeneman, Wole Adeoye, Emily Power, Delaney Ragusa, Julia Stumbo, Olivia Theders, Jackson Ward, Jude Weis, and Grace Yearout. You inspire me with your music and smiles!

And finally, I want to acknowledge a childhood sitter who I only remember by the first name of Joy, but to whom I owe much gratitude for giving me my first guitar shortly after my mother died when I was ten years old. Throughout the instability of my childhood, that sunburst Sears Silvertone guitar became the one thing that I could always count on being there for me. Ever since, making music has been with me through all the joys and sorrows that comprise a full and vibrant life.

Introduction for Classroom and Private Guitar Educators

If you want to teach guitar, you have found the curriculum you have been looking for—*The Best Guitar Method!* I wrote *The Best Guitar Method* because I know there is a need for a new beginning guitar curriculum: one that is grounded in music education theory, teaches modern notation, includes popular techniques used by today's guitarists, and supports a variety of student learning styles. *The Best Guitar Method* is an innovative and comprehensive beginning guitar multi-media curriculum for use in classrooms, private lesson studios, and self-instruction. *The Best Guitar Method* includes a stand-alone textbook, videos for reinforcement of every lesson, and audio recordings of every song. Students can access video and audio at home or in the classroom at *www.bestmusicpublications.com*.

The Best Guitar Method is not just another "start on the first string" guitar book with a new cover—it bridges the worlds of classroom music educator, private guitar instructor, and guitar player. Below is a brief list of why *The Best Guitar Method* is an innovative advancement in guitar education.

Instructional Sequence, Differentiated Curriculum, and Instructional Approach

- Students first learn right-hand techniques, enabling early success.
- Students then learn chords and accompaniment skills since the guitar is a rhythm section instrument.
- Students learn to sight-read starting on the third string in the key of G. This curricular innovation departs from most guitar texts and significantly accelerates student progress. Starting on the third string promotes proper left-hand technique.
- Differentiated curriculum through simplified and challenge options for many of the lessons keeps students engaged and successful in a group or individual setting.
- Textbook lessons include **clear instruction** and *Play and Do* sections to guide student practice.
- Standard notation, TAB, chord grids, and photos are used throughout the textbook.
- Innovative chord grids—fingerings show the "how" and **note names + scale degrees** show the "why."
- Music theory concepts are integrated into lessons.

Classroom Management and Assessment

- Most songs include separate accompaniment and melody parts, enabling all students to always play.
- No need to set-up A/V or access computer systems during group instruction, the textbook is comprehensive.
- Online video and audio content support student practice at home or during in-class independent study.

Free Online Teacher Resources - www.bestmusicpublications.com

- Classroom music educators can access lesson ideas that are easily aligned to national school music standards.
- Classroom music educators who are new to guitar instruction can access guitar-specific teaching tips.
- Private guitar instructors can access lesson ideas and teaching strategies for engaging students.
- Instructional videos are available for all lessons.
- Audio examples are available for all the songs.

I developed *The Best Guitar Method* because I am passionate about increasing access to guitar education. I recognized that a comprehensive guitar curriculum opens the door for music educators to start classroom guitar programs and provides private instructors with a curriculum that supports musical literacy. To the seasoned and emerging guitar educators, welcome, and enjoy!

Yours Truly, Brian

Introduction for Students

Welcome to *The Best Guitar Method!* I have taught hundreds of students how to play guitar, and one thing I know for sure—you want to learn how to play your favorite songs, and you want to get there fast! Other guitar books or websites might try to sell you the "easy way," but in reality, the fastest way to play the songs you love is to first learn the basics. Don't waste your time looking for a shortcut that doesn't exist. You will be amazed at how easily all of your favorite songs arise from the same basic foundation. Whether you prefer to learn from a private instructor, textbook, online video, or a combination of these, *The Best Guitar Method* has an instructional style that matches your learning style. See online instructional videos and audio examples at www.bestmusicpublications.com.

My goal is the same as your goal—I want you to learn to play the songs you love as quickly as possible. That is why *The Best Guitar Method* includes an online database of popular songs that you will be able to play as you progress through the lessons. I am continually updating the database, so please submit your song suggestions to www.bestmusicpublications.com. No matter the style of music—Pop, Blues, Rock, Country, Jazz, R&B, Hip-Hop, Classical or any other style—*The Best Guitar Method* teaches you the essential rhythm, chord, and single-note skills in both standard and TAB notation. All this and more is why *The Best Guitar Method* will quickly become your new best friend.

The website www.bestmusicpublications.com is also where you can ask questions and get helpful tips about songs to learn, so be sure to register now.

Free Online Student Resources - www.bestmusicpublications.com

- Video instruction for each lesson designed for use at home or in the classroom
- Audio examples designed for use at home or in the classroom
- A database of popular songs organized by the chords you have learned

You are encouraged to study with a teacher. The internet and books are sometimes excellent sources of one-way information, but these sources vary tremendously in quality. Even if you happen to stumble upon a source that uses correct information, the source is never able to give you feedback about what you are doing. The professional feedback you receive from a quality instructor helps you progress further and faster. I have been a successful guitarist and teacher for a long time and have learned that anyone can learn to play the guitar if they practice the correct techniques in the correct order, on a regular basis.

If you want the technical details about why *The Best Guitar Method* is for you, read *Introduction for Teachers*; otherwise, let's get started playing the guitar!

Yours Truly, Brian

UNIT 1

About the Guitar
The Types of Guitars, Holding, Playing, Practicing and Notation

LESSON 1

The Most Important Lesson in the Book

Lesson Concepts
- Patience
- Overcoming Difficulty
- Practice Strategies

Patience

Patience is your friend. You may be tempted to go straight to Unit 2 because that is when you start to learn chords and songs *but don't do it!*

Be patient. I have been teaching guitar for over forty years, and I promise that you will go further faster if you do not skip Unit 1. Guitar requires a great deal of physical strength in the left hand and very specific techniques for both hands. Unit 1 focuses on developing hand strength and technique which will take a few weeks. If you skip ahead, you will not have the strength or hand technique, and so you are very likely to develop bad habits!

Overcoming Difficulty

Learning guitar can be difficult at times, and when it gets difficult, you need to remember patience is your friend. There will be times when you are trying to play something, and it seems impossible, and most of the time it is just a matter of repetition and time for muscles to develop, so just keep trying.

Practice Strategies

Here is a short list of practice strategies to help you learn quicker and faster:

- Use your ears; listen to the recording before you try to play the exercises and songs.
- Practice slowly and correctly with a steady beat, so you learn the technique or song properly.
- Separate tasks into the smallest possible parts, focusing on one hand while simplifying or omitting the other hand.
- Separate the task of reading music from the task of playing music.

More detailed practice strategies are available at *www.bestmusicpublications.com*

LESSON 2

Getting Ready to Play the Guitar

> **Lesson Concepts**
> - Fingernails
> - Two Broad Categories of Guitars: Acoustic Guitars (Steel-String or Nylon-String) and Electric Guitars (Solid-Body, Semi-Hollow-Body, and Hollow-Body)
> - Casual Posture — Sitting and Standing
> - Classical Posture — Sitting and Standing
> - String Numbers
> - Left-Hand Finger Designations
> - Right-Hand Finger Designations
> - Tablature Notation

Fingernails

Your left-hand fingernails should be cut short. You can grow your right-hand fingernails out so you can use the fingernail to pluck a string. Plucking the strings with your fingernails is very common when playing the nylon string guitar.

Two Broad Categories of Guitars:

Acoustic Guitars (Steel-String or Nylon-String) and *Electric Guitars* (Solid-Body, Semi-Hollow-Body, and Hollow-Body).

The Acoustic Steel-String Guitar

The acoustic steel-string (Figure 1.2.1) is the most common type of acoustic guitar and is used for all styles of music except classical. They are strung with ball-end steel (bronze) strings. The guitar pictured in Figure 1.2.1 is a cutaway acoustic steel-string guitar.

The Acoustic Nylon-String Guitar

The acoustic nylon-string guitar (Figure 1.2.8) (often called a "classical guitar") is used primarily for classical and Latin music. Nylon-string guitars are designed to be played without a pick, but many use a pick when playing the nylon-string guitar. They are strung with nylon strings.

Parts of the Acoustic Guitar

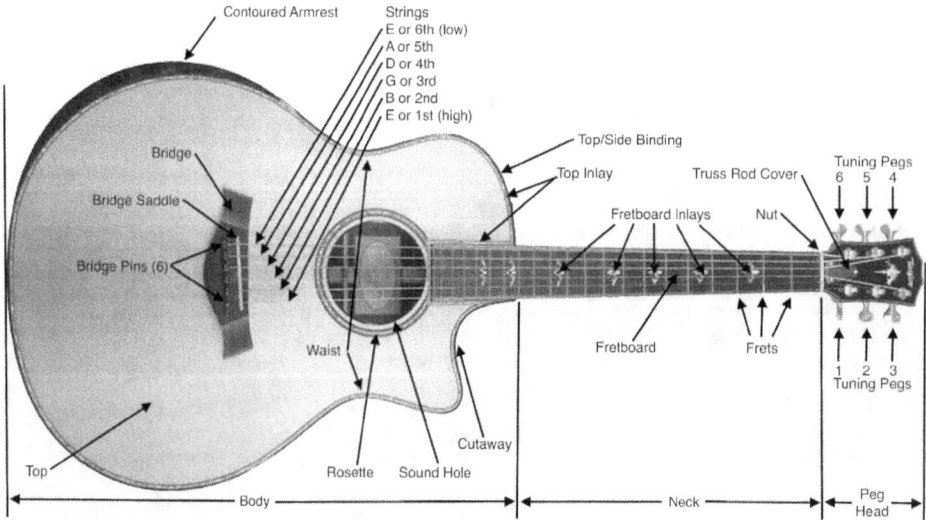

Figure 1.2.1

2

UNIT ONE • LESSON 2

THE ELECTRIC GUITAR

The solid-body electric is the most common and least expensive type of electric guitar. All electric guitars use steel strings (nickel) that are thinner than acoustic steel strings. Electric guitars require a separate amplifier and are used in all styles of music except classical. They come in a wide variety of body and neck sizes and fall into three subcategories: solid-body, semi-hollow, and hollow-body.

Parts of the Electric Guitar

Figure 1.2.2

Solid-body electric, Figure 1.2.3

Semi-hollow electric, Figure 1.2.4

Hollow-body electric, Figure 1.2.5

More detailed information about guitars and accessories is available at ***www.bestmusicpublications.com***

THE BEST GUITAR METHOD

Casual Posture

Sitting (Figure 1.2.6) and Standing (Figure 1.2.7) (Contemporary)

Figure 1.2.6

Figure 1.2.7

Classical Posture

Sitting (Figures 1.2.8 and 1.2.9) and Standing (Figure 1.2.10) (Traditional)

Figure 1.2.8

Figure 1.2.9

Figure 1.2.10

Finger Indications

Left-Hand (Figure 1.2.11), Right-hand (Figure 1.2.12)

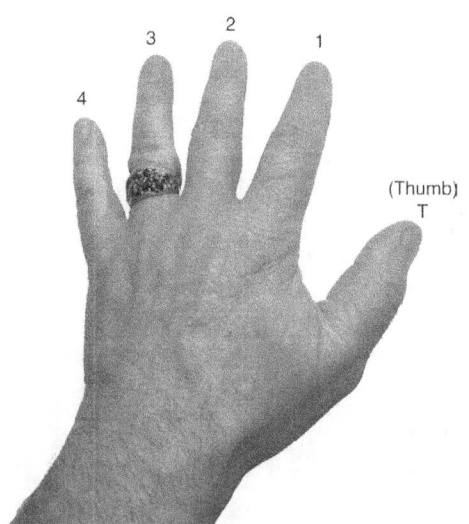
Figure 1.2.8

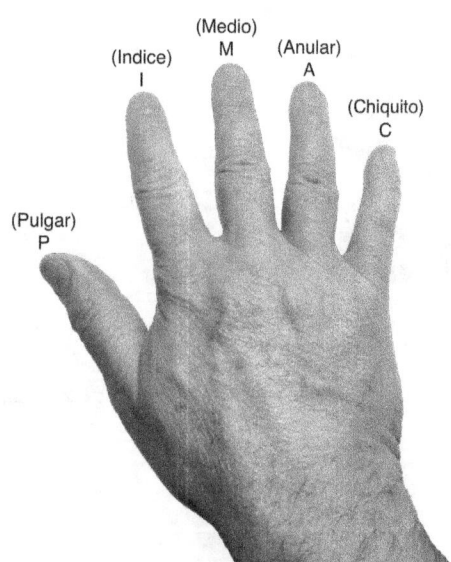
Figure 1.2.9

4

Tablature Notation

Tablature notation for guitar has six horizontal lines that each represent a string on the guitar. The bottom line in tablature (TAB for short) represents the low sixth string on the guitar. The low sixth string is the fattest string on the guitar and is closest to your nose when you are holding the guitar in the playing position. (Refer to Figure 1.2.1 if you are confused regarding which string is the sixth string.)

In TAB, numbers on the lines (strings) indicate the fret where you should place your left-hand finger. If the number is a zero, that means you don't have to use a left-hand finger to press a string down — just pluck the string as an "open" string with your right hand.

Figure 1.2.13 shows how we would indicate plucking each open string four times starting on the first string and working across the guitar to the open sixth string.

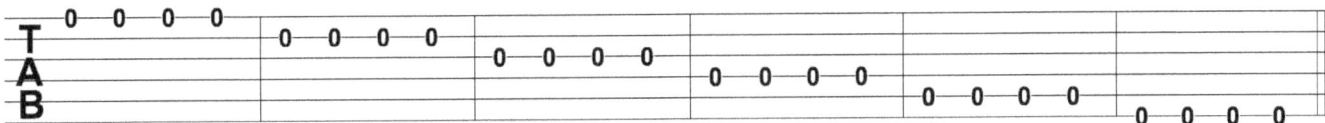

Figure 1.2.13

Play & Do… Video examples at *www.bestmusicpublications.com*

- Point to the parts of your guitar and say the name for each of the parts. Point to each string and say the letter name and number.
- Move your thumb and fingers of your left-hand and say the letter and names and numbers for each.
- Move your thumb and fingers of your right-hand one at a time and say the letter and name for each.

LESSON 3

Right-Hand — Plucking Individual Strings Using the Fingers and Thumb

Lesson Concepts
- Hand Position for Plucking Single Strings with Thumb or Fingers
- Planting
- Free Stroke
- Rest Stroke
- Standard Finger Assignment
- Alternating Fingers

Hand Position for Plucking Single Strings with the Thumb and Fingers

- Your thumb is stiff and straight. The thumb plucks downward. When you pluck down, it is called a *downstroke*. (Figure 1.3.1)
- Your fingers are curved, pointing toward the wrist. The fingers will pluck upward. When you pluck up, it is called an *upstroke*. (Figure 1.3.1)

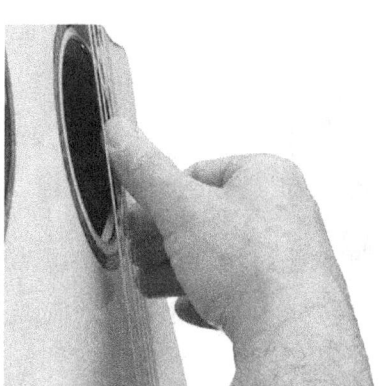

Figure 1.3.1

Planting

Planting describes what happens *before* you pluck a string. *Planting* is when the thumb or fingers rest on a string before plucking the string. (Figure 1.3.2)

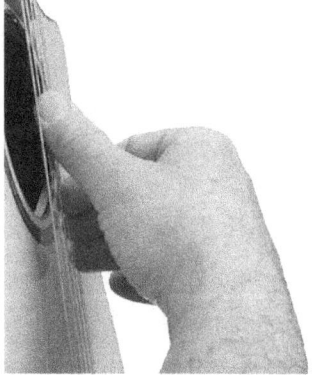

Figure 1.3.2

Free Stroke

A free stroke describes what happens *after* you pluck a string. A free stroke is when your finger or thumb does not contact a string after the string is plucked. (Figure 1.3.3)

Figure 1.3.3

Rest Stroke

A rest stroke describes what happens *after* you pluck a string. When you play a rest stroke your thumb or finger will contact (rest) on the next string after you pluck a string. Your thumb will rest on the next higher string (you can't play a rest stroke on the first string with your thumb). Your finger will rest on the next lower string (you can't play a rest stroke on the sixth string with your fingers).

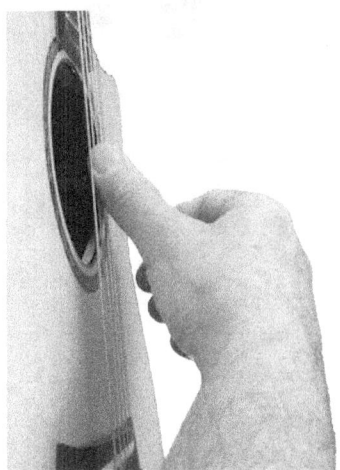

Figure 1.3.4 – Thumb Rest Stroke

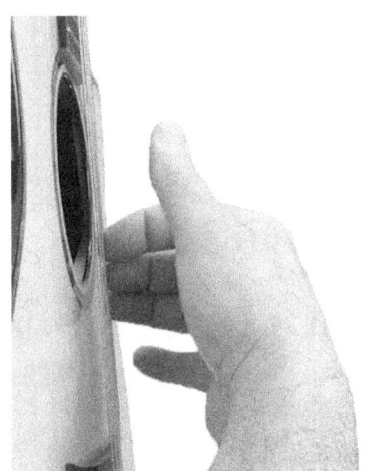

Figure 1.3.5 – Finger Rest Stroke

Standard Finger Assignment

When using the standard finger assignment, the thumb plucks the fourth, fifth, and sixth strings with a downstroke. The index finger plucks the third string, the middle finger plucks the second string, and the ring finger plucks the first string using an upstroke.

Alternating Fingers

The *alternating fingers* technique uses up strokes to pluck individual strings alternating between the index and middle fingers. The alternating finger technique is commonly used for single-note passages and melodies that fall on the first, second, and third strings, but it can be used on all strings. Your thumb plays the fourth, fifth or sixth strings.

Play & Do... Video examples at *www.bestmusicpublications.com*

- Practice plucking the fourth, fifth and sixth string individually with your thumb while planting your fingers on the first, second and third string as if using standard finger assignment. Practice both rest strokes and free strokes.
- Practice assigned fingering by planting your index finger on the third string, your middle finger on the second string and your ring finger on the first string. While planting your thumb on either the fourth, fifth or sixth string, use a free stroke to pluck the third string with your index finger, then the second string with your middle finger and the first string with your ring finger. Try plucking each string repeatedly with each finger before going to the next finger. Try planting and not planting before you repeat the notes.
- Practice alternating plucking by plucking each string first with your index finger and then with your middle finger repeatedly before moving to the next string.

LESSON 4

Picking Individual Strings Using a Pick

Lesson Concepts
- Pick Grip
- Single String Technique

Pick Grip

- Between your thumb and index finger (Figure 1.4.1)
- Your thumb is perpendicular to the pick and your index finger curls behind it
- 25% of the pick is exposed, and the grip is firm

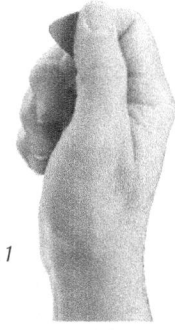

Figure 1.4.1

Single String Picking Technique

Lightly rest your middle, ring, and little fingers on the top of the guitar when you use a pick to steady your right hand. When you pluck a string with a pick, the tip of the pick extends slightly beyond the string, just enough to make the string sound when it is plucked. The most common picking technique is called *alternate picking*. When you alternate pick, the pick moves alternately up and down across the string.

Figure 1.4.2 – Ready position
(down on the sixth string)

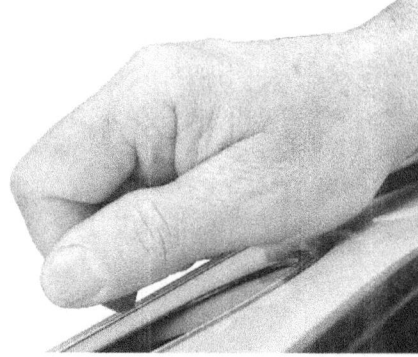

Figure 1.4.3 – Ready position
(up on the sixth string)

Play & Do... Video examples at *www.bestmusicpublications.com*

- Hold the pick between your thumb and index finger as described above and pick single strings in a down/up repeated motion.
- As you pick, experiment with the firmness of your grip and note how the sound changes.

LESSON 5

The Three P's of Tone Production

> **Lesson Concepts**
> - Placement, Positioning, and Pressure
> - Finger Positions on the Neck
> - Four-Finger Exercise
> - Warm-Ups

Good Tone = Placement, Positioning, and Pressure

Placement

Proper fingertip placement is just behind the fret. (Figure 1.5.1)

Positioning

Hand shape, finger shape, thumb shape and wrist mechanics are all part of "positioning." If you pretend you are holding a tennis ball in your left hand, you have the correct hand shape. Keep the hand shape and turn your hand palm up and place your hand around the guitar neck from below. Fingers are held close to the strings and fretboard. The knuckles where the finger joins the hand should be in line or slightly forward of the fretboard. The tip knuckles of fingers should be bent, so the fingertips are coming straight down on the strings and fingerboard. Only the fingertips and thumb come in contact with the guitar. The thumb is placed on the upper back (shoulder) of the neck with the end knuckle of the thumb bent backward a bit. (Figure 1.5.2) The wrist should be relaxed and slightly bent.

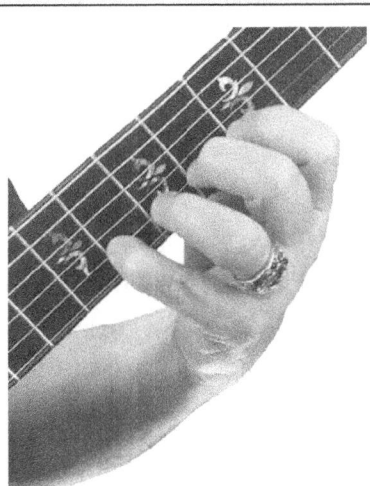

Figure 1.5.1

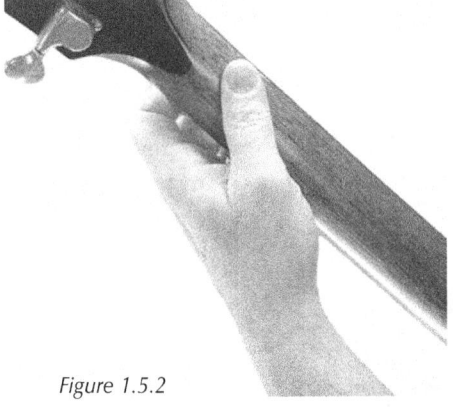

Figure 1.5.2

Pressure

If you have properly considered your placement and positioning, less pressure is needed to get a good sound from the guitar. Sometimes you need to use more pressure on a string (finger) due to compromises in placement and positioning when playing chords.

In summary, for beautiful tone production remember the three P's: placement, positioning, and pressure.

Finger Positions on the Neck

Assigning your four left-hand fingers to four consecutive frets on the fretboard is a *fingering position*. When you are in the first position, your first finger plays the notes on the first fret, the second finger plays the notes on the second fret, the third finger plays the notes on the third fret, and the fourth finger plays the notes on the fourth fret. When you shift your four fingers up one fret, your first finger is now on the second fret, your second finger is on the third fret, and now you are in the second position. The idea of finger position continues up the neck. The fret number of your first finger determines the "position." Figure 1.5.3 shows how your four fingers would be assigned when playing in the fifth position. (The first finger is on the fifth fret.)

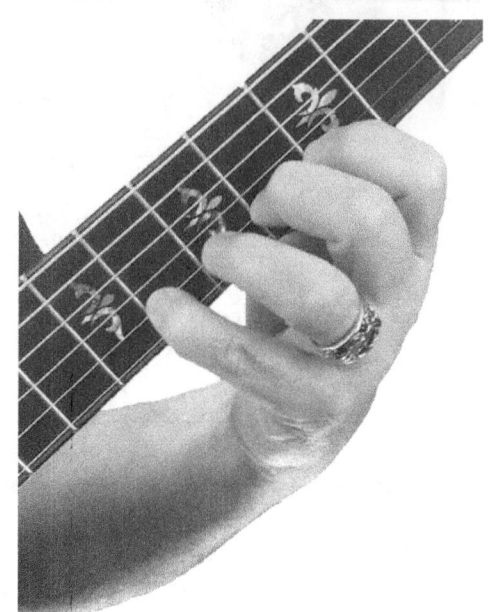

Figure 1.5.3

The Four-finger Exercise (in Fifth Position)

To play the four-finger exercise in the fifth position, start with your first finger on the second string on the fifth fret. Be careful not to interfere with the first or third string and pluck the second string. If you are mindful of the three P's of tone production and pluck the string correctly, using one of the right-hand plucking techniques, you should hear a nice clear note. While holding the second-string note with your first finger, pluck the adjacent open first string, pluck the fretted second string again, and then pluck the open third string. If your first-, second-, and third- string notes don't sound clear when fretting the second string, adjust your left-hand and try again. Once you have succeeded getting clear notes with your first finger holding the second string, add your second finger on the sixth fret and pluck the second, first, second and third strings as you did previously to check that they all sound good. Repeat the process, adding your third finger to the seventh fret second string, and then finally your fourth finger to the eighth fret second string. (Figure 1.5.3) You can then repeat the process for the third, fourth, and fifth strings.

Figure 1.5.4 shows the TAB for the four-finger exercise in the fifth position for the second string:

```
    0       0       0       0
T 5   5   6   6   7   7   8   8
A       0       0       0       0
B
```

Figure 1.5.4

Play & Do... Video examples at *www.bestmusicpublications.com*

- Play the four-finger exercise at the fifth position, be sure to keep the three P's of tone production in mind as you do. When doing the four-finger exercise, try to do it three times with each of the three right-hand techniques, thumb, fingers, or pick.

LESSON 6

Tuning

Lesson Concepts
- Adjusting the String Tension
- Tuning with an Electronic Tuner or Application

Adjusting the String Tension

The first step to learning to tune is to be able to change the string tension. One rule when adjusting the string tension: you should always listen to the sound of the string as you adjust the tension!

To change the tension, follow these steps:

1. Identify the string you want to adjust and follow that string to the end of the neck to identify which tuning pegs to adjust.

2. Grab that tuning peg's adjustment peg firmly between your thumb and index finger with your left hand, but do not turn it yet! Note the position of the tuning peg in case you want to return to that position.

3. Pluck the chosen string with your right hand

4. Steadily turn the tuning peg one way or the other no more than a quarter turn, and listen to the sound of the string. You should hear the pitch or sound of the string go higher or lower depending on which way you turned the tuning peg. If you do not hear the sound of the string changing, then you are not adjusting the correct tuning peg!

Tuning with a Clip-On Electronic Tuner or Application

All beginners should get a clip-on style electronic tuner. Clip-on electronic tuners sense the physical vibrations (they work in noisy environments) and use lights that indicate the note you are playing and if it is in tune or sharp of flat. Also, there are apps available that display like clip-on tuners, but they rely on "hearing" the sound, so they work best in a quiet environment.

The strings are tuned E-A-D-G-B-E from the lowest (fattest) string. The strings are numbered from the lowest 6-5-4-3-2-1 (Figure 1.6.1). Be sure your tuner is displaying the proper note name for the string you are trying to tune. The tuner display will indicate if the note is in tune, too low or too high. Adjust the string tension until the tuner indicates the string is in tune.

Go to the website: *www.bestmusicpublications.com* to find detailed videos describing these and other tuning techniques.

Play & Do... Video examples at *www.bestmusicpublications.com*

- Find someone who can tune your guitar (preferably your teacher). While you are with this person, practice tuning your guitar by the method of your choice. Tuning takes practice just like anything else about the guitar, but practicing with an individual who can supervise you is important because they can be sure your guitar gets in tune and you do not break a string trying to learn how to tune!

LESSON 7

Guitar Chord Notation and Notes on the Guitar

Lesson Concepts
- Chord Grids
- Standard Notation
- TAB (Tablature) Notation
- Notes on the Guitar

Chord Grids

Chord grids are visual representations of the first few frets of the guitar neck. Below is a C chord grid (Figure 1.7.1) and photo (Figure 1.7.2) as an example of what is used throughout this book. In the example below, you would strum the five highest strings.

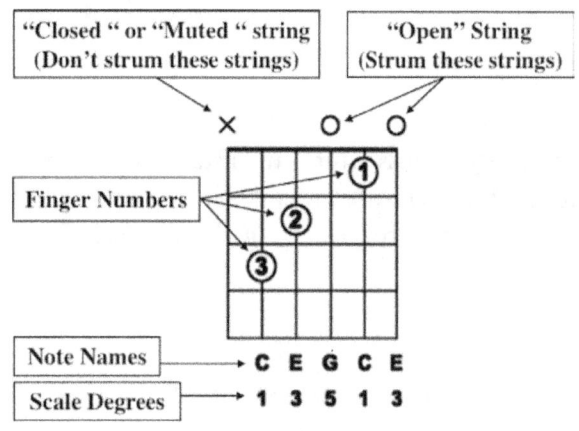

Figure 1.7.1

Figure 1.7.2

Standard Notation

Standard notation is the system of notation used for virtually all musical instruments. Chords can also be notated in standard notation. Figure 1.7.3 shows the C chord in standard notation. For a more detailed explanation of standard notation visit *www.bestmusicpublications.com*.

Figure 1.7.3

TAB (Tablature) Notation

Chords can also be notated in TAB. Figure 1.7.4 shows the C chord in TAB notation. For a more detailed explanation of tablature notation visit *www.bestmusicpublications.com*.

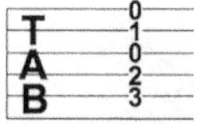

Figure 1.7.4

UNIT ONE • LESSON 7

The Notes on the Guitar

Below is a picture of the guitar neck oriented like a chord grid with the names of all the notes.

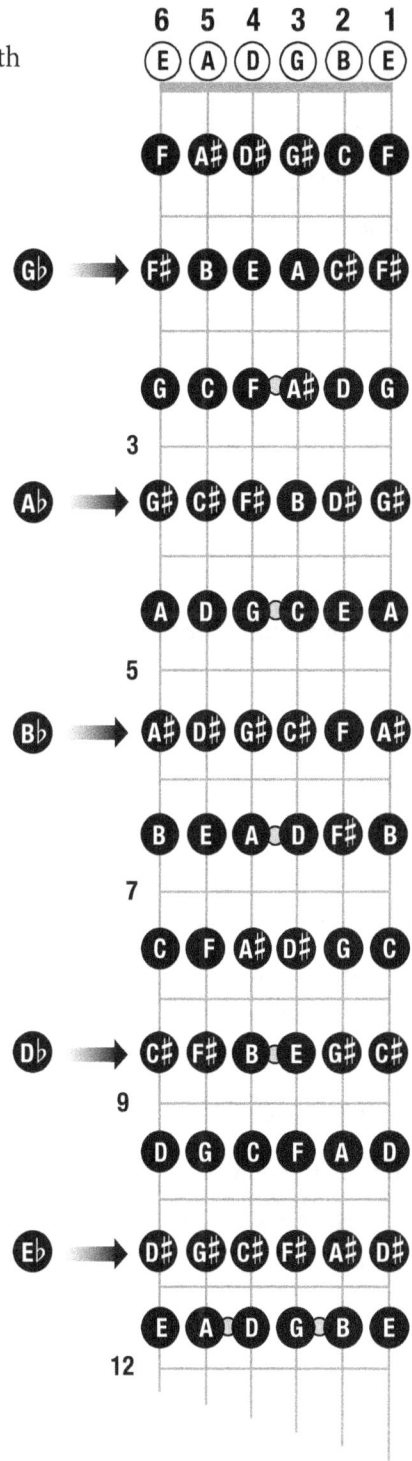

Play & Do... Video examples at *www.bestmusicpublications.com*

- Finger the C chord and pick each string one at a time. As you play the note say the note name.
- Finger the C chord and pick each string one at a time. As you play the note, say the scale degree number.
- Play the open strings and say each note name and string number.

13

Review and Summary

You should be able to demonstrate your knowledge of the following:

Identify the type of guitar you own

Identify the parts of your guitar

Classical sitting posture

Contemporary sitting posture

Classical or contemporary standing posture

Right-hand numbering

Right-hand plucking techniques:
- Planting
- Free stroke
- Rest stroke

Right-hand, single string picking technique with a pick:
- Pick grip
- Arm motion

Left-hand numbering

Left-hand finger position

Four-finger exercise

Outline a practice routine

Change the tension of a string

Tune with an electronic tuner

Tune by ear

Right-hand finger numbering system

Read guitar chord grid notation
- Identify open strings and muted/unused strings
- Identify note names
- Identify scale degrees

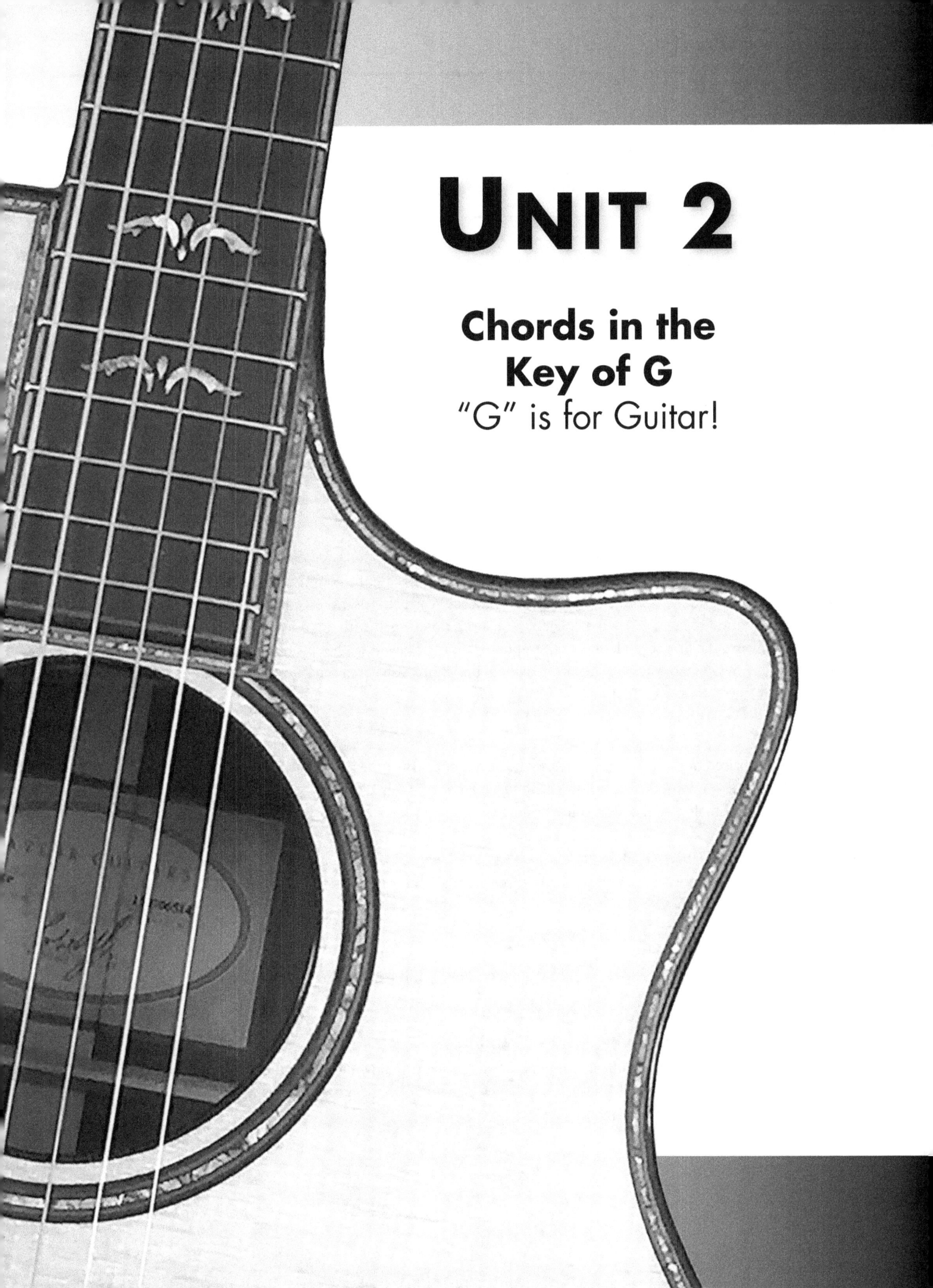

UNIT 2

Chords in the Key of G
"G" is for Guitar!

LESSON 1

Primary Chords in the Key of G — G, C, D, and D7 (I, IV, V, V7)

> **Lesson Concepts**
> - Chord Presentation
> - Chords
> - Primary Chords in the Key of G — G, C, D and D7
> - Upper Case Roman Numerals
> - Primary Chords in the Key of G — I, IV, V and V7
> - Standard Fingerings for the Primary Chords in the Key of G
> - Simplified and Challenge Chord Fingerings
> - Catch and Release
> - Economy of Motion — Changing Chords

Chord Presentation

Chords are presented at three different levels — *Standard* in the unit lessons and *Simplified*, and *Challenge* on the website at *www.bestmusicpublications.com*. Standard chords are the commonly accepted chord forms for beginning guitar players to learn. In this book, you learn chords, notes, and songs by *key*. Here is a quick explanation of keys: A key is a collection of seven notes, each with an individual letter name. In music, you only use the first seven letters of the alphabet. For the key of C, the seven notes are C–D–E–F–G–A–B. The key of G where you will start in this book, and it has a sharp in the key. The seven note names for the key of G are G–A– B–C–D–E–F♯.

Chords

Chords are comprised of three or more notes sounded together. The notes in a G chord are G, B, and D. To indicate a G chord, you write "G." All chords with just a letter name are major chords. For the G chord, you could say "G" or "G major," and either would be correct.

Primary Chords in the Key of G — G, C, D, and D7

In any major key, there are four primary chords: three are major chords and one is a dominant 7 chord. In the key of G, the major chords are G, C, and D. The dominant 7 chord is D7.

Uppercase Roman Numerals

Uppercase Roman numerals are used to indicate major chords, and when followed by a 7 they indicate dominant 7 chords.

Primary Chords in the Key of G — I, IV, V, and V7

Roman numerals can be used to indicate primary chords in a key. In any major key, the primary chords can be indicated as I, IV, V, and V7. As you learn new keys, you will notice the chord names will change, but the Roman numerals will remain the same.

Standard Fingerings for the Primary Chords in the Key of G – G, C, D, and D7 (I, IV, V, V7)

Simplified and Challenge Chords Fingerings

Simplified and challenge chords fingerings for all the chords in this book can be found at *www.bestmusicpublications.com*

Catch and Release

"Catch and Release" is a practice technique that helps you learn to properly finger chords. Initially, you will try to form a chord one finger at a time. That is perfectly fine—ONCE! After you have your fingers on the correct strings, *do not remove them from the strings*. Just *release* the finger pressure while keeping your fingers touching the strings and then catch the chord again by pushing all the fingered strings down *at the same time!* Doing this will help you develop muscle memory, so all your fingers come down at once. Do this at least 25 times, if not more, for each chord. Eventually, when you can change between chords, all your fingers will simultaneously land on the correct strings for each chord.

Economy of Motion — Changing Chords

Economy of motion is about minimizing motion. When changing chords, your fingers should all move together just above the strings and straight to the next chord. When you are fingering chords, make sure the unused fingers are hovering just over the strings in a comfortable position so that when you change to the next chord, they are close to the strings.

Play & Do... Video examples at *www.bestmusicpublications.com*

- Finger (play) each chord and make sure you are mindful of the three P's of tone production. Pick each string of the chord to be sure each string is making a good sound. As you play the chord, say its name (for example, "G").

- "Catch and release" each chord. Strum the chord as you apply pressure and then check that each string is still sounding good. If it does not sound good, go back and check the three P's of tone production. Recite the specific names and universal names for the primary chords in the key of G. Say, "The primary chords in the key of G
  are: G, also known as the I chord, C, also known as the IV chord and D, also known as the V chord."

- Fill in the universal chord names for the key of G in the spaces:

  G =_____   C = _____   D = _____   D7 = _____

- Memorize the names and universal numbers for the primary chords in the key of G.

Lesson 2

Strumming the Strings Using the Fingers and Thumb

> **Lesson Concept**
> - Strumming Multiple String with Fingers or Thumb

Strumming Multiple Strings with the Thumb and Fingers

When strumming with your thumb, there is more forearm/elbow motion involved than when you plucked single strings. Relax your right hand and drag your thumb down across the desired strings *moving from your elbow* and with a slight twisting motion of your forearm and wrist (Figure 2.2.1). Your arm should make a continuous down-motion from your elbow (Figure 2.2.2). At slower speeds, your arm will move across the entire width of the guitar top (Figure 2.2.3), and as the speed of the motion increases, your arm will travel less distance. On the up strum, turn your hand so your thumb points slightly downward and engage your thumbnail as you strum with an up motion.

Figure 2.2.1 *Figure 2.2.2* *Figure 2.2.3*

A variation is to use the same motion only using your index finger or combinations of the index, middle and ring fingers. When using your fingers instead of your thumb, it is common to use your fingernail on the down strum. When you strum downward with your fingernails, it is called a *nail stroke* (Figure 2.2.4). When you strum upward with your fingers, it is called a *brush stroke* (Figure 2.2.5). The fingers will point slightly downward on the up strum.

Figure 2.2.4 *Figure 2.2.5*

Play & Do... Video examples at *www.bestmusicpublications.com*

- Strum the correct strings for each of the primary chords in the key of G using your thumb, using all down strokes and then alternating down and up strokes.

- Strum the correct strings for each of the primary chords in the key of G with your index finger, using all down strokes and then alternating down and up strokes.

- Strum the correct strings for each of the primary chords in the key of G with multiple fingers, using all down strokes and then alternating down and up strokes.

LESSON 3

Strumming the Strings Using a Pick

> **Lesson Concepts**
> - Pick Grip
> - Strumming Technique

Pick Grip

The pick should be held between your thumb and index finger. Your thumb is perpendicular to the pick, and your index finger should curl behind it, so it does not interfere with the pick and strings. About half the pick is exposed, and the grip is relaxed (Figure 2.3.1). If you hold the pick too firmly, you will produce a harsh sound and the pick will tend to stay on the string. A relaxed grip will produce a better sound, and the pick will adjust naturally.

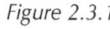

Figure 2.3.1

Strumming Technique

Move the pick up and down across the desired strings *moving from your elbow* and with a slight twisting motion of your forearm and wrist as you did when strumming in the previous lesson. The tip of the pick should just barely extend beyond the string, (Figure 2.3.2) so it plucks but doesn't hang up on the string. Your arm should make a continuous down/up motion from your elbow. At slower speeds, your arm will move across the entire width of the guitar top, and as the speed of the motion increases, your arm will travel less distance. On the down strum, the point of your pick will point slightly upward, on the up strum the point of your pick will point slightly downward. Strum the strings over the sound hole about an inch from the end of the fretboard.

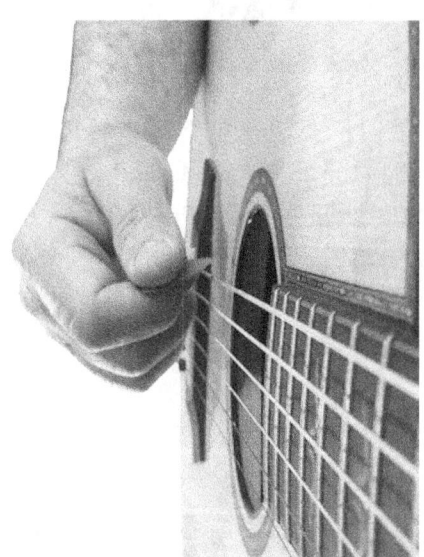

Figure 2.3.2

Play & Do... Video examples at *www.bestmusicpublications.com*

- Hold the pick between your thumb and index finger as described above and strum the correct strings in a down/up repeated motion for each of the primary chords in the key of G.

- As you strum, experiment with the firmness of your grip and note how the sound changes.

LESSON 4

Strumming the Strings with a Steady Beat

> ***Lesson Concepts***
> - Steady Beat and Strumming
> - Meter: 4/4 Time
> - Barlines, Measures, and Bars
> - Strumming Frame: Quarter Note
> - Economy of Motion
> - Emphasizing Beat 1 to Establish Meter

Steady Beat and Strumming

A *steady beat* is a pulse that does not slow down or speed up. The ticking of a clock is an example of a steady beat. *Tempo* is the musical term for *speed*. Clocks all have a steady beat and the same *tempo* (60 beats per minute).

The basic motion for strumming is to move your right arm in a smooth and constant down/up motion from your elbow. It is important to move your forearm up and down with a steady beat.

Video examples at ***www.bestmusicpublications.com***

Meter: 4/4 Time

In music, the steady beat is commonly grouped into groups of four. When you group the steady beat, you are applying a *meter* to the steady beat. The most common meter in music is 4/4 time. Without the meter, the steady beat sounds like a clock continuously ticking. When a meter is added, this ticking is still steady like a clock, but the first beat of each group of four is emphasized slightly (1-2-3-4, 1-2-3-4, etc.).

Barlines, Measures, and Bars

Barlines are vertical lines on the music staff that divide the music into bars of music. In 4/4 time there are four beats in a bar. The term "measure" is just another word for a bar; they mean the same thing. Measures or bars are the space between the barlines. Most barlines are single thin lines, but there are also special barlines like the double one at the end of Figure 2.4.1. In 4/4 time the top number indicates the number of beats in a measure. The bottom number indicates what kind of note is used to represent one beat; in this case, the 4 on the bottom represents a quarter note. (Figure 2.4.2) A quarter note can have a solid oval note head, and a stem or the note head can be replaced by a line.

Figure 2.4.1

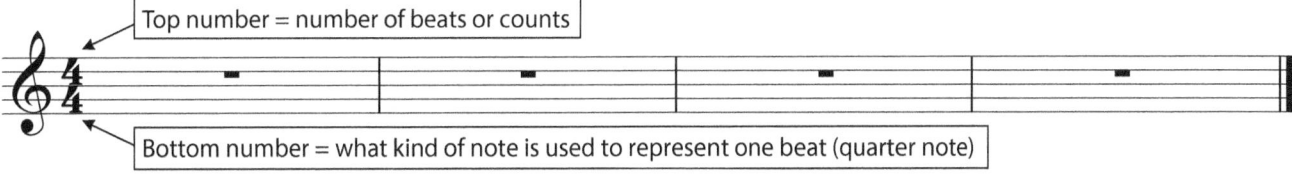

Figure 2.4.2

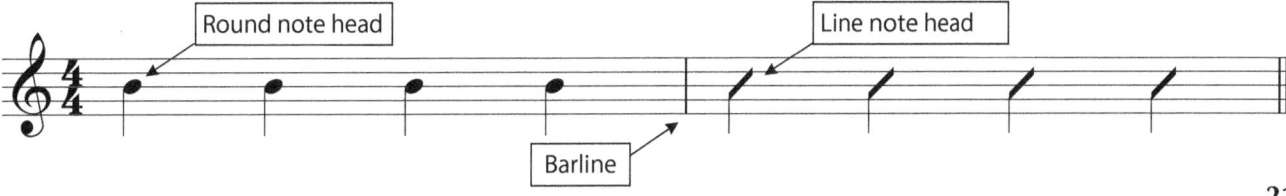

21

Strumming Frame: Quarter Note

When your downward right arm motion is aligned to the quarter note, you are using a *quarter note strumming frame*. It is a "frame" because you are not necessarily strumming the strings on the quarter note; you are simply moving your arm in a downward motion on every quarter note. This constant *strumming frame* motion is the key to playing strum *patterns!*

Economy of Motion

When you are strumming, move your arm just beyond the strings in each direction.

Emphasizing Beat 1 to Establish Meter

Try to strum more strings or even the lowest few strings on beat 1, and then strum higher strings on the remaining beats. Playing more or lower strings adds a sense of *meter*, especially when playing a simple quarter note rhythm.

When you play *quarter note rhythms* with a *quarter note frame*, you will strum the strings every time you move your hand in a downward motion. The (⊓) indicates a downstroke. Figure 2.4.3 shows how this strum pattern is notated:

Figure 2.4.2

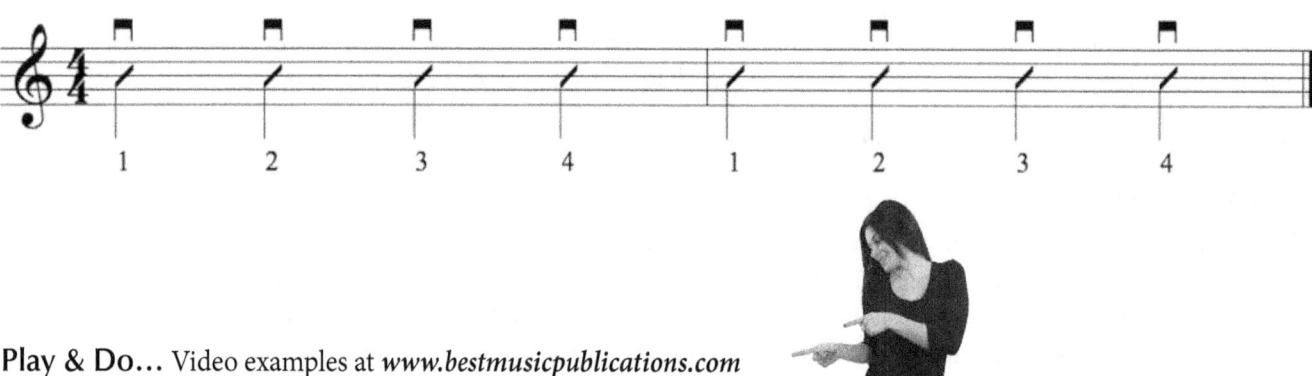

Play & Do... Video examples at *www.bestmusicpublications.com*

- Say it don't play it. Move your right arm in a steady up and down motion without strumming the strings and while you do so, say either "down-down-down-down" or "1-2-3-4" as you move your arm in each downward motion.
- Now say it while you play it. As you move in a downward motion strum the strings of the G chord and say either "down-down-down-down" or "1-2-3-4" with each downward motion of your arm.
- Now finally play it, but don't say it. That means strum the strings, but instead of saying either "down-down-down-down" or "1-2-3-4" out loud, think it silently as you strum the strings.

To sum up the three-step sequence:

Step 1 — "Say it, don't play it."

Step 2 — "Say it while you play it."

Step 3 — "Play it while you think it silently."

LESSON 5

Playing Songs — "Hot Cross Buns" and "Merrily We Roll Along" (Songs)

Lesson Concepts
- Counting and Following Written Music
- Anticipating the Chord Change
- Economy of Motion

Counting and Following Written Music

Being able to follow the written music while counting the steady beats is an important skill. Because following and counting are separate skills from playing the steady beat, you should practice counting and following the written notation *before* you try to play it!

Steps before trying to play along with the pre-recorded examples:

- Listen to the recording.
- Point to the music and count out loud "1-2-3-4" for each measure as you follow the written music with your finger.

Counting without playing allows you to focus on steady beat and gets you used to what the song is supposed to sound like before trying to play it.

Anticipating the Chord Change

To play these songs at full speed, you need to be able to anticipate the chord change. To anticipate the next chord change, think about it before you play it. The best way to do this is to "shortchange" the last beat preceding the chord change, that is, don't sustain it, but instead strum the chord and then start changing to the next chord right away!

Economy of Motion

Now you want to consider the motion *between* the chords. When you change from the G chord to the D chord, all your fingers must move. You want to move all your fingers simultaneously from one chord to the other. When you move between chords, try to keep your fingers right above the strings. Make sure to consider individual finger movements between chords. For example, when changing from G to D the first finger stays on the same fret but moves from the 5th string to the 3rd string. The second finger moves from the 6th string to the 1st string and moves to the second fret. The third finger moves from the 1st string to the 2nd string and stays in the same fret.

Remember the Basic Three-Step Learning Process

Step 1 — "Say it, don't play it." (While moving your arm using a quarter note frame.)

Step 2 — "Say it while you play it."

Step 3 — "Play it while you think it silently."

THE BEST GUITAR METHOD

"HOT CROSS BUNS" WITH G-C-D CHORDS *(TRADITIONAL)*

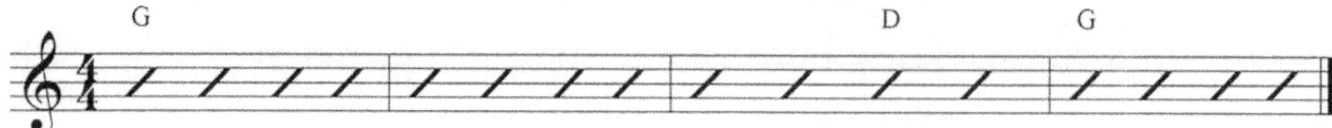

"HOT CROSS BUNS" WITH G AND D7 CHORDS *(TRADITIONAL)*

"MERRILY WE ROLL ALONG" WITH G AND D CHORDS *(TRADITIONAL)*

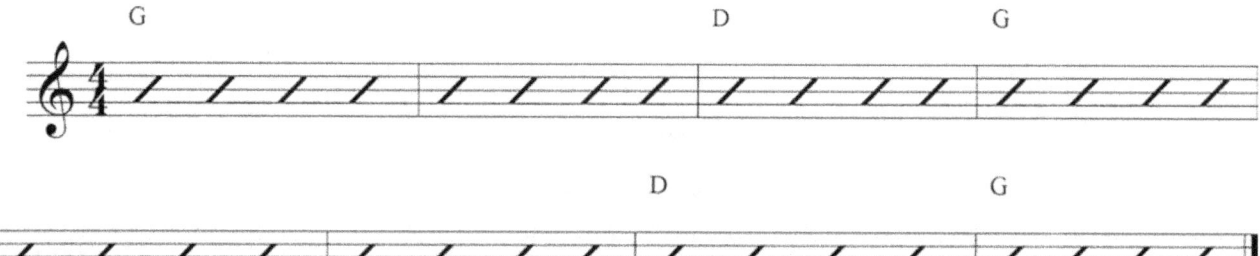

"MERRILY WE ROLL ALONG" WITH G AND D7 CHORDS *(TRADITIONAL)*

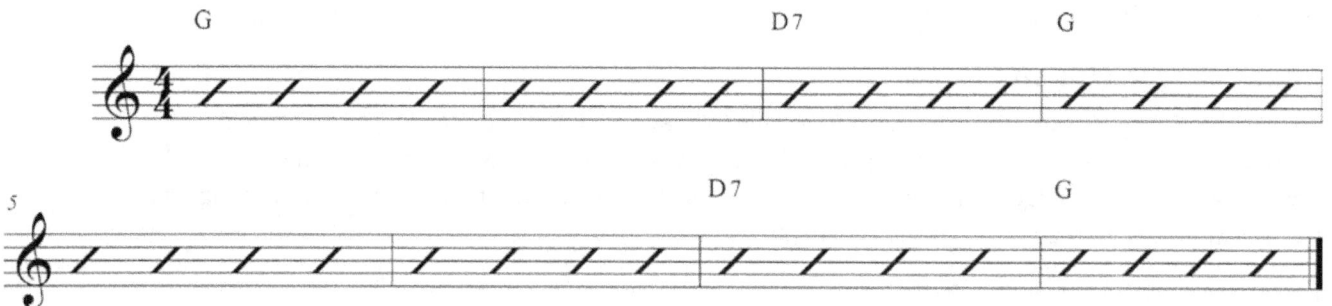

About the Songs

Once you can play these songs, visit **bestmusicpublications.com** and follow the links to "online content." Click the "songs you can play with the chords you know" button, and you will find a list of popular songs that you can learn to play in addition to the songs printed in the book.

Play & Do... Video examples at *www.bestmusicpublications.com*

- Listen to the recording of "Hot Cross Buns" in the key of G and "Merrily We Roll Along" in the key of G and count "1-2-3-4" for each measure as you point to and follow the written music.
- Listen to the recording of "Hot Cross Buns" in the key of G and "Merrily We Roll Along" in the key of G and say the chord names as you point to and follow the written music.
- Listen to the recording of "Hot Cross Buns" in the key of G and "Merrily We Roll Along" in the key of G and play the chords and strum pattern as shown in the written music.

LESSON 6

Standard Strum Patterns in 4/4 Time

Lesson Concepts
- Quarter Notes and Eighth Notes
- Directional Notation
- Standard Strum Patterns

Quarter Notes and Eighth Notes

In Unit 2 / Lesson 4 you learned about *quarter notes* and the *quarter note* frame. To play a quarter note rhythm, you move your arm up between each down strum. If you were to strum the strings as you moved your arm upward, you would be playing twice as many notes. When you play the up strums, you are now playing *eighth notes*. The (V) indicates an upstroke. Figure 2.6.1 shows how they are notated:

Figure 2.6.1

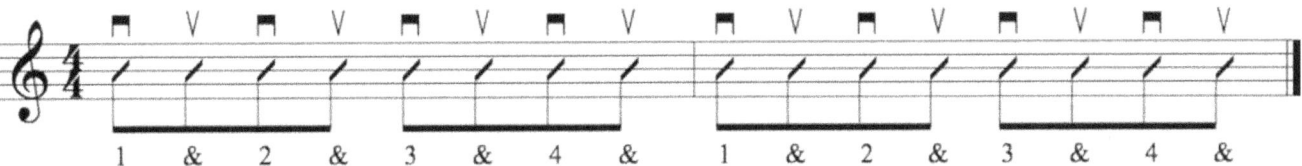

Directional Notation

There are many ways to notate downstrokes and upstrokes in guitar notation. The standard way is to use a 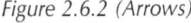 symbol to represent a downstroke and a V symbol to represent an upstroke. (Figure 2.6.1) These symbols originated in violin notation (downbow and upbow) and have been adopted in guitar notation. Beginning guitar players often find this standard directional notation confusing because the symbol for up appears to point down. This standard notation (Figure 2.6.1) is used throughout this book.

Figures 2.6.2 and 2.6.3 show some other common ways that downstrokes and upstrokes are notated.

Figure 2.6.2 (Arrows)

Figure 2.6.3 (D and U)

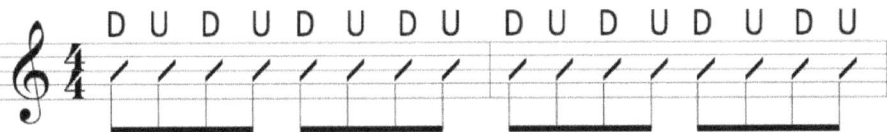

THE BEST GUITAR METHOD

Standard Strum Patterns

Patterns #1 and #2 have steady quarter and eighth note rhythms that are even like the ticking of a clock. Patterns #3–#7 have varied rhythms combining quarter and eighth notes. Choose a G, C or D chord, and play each example until you can do it without pausing. Refer to the video and audio examples for help.

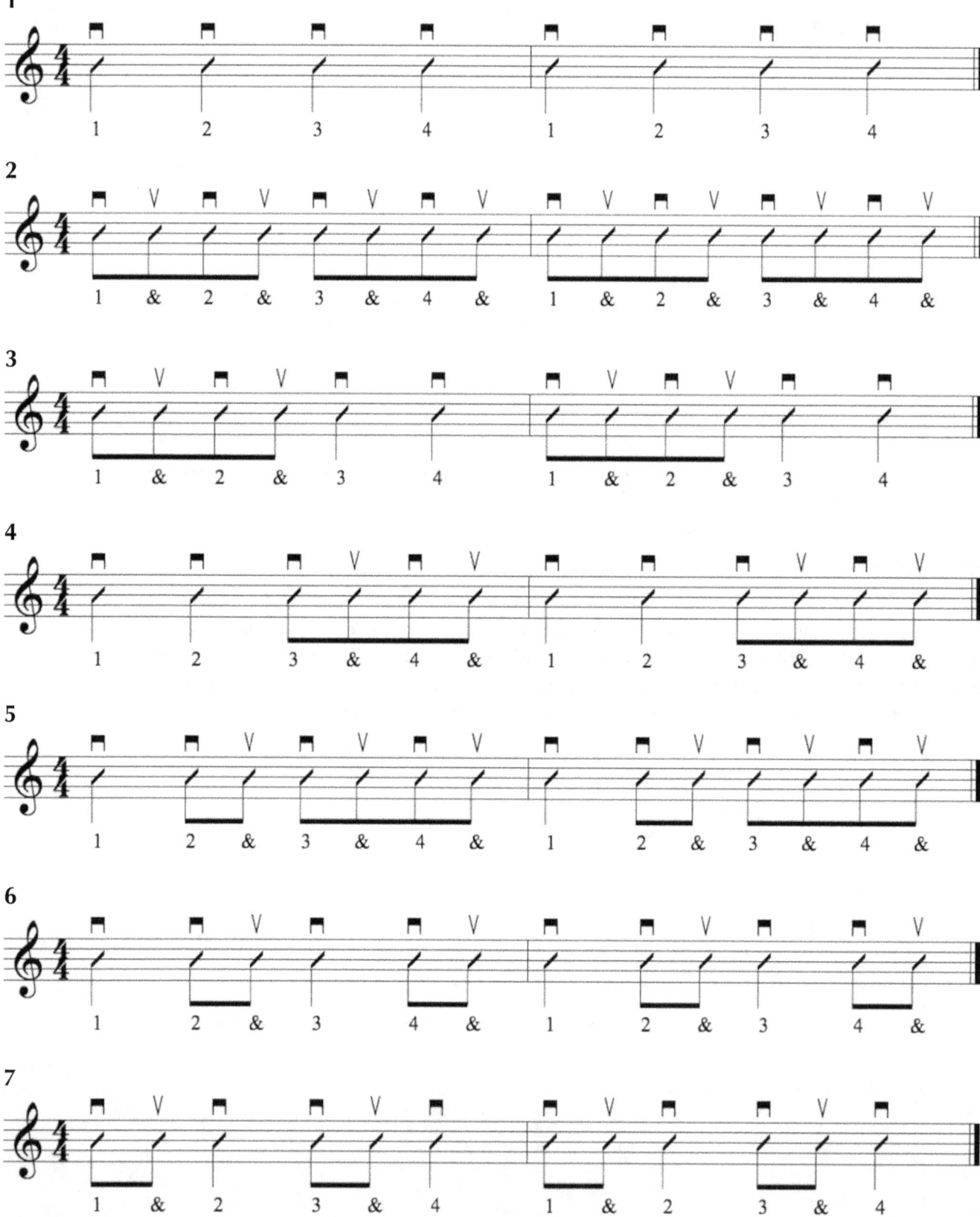

UNIT TWO • LESSON 6

Play & Do... Video examples at *www.bestmusicpublications.com*

Note: All the strum patterns use a "quarter note frame" motion of your right arm.

- Start with the simple pattern #1 and say *but don't play* the rhythm while continuing to move your right arm in a steady up and down manner (quarter note frame). You can say either "down-down-down-down" or "1-2-3-4" as you move your arm in each downward motion.
- Now *say it while you play it*. Choose one of the chords from the key of G and say pattern #1 as you play it. Say either "down-down-down-down" or "1-2-3-4" as you move your right arm while strumming the strings.
- Now *play it, but don't say it*. That means strum the chords, but instead of saying either "down-down-down-down" or "1-2-3-4" out loud, say it silently inside your head as you strum the strings.

To sum up the three-step sequence:

- *Say it don't play it, while moving your right arm using a quarter note frame.*
- *Say it while you play it.*
- *Play it while you think it silently.*

LESSON 7

"Down by the Riverside" (Song)

Lesson Concept
- Song – "Down by the Riverside"

DOWN BY THE RIVERSIDE (Traditional)

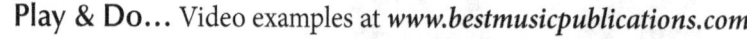

Play & Do... Video examples at *www.bestmusicpublications.com*

Note: All the strum patterns use a "quarter note frame" motion of your right arm.

- Listen to "Down by the Riverside" while counting and following the music.
- Play "Down by the Riverside" while counting.
- Play "Down by the Riverside" while counting silently inside your head.
- Play "Down by the Riverside" with the recorded version.

LESSON 8

Other Strum Patterns in 4/4 Time

Lesson Concepts
- Whole Notes and Half Notes
- Strum Patterns with Whole Notes and Half Notes
- Ties
- Strum Patterns with Tied Notes

Whole Notes and Half Notes

You have learned *quarter notes* that are held for one beat in 4/4 time. *Whole notes* (Figure 2.8.1) and *half notes* (Figure 2.8.2) are used to notate notes that are held longer than one beat. A whole note is held for four beats, and a half note is held for two beats.

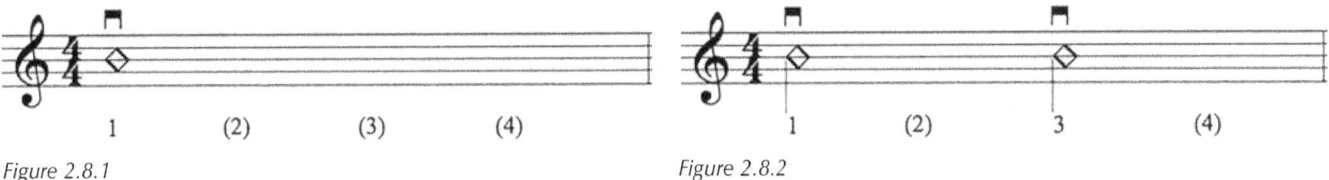

Figure 2.8.1   Figure 2.8.2

Strum Patterns with Whole Notes and Half Notes

#1 and #2 are non-mixed quarter and eighth notes and have a steady even beat like the ticking of a clock. #2–#6 have varied rhythms combining whole, half, and quarter notes. Choose a G, C or D chord, and play each example until you can do it without pausing. Refer to the video and audio examples for help.

Remember the basic three-step learning process…

Step 1 — "Say it out loud."

Step 2 — "Play it while you say it out loud."

Step 3 — "Play it while you say it silently inside your head!"

STRUM PATTERNS WITH WHOLE NOTES AND HALF NOTES

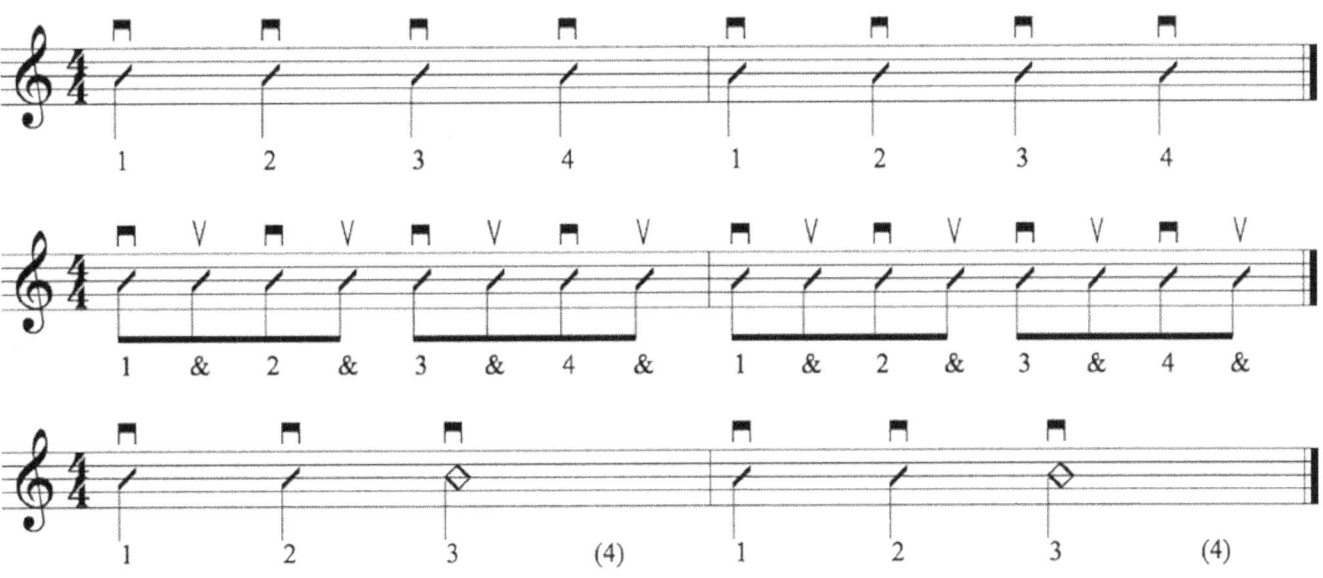

29

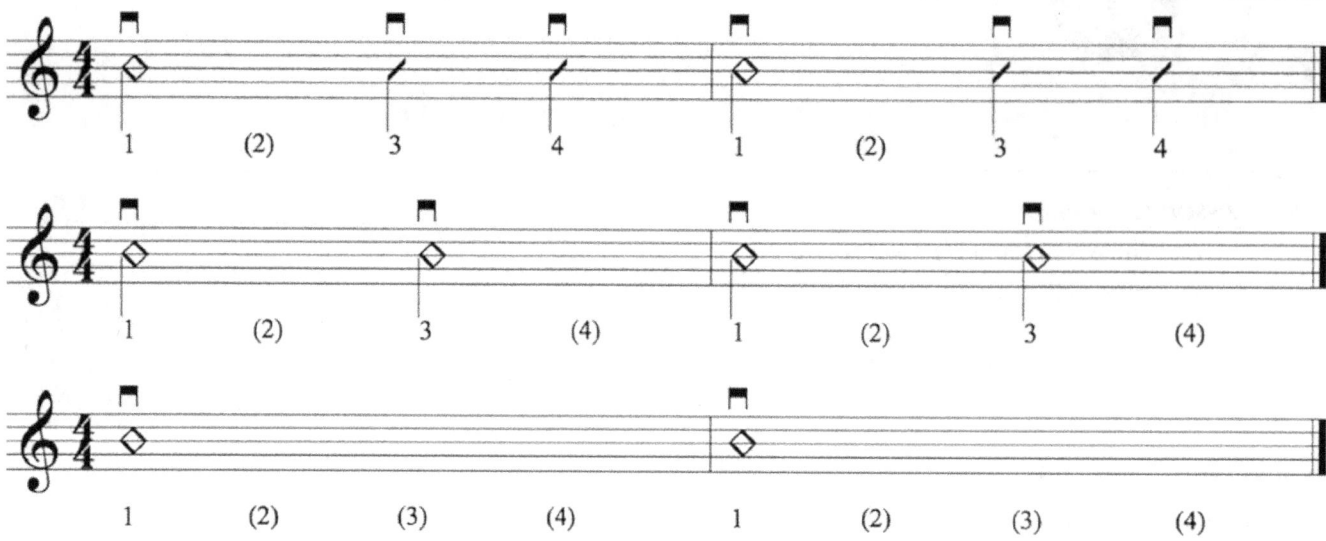

Ties

A *tie* is used to combine the rhythmic value of two notes. In tied strum pattern example #1, beat 2 is tied to beat 3. What this means is that you will move your arm in a downward motion on each beat keeping a quarter note frame, but you will only strike the strings on beat 1, 2 and 4. Let the sound of beat 2 ring through beat 3. Ties can be used with strum patterns and with single notes when they are the same note. Choose a G, C or D chord, and play each example until you can do it without pausing. Refer to the video and audio examples for help.

Strum Patterns with Tied Notes

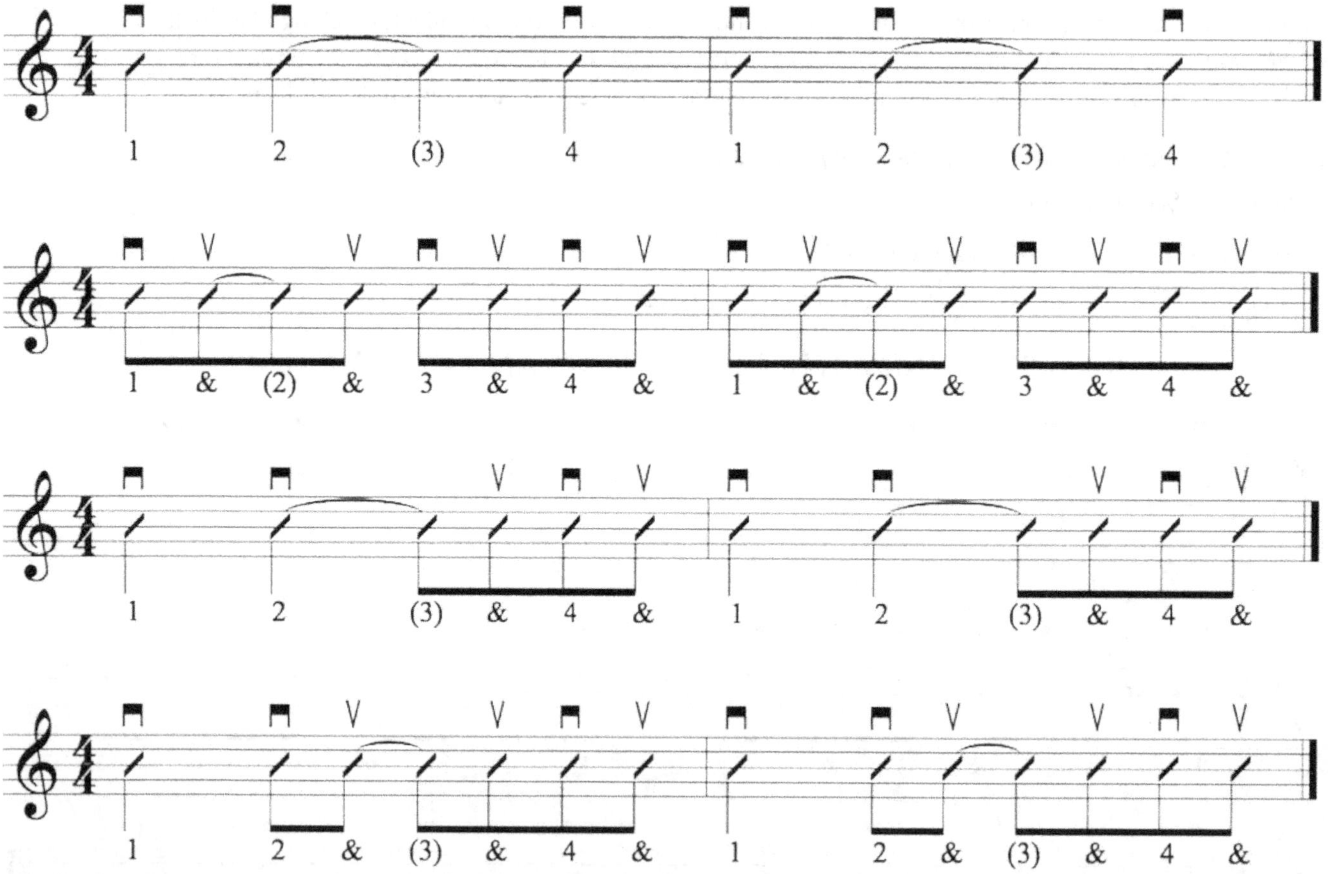

UNIT TWO • LESSON 8

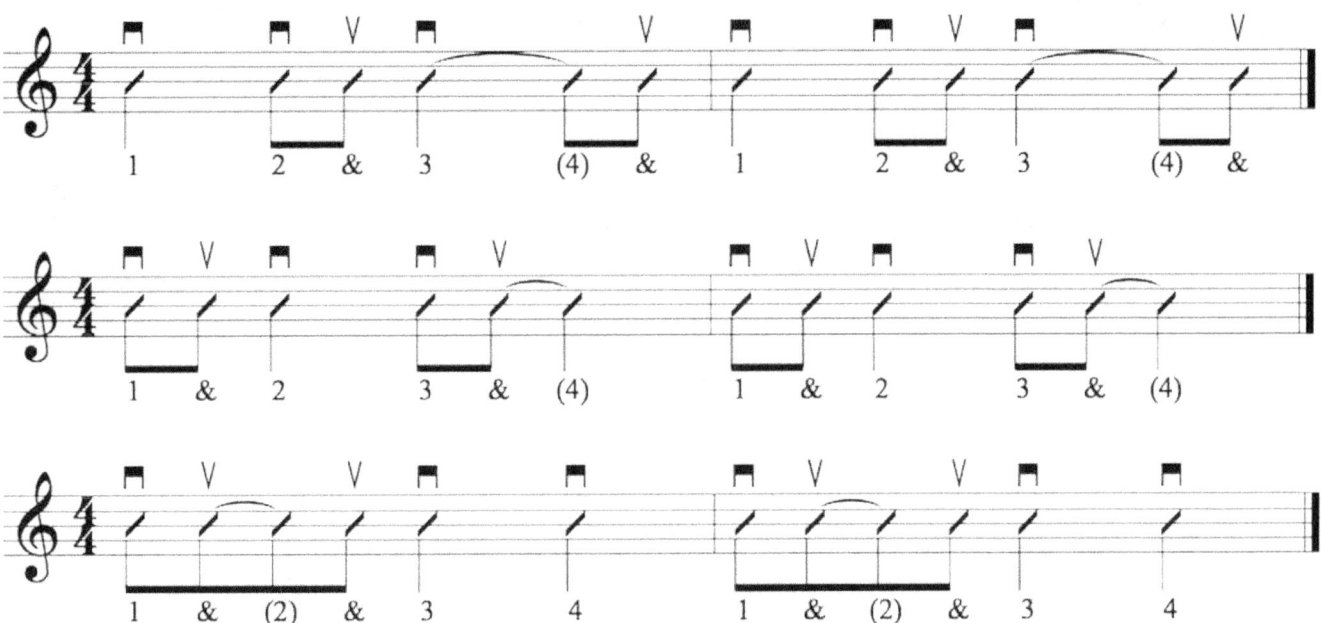

 **Play & Do…** Video examples at *www.bestmusicpublications.com*

Note: All the strum patterns use a "quarter note frame" motion of your right arm.

Step 1) Start with the simple pattern #1 and *say but don't play* the rhythm while continuing to move your right arm in a steady up and down manner (quarter note frame). You can say either "down-down-down-down" or "1-2-3-4" as you move your arm in each downward motion.

Step 2) Now *say it while you play it*. Choose one of the chords from the key of G and say pattern #1 as you play it. Say either "down-down-down-down" or "1-2-3-4" as you move your right arm while strumming the strings.

Step 3) Now *play it, but don't say it*. That means strum the chords, but instead of saying either "down-down-down-down" or "1-2-3-4" out loud, say it silently inside your head as you strum the strings.

    Step 1 — "Say it out loud."
    Step 2 — "Play it while you say it out loud."
    Step 3 — "Play it while you say it silently!"

- Repeat the three-step sequence for each of the six simple strum patterns
- Repeat the three-step sequence for each of the seven standard strum patterns
- Repeat the three-step sequence for each of the seven challenge strum patterns

LESSON 9

3/4 Time

Lesson Concepts
- Emphasizing Beat 1 to Create a Sense of Meter
- Three-Four (3/4) Time Strum Patterns

Emphasizing Beat 1 to Create a Sense of Meter

Music can be divided into a group of 3 or 4 beats by placing a bar-line (or a "measure line") to show the *meter*. The most standard *meters* are groups of 4 (4/4 time) or 3 (3/4 time) beats per measure. So far, all the strum patterns have been in 4/4 time, meaning you've been counting "1-2-3-4" for each measure. Three-Four (3/4) time has a meter of three (three quarter notes,) so that you will count "1-2-3" for each measure.

Accenting beat 1 in a strum pattern is important, especially if the strum pattern is a quarter note rhythm because the accented beat one gives the listener and player a clear indication of the meter. (Either 3/4 time or 4/4 time.)

Strum more or the lower strings on beat one and then fewer or the higher strings of the chord on the remaining beats. *The basic concept is that something needs to be different about beat one from the other beats to make the music sound like it has a meter.*

Figure 2.9.1 shows the accent symbol over a quarter note.

Figure 2.9.1

Three-Four (3/4) Strum Patterns

Here are some basic 3/4-time strum patterns with accents added to remind you to accent beat 1:

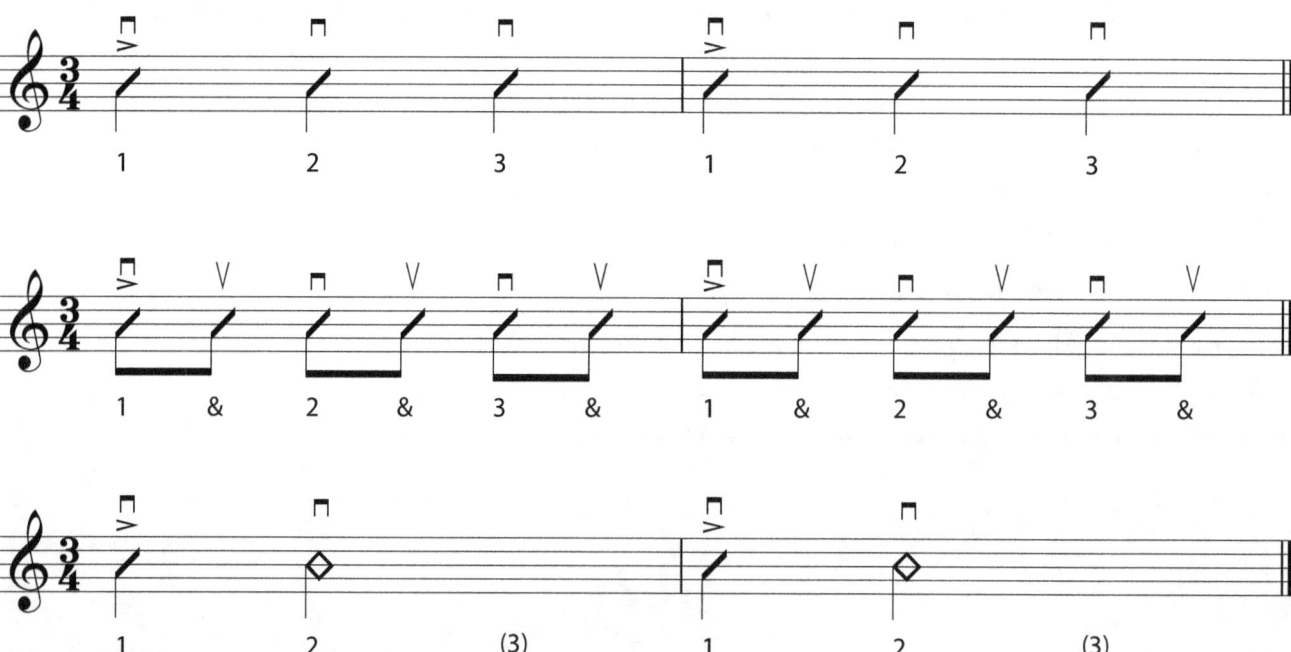

UNIT TWO • LESSON 9

Play & Do... Video examples at *www.bestmusicpublications.com*

Note: All the strum patterns use a "quarter note frame" motion of your right arm.

- Step 1 — Start with the Simple Pattern #1 and say but don't play the rhythm while continuing to move your right arm in a steady up and down manner (quarter note frame). You can say either "down-down-down" or "1-2-3" as you move your arm in each downward motion.
- Step 2 — Now say it while you play it. Choose one of the chords from the key of G and say pattern #1 as you play it. Say either "down-down-down" or "1-2-3" as you move your right arm while strumming the strings.
- Step 3 — Now play it, but don't say it. That means strum the chords, but instead of saying either "down-down-down" or "1-2-3" out loud, say it silently as you strum the strings.

Lesson 10

Pickup Measures, Changing Chords, and Repeats Signs

Lesson Concepts
- Song Form
- Chord Progression
- Pickup Measure
- Repeat Signs

Song Form

Song form refers to the overall structure of the song. The terms verse, chorus, and bridge are commonly used to identify the various sections of a song. The order of the sections in a song and the length of each section in measures are all part of the song and go together to create the overall *song form*.

Chord Progression

The chord progression is the sequence of chords. The chord progression is part of the accompaniment and starts at the beginning of the song form.

Pickup Measure

A *pickup measure* is an incomplete measure at the beginning of the music where the melody (words) starts before the song form and chord progression. When there is a pickup measure, you start strumming in the first complete measure after the pickup measure when the song form starts.

Repeat Signs

Figure 2.10.1 shows a *left repeat*.   Figure 2.10.2 shows a *right repeat*.

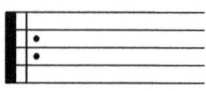   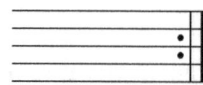

Figure 2.10.1   *Figure 2.10.2*

Any music that is notated between the *left* and *right* repeats is repeated. It is assumed only to be repeated one time. If more repetitions are needed, there is often a notation like this: "4xs." "4xs" is short for "play four times."

Play & Do… Video examples at *www.bestmusicpublications.com*

- Locate the pickup measure and repeat signs in the next lesson in the song "The Streets of Laredo."

LESSON 11

"The Streets of Laredo" (Song)

Lesson Concept
- Changing Chords Within a Measure
- "The Streets of Laredo" (Song)

Changing Chords within a Measure

Notice in measure 15, you play the G chord for beats 1 and 2, and then switch to the D7 chord on beat 3. You only play the D7 chord for one beat in measure 15, because you switch right back to the G chord on beat one of measure 16.

"The Streets of Laredo" is a classic cowboy song in 3/4 time, yippee-tie-yea! This song has a *pickup measure* and *repeat signs*.

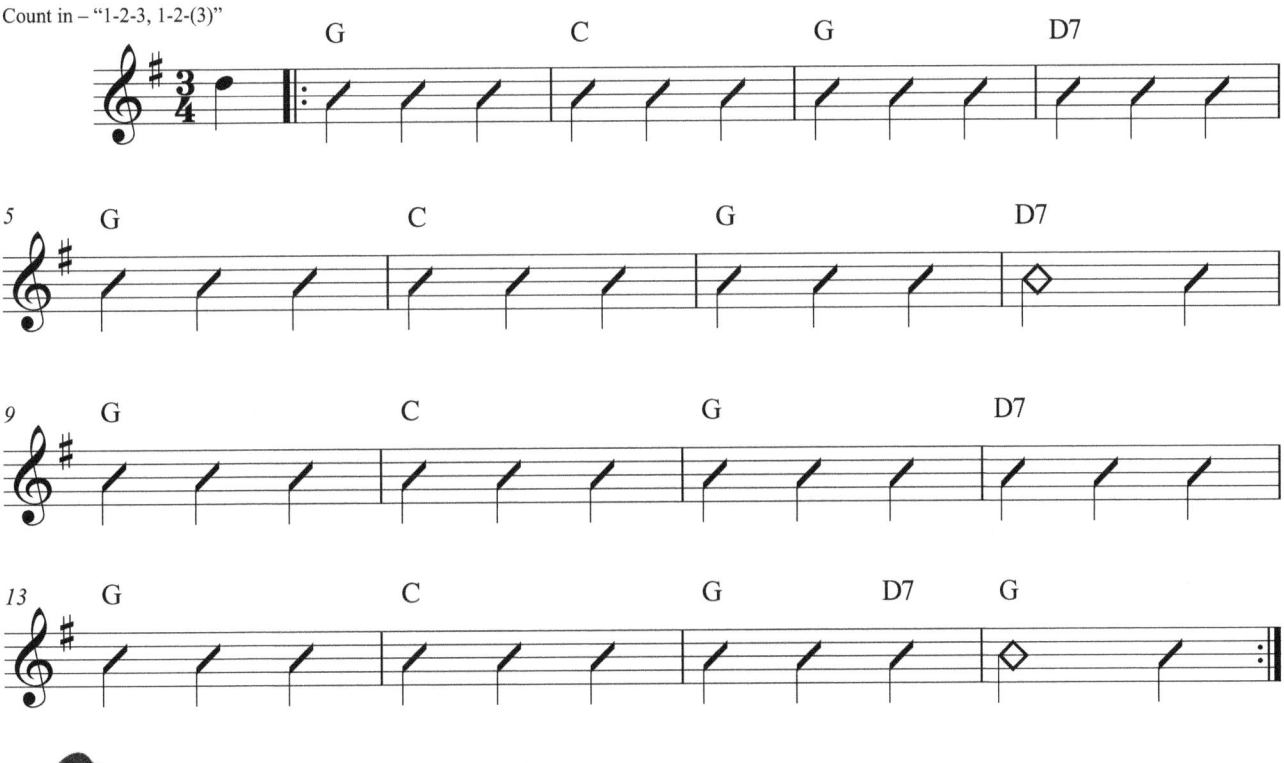

Play & Do... Video and audio examples at www.bestmusicpublications.com

- Listen to any of the recorded versions of "The Streets of Laredo" and count "1-2-3" as you point to and follow the written music.
- Listen to any of the recorded versions of "The Streets of Laredo" and say the chord names as you point to and follow the written music.
- Play "The Streets of Laredo" chords and strum pattern as shown in the written music.
- Play along with the recorded version of "The Streets of Laredo."

LESSON 12

12-Bar Blues (Chord Progression)

> **Lesson Concepts**
> - Counting Beats and Measures Together
> - Saying Chord Names While Counting Beats and Measures
> - Chord Chart
> - 12-Bar Blues Form

Counting Beats and Measures Together

- "**1**–2–3–4" (measure 1) "**2**–2–3–4" (measure 2) "**3**–2–3–4" for (measure 3), "**4**–2–3–4" (measure 4), "**5**–2–3–4" (measure 5), "**6**–2–3–4" for (measure 6) "**7**–2–3–4" (measure 7), "**8**–2 –3–4" (measure 8)

Play & Do… Video examples at *www.bestmusicpublications.com*

- Practice counting the measures using the measure counting method for eight measures:
- Say: "**1**–2–3–4" (measure 1) "**2**–2–3–4" (measure 2) "**3**–2–3–4" for (measure 3),
- "**4**–2–3–4" (measure 4), "**5**–2–3–4" (measure 5), "**6**–2–3–4" for (measure 6) "**7**–2–3–4" (measure 7), "**8**–2 –3–4" (measure 8)

Saying Chord Names While Counting Beats and Measures

Keeping track of the chord changes and counting beats at the same time is an essential musical skill for a guitar player. Substitute the chord name for beat 1 of measure 1 and then count the remaining beats and measures using the measure counting method. You will restart the measure count at each chord change! If there are four measures of G you would count: "**G**–2–3–4" (measure 1,) "**2**–2–3–4" (measure 2), "**3**–2–3–4" (measure 3), "**4**–2–3–4" (measure 4).

Chord Chart

Many of the songs you have played and the next few songs are notated as *chord charts*. *Chord charts* are a common way to notate music for guitar. It is assumed that you will choose an appropriate strum pattern.

12-Bar Blues Form

The *12-bar blues* is a 12-bar song form is an important part of American music and is commonly found in blues, pop, rock, country, jazz, funk and folk styles.

Here is an example of a 12-bar blues with Roman numerals:

12-BAR BLUES — UNIVERSAL CHORD NOTATION *(Chord Progression)*

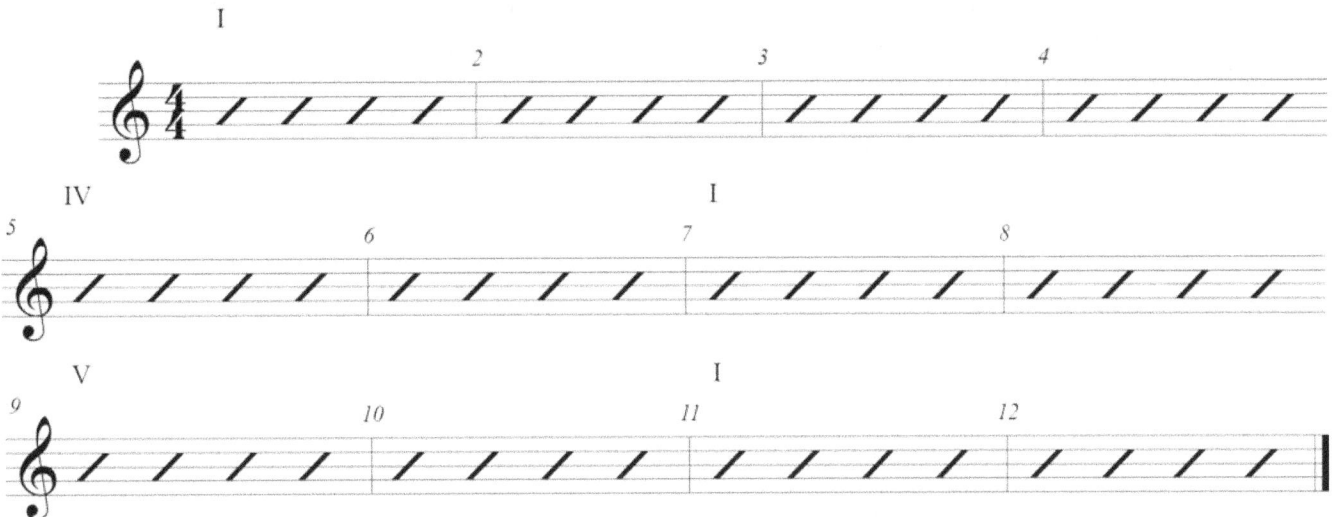

In the key of G, the I chord = G, the IV chord = C, and the V chord = D, so the universal progression translated to the key of G looks like this:

12-BAR BLUES — KEY OF G *(Chord Progression)*

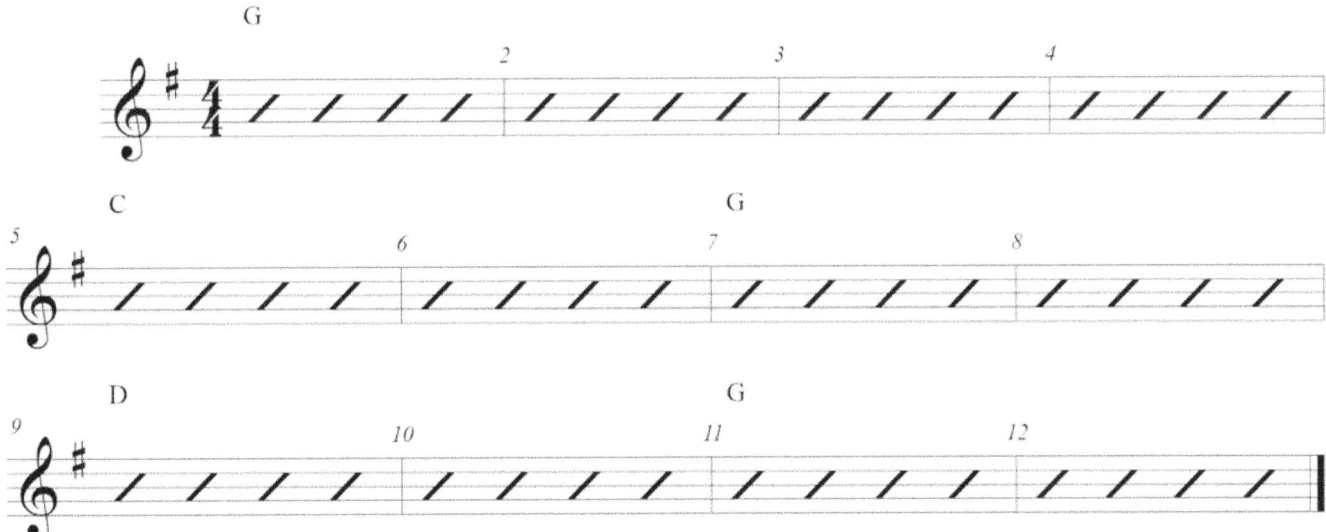

Play & Do… Video examples at *www.bestmusicpublications.com*
- Listen to the recorded version of "12-Bar Blues in the key of G" — *counting the measures* and say the count using the measure counting method.
- Listen to the recorded version of "12-Bar Blues in the key of G" — *saying the chord names while counting* and substitute the chord name for beat 1. Then count the remaining measures using the measure counting method.
- Play "12-Bar Blues in G."
- Play along with the recorded version of "12-Bar Blues in G."

Adding *Stops* to the 12-Bar Blues

A common variation to a 12-bar Blues is to add stops to the form. *Stop(s)* is the term we use to describe having the accompaniment part *stop* (rest) at certain times to allow for a soloist to fill the space left by the stop or rest. Stops usually occur in the first four measures of the 12-Bar Blues form. The accompaniment will only play on beat one of each of the first four measures. *Stops* are often added for solos or variation. Here is a 12-bar form in the key of G with *stops*:

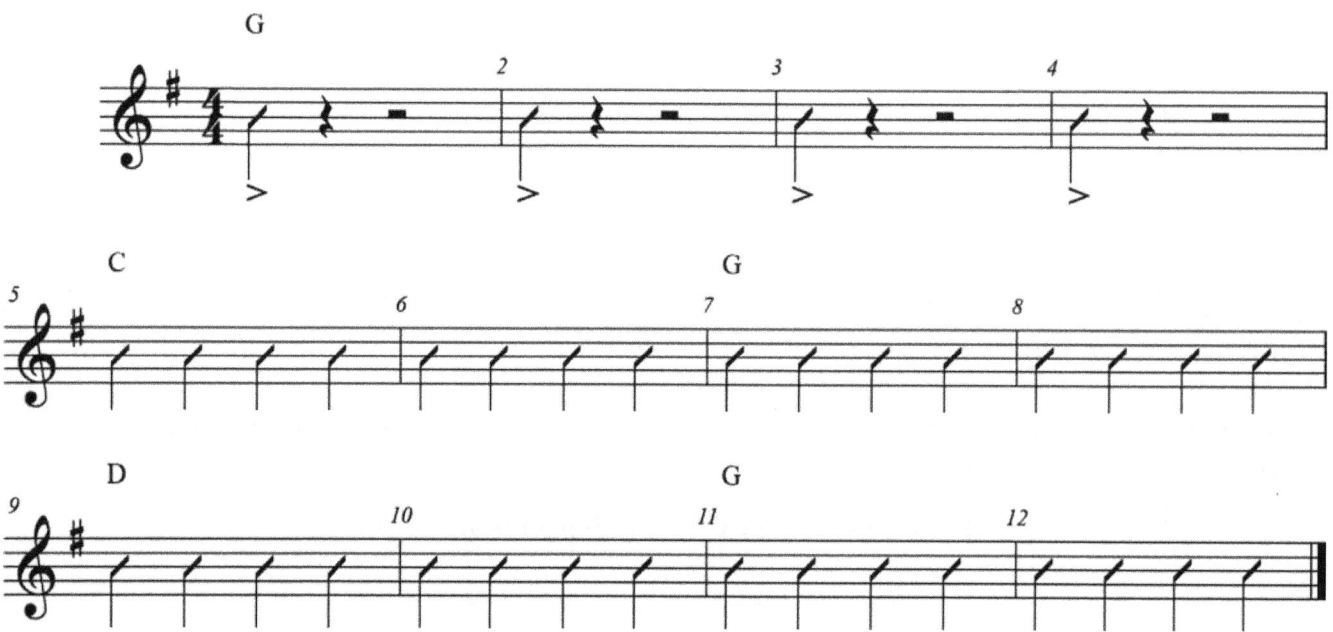

Examples of common songs that follow the 12-bar blues form and have stops are:

- "Johnny B. Goode" by Chuck Berry
- "Sweet Home Chicago" by Robert Johnson (listen to the Blues Brothers recording)
- "Kansas City" by Jerry Leiber and Mike Stoller (listen to the Little Richard recording)

 **Play & Do...** Video examples at *www.bestmusicpublications.com*

- Listen to the recorded version of "12-Bar Blues in G" with stops and play along.

LESSON 13

Adding Root Notes to any Song

Lesson Concept
- Adding Root Notes on Beat 1

Adding Root Notes on Beat 1

A common technique to add variation to a strum pattern and to highlight beat 1 is to substitute the root note of the chord for beat 1 in the pattern. Here are examples of the first three strum patterns you learned, but now showing how you would notate (and play) the root (bass) note of a standard G chord:

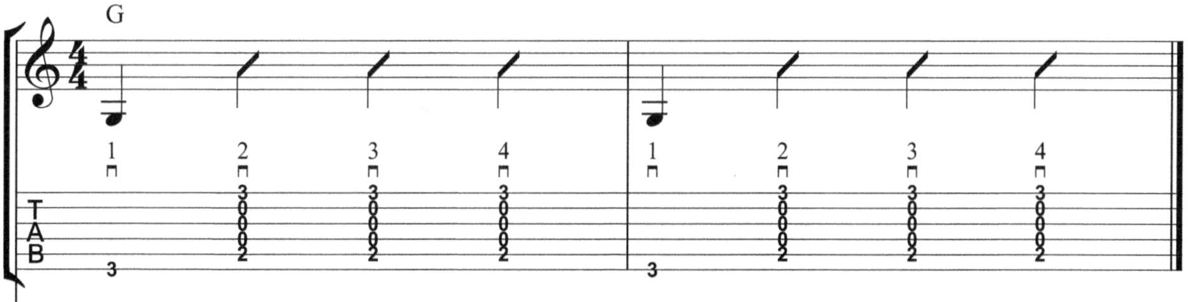

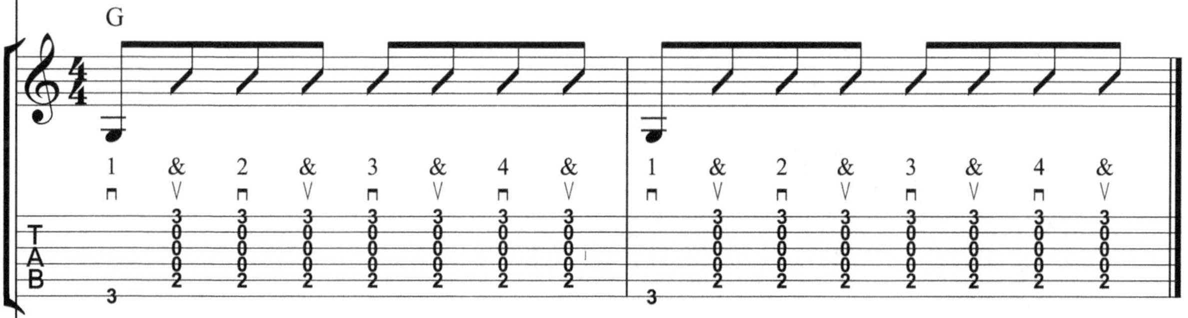

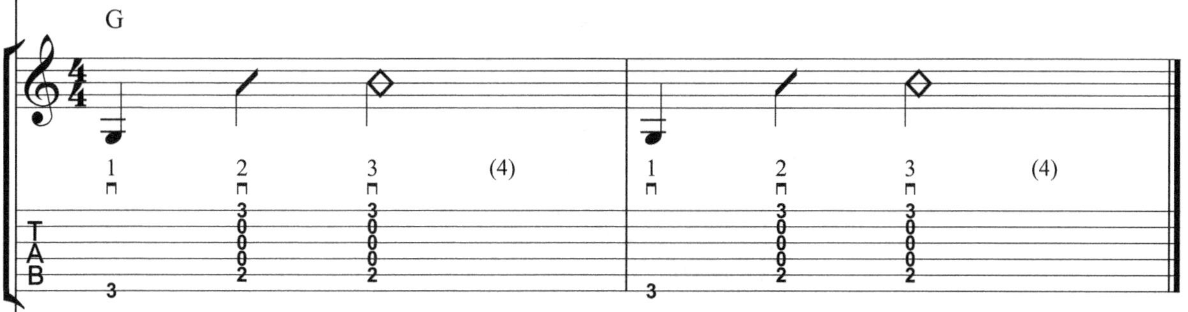

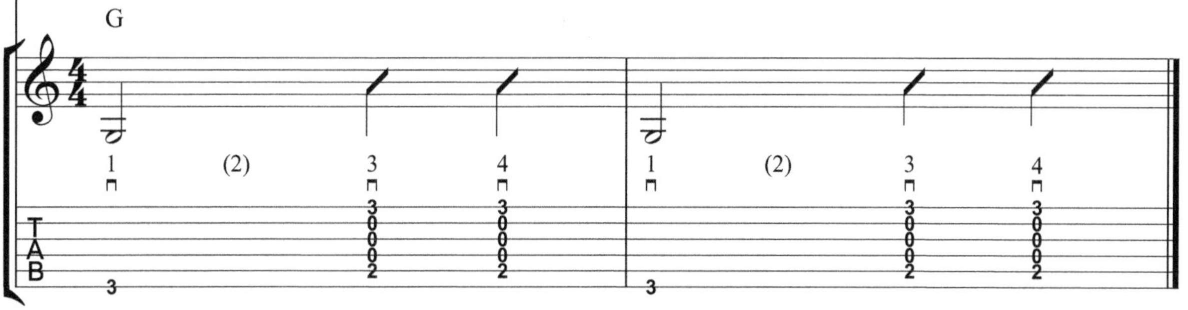

THE BEST GUITAR METHOD

Play & Do... Video examples at *www.bestmusicpublications.com*

- Listen to the recorded version of *Strum Pattern #1 with bass notes on beat 1*.
- Play along using a G chord with the recorded version of *Strum Pattern #1 with bass notes on beat 1*.
- Repeat the previous steps for with patterns 2–4.

LESSON 14

Finding the Root Note of a Chord

Lesson Concept
- Root Notes

Root Notes

In the previous section, you learned the root note for G chord is on the sixth string. From now on, whenever you learn a new chord, *you must also memorize which note is the root* of each chord. Usually, the lowest string that you play is the root note if that note is the same as the letter name of the chord. In the case of the G chord, the lowest note that you strum is a G note.

If you look closely at the standard chord fingerings below, you will notice at the bottom of each fingering there is a row of letters and below that, a row of numbers. The row of letters indicates the note names of each of the notes you play in a chord. The numbers are another way of thinking about the note which you will learn about in the future.

Standard

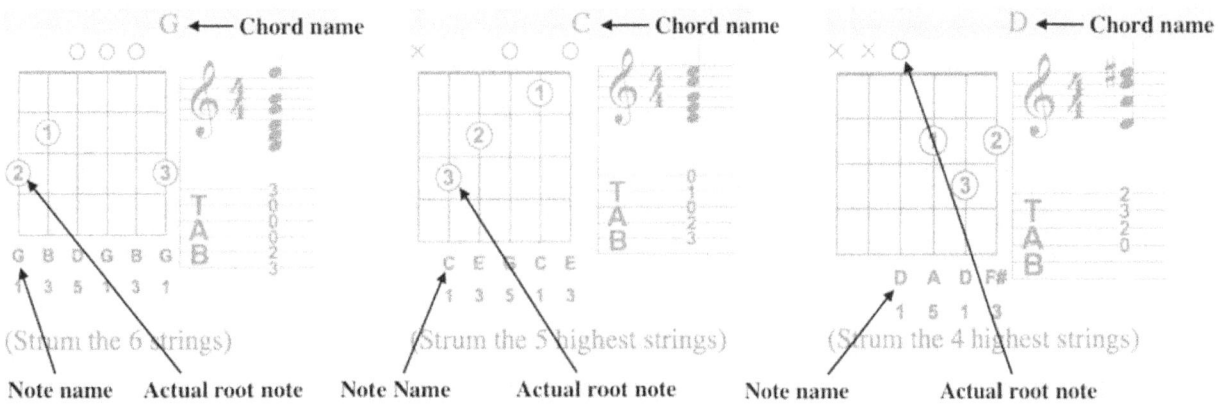

For the primary chords in the Key of G, you pluck the fretted sixth string as the root note of a G chord, the fretted fifth string as the root of the C chord and the open fourth string as the root of the D chord. If you are still using the simplified versions of the chords, it is time to start using the standard forms because the simplified forms of the G and C chord, because the simplified forms do not have the root note as the lowest note!

Play & Do... Video examples at *www.bestmusicpublications.com*

- Practice playing the root note of each of the primary chords in the Key of G.

LESSON 15

"Oh My Darling, Clementine" (Song)

Lesson Concept
- "Oh My Darling Clementine" (Song)

OH MY DARLING, CLEMENTINE
WITH ROOT NOTES

(Percy Montrose)

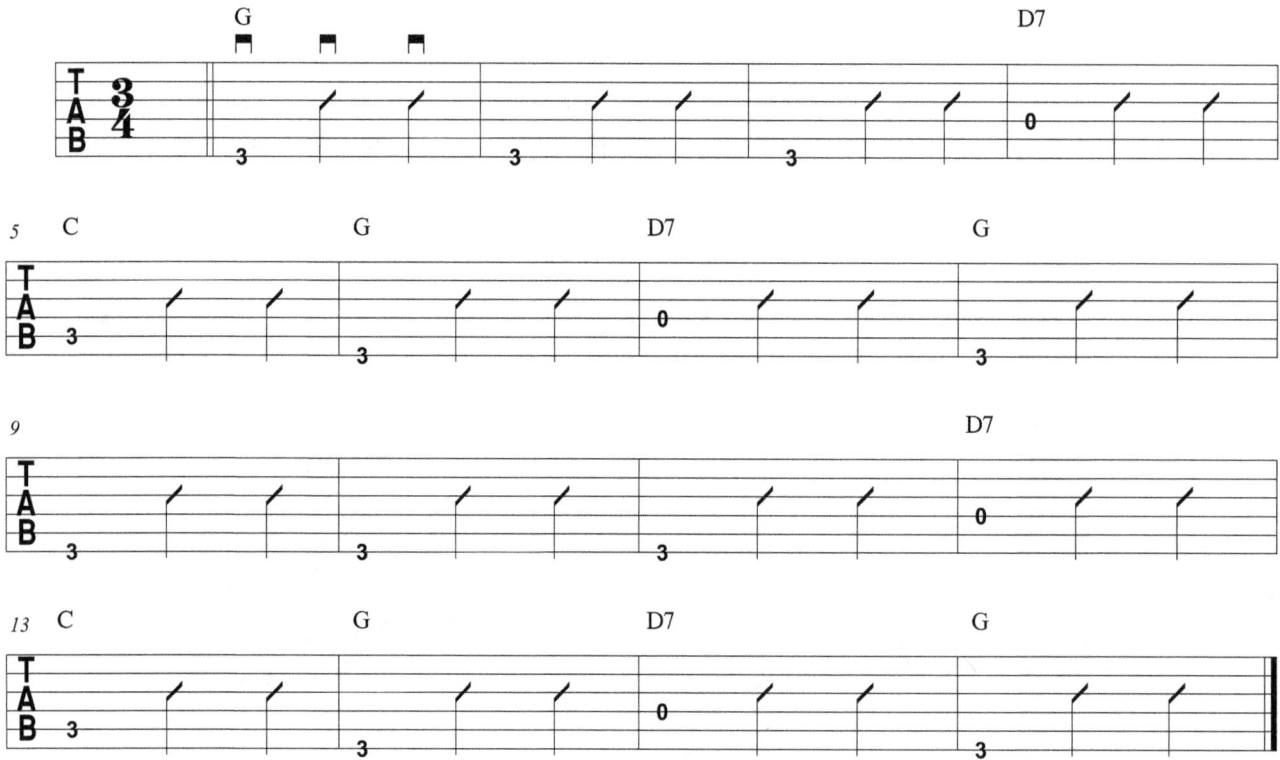

Play & Do... Video examples at *www.bestmusicpublications.com*

- Listen to the recording of "Oh My Darling Clementine."
- Play "Oh My Darling Clementine" as shown in the written music.
- Play along with the recording of "Oh My Darling Clementine."
- Play "Oh My Darling Clementine" and try using pattern #6 of the basic 3/4 strum patterns from Unit 2 / Lesson 9.
- Play "Oh My Darling Clementine" and try using pattern #6 of the basic 3/4 strum patterns from Unit 2 / Lesson 9 and substitute the root note of each chord for beat one.

UNIT TWO • REVIEW AND SUMMARY

Review and Summary

You should be able to demonstrate and identify the following skills:

- Primary chords in the key of G with their Roman numeral equivalents
- Count and play all the strum patterns from Unit 2
- Count and keep track of up to 8 measures
- Explain the form and play the "12-Bar Blues in the Key of G"
- Play any song from Unit 2 with the recordings
- Play all songs using root notes on beat one

Right-hand strumming techniques:

- Thumb (down and up)
- Brush stroke
- Nail stroke

Right-hand strumming technique with a pick:

- Pick grip
- Arm motion

UNIT 3

Notes in the Key of G on the Highest Three Strings

LESSON 1

Notes — B, A, and G

> **Lesson Concepts**
> - 5-Line Staff
> - Treble Clef
> - Lines and Spaces
> - Rhythms — Notes and Rests
> - Notes: B, A, G
> - Left-Hand Position

5-Line Staff — Treble Clef

Standard notation uses a *5-line staff*. The staff itself has no note reference until it has a *clef* is added to the staff. The guitar is written in the *treble clef*. (Figure 3.1.1)

Figure 3.1.1

Lines and Spaces

In *standard notation*, the lines and spaces of the staff represent note names. In treble clef, the note names are shown in Figure 3.1.1

Rhythms — Notes and Rests

There is a parallel and relative system of symbols to represent notes (sound) and rests (silence). Figure 3.1.2 shows the symbols for notes and rests and the relative relationships between the symbols.

Figure 3.1.2

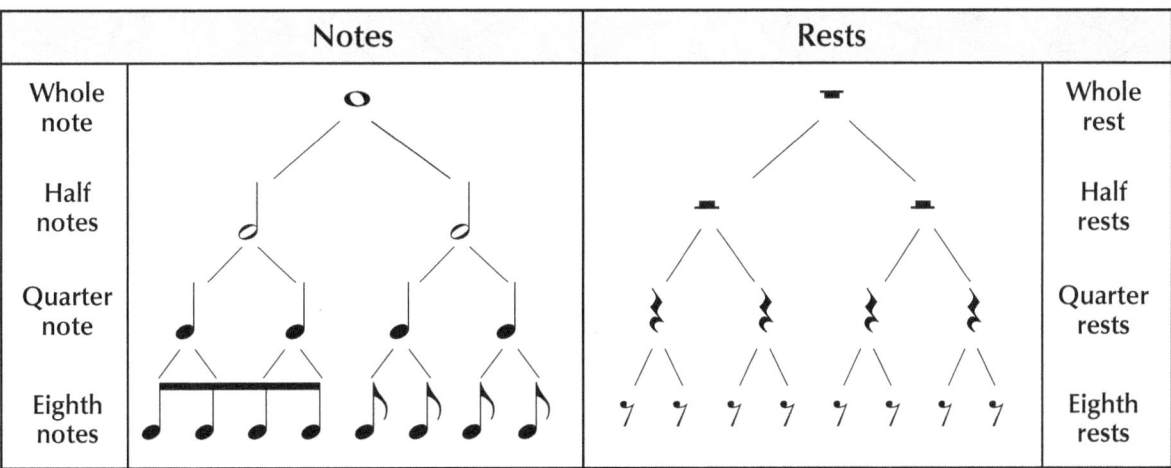

Notes B, A, G

Notes are the symbols for individual pitches. For example, when you pluck the third string open, you are playing the *open note* "G." If you push the string down the third string on the second fret and pluck that string, you are playing the *fretted note* "A."

45

In standard notation, you will notice that:

- The B note is written on the center *line* on the staff.
- The A note is written on the *space* below the center *line* on the staff.
- The G note is written on the *line* that is second from the bottom on the staff.

The first three notes you will learn are B, A, and G, shown four different ways: as a picture, as a *neck grid*, in *standard notation*, and in *tablature notation*. Here is how you play them:

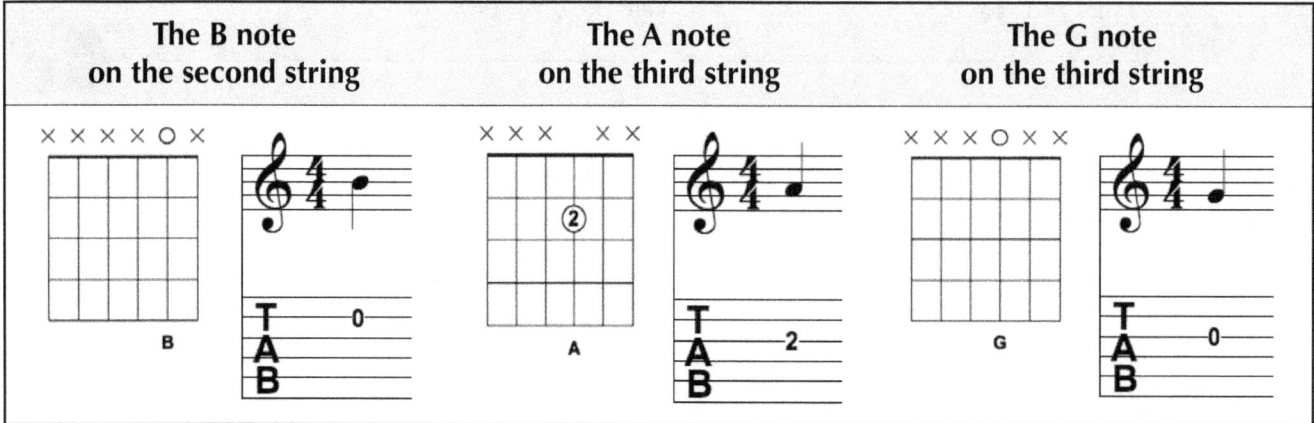

Left-Hand Position

Keep your left-hand fingers "ready" to play any note even if the note you are playing is an open note like B or G. Figure 3.1.2 shows how to hold your left-hand fingers above the strings when you play a B or G note, so you are "ready" to finger the A note. Figure 3.1.3 shows how your left-hand fingers should be held when fingering an A note.

Figure 3.1.3

Figure 3.1.4

Play & Do... Video examples at *www.bestmusicpublications.com*

- Play the B note and pluck with either a pick, finger or thumb. Say or sing the note name as you play it. Look at the standard notation for the B note as you do this exercise.
- Repeat the first two steps with the A and G notes.
- Randomly play the notes B, A, and G in any order. You can repeat notes. Say the names as you play them! Be sure to use the correct finger for fretted notes. Use a variety of right-hand techniques including: pick, standard finger assignment, alternating index and middle fingers, and thumb.

LESSON 2

How to Practice Song Melodies and Chords from Written Music

> **Lesson Concepts**
> - Chords and Melodies
> - Breaking Down the Learning Process into Small Steps

Chords and Melodies

All the songs in this book now include chords and often include notated melodies. When the melodies are notated, they use notes and rhythms that you have already learned. Be sure to *practice playing both the chords* (choose a strum pattern, if one isn't provided!) *and the single note melodies*. When playing the melodies, you should play them with and without a pick. As you play these songs, keep your eyes on the printed music. Each recorded example repeats four times.

Breaking Down the Learning Process into Small Steps

When trying to learn to read standard notation on the guitar, breaking the music reading process into smaller steps will help you learn faster. Remember, when trying to learn new songs, always break down the process using this 10-step technique:

Step 1: Listen to the recording of the song and become familiar with the song.

Step 2: Listen to the recording of the song and count out loud while you are listening.

Step 3: Listen to the recorded version of the song and count out loud while you follow the written music notation by pointing to the notes as they are played.

Step 4: Say the names of the notes as you point to the notes and look for any repeating patterns or measures.

Step 5: Listen to the recorded version of the song and say the names of the notes as they are played while you point to the notes.

Step 6: Play the rhythms on one note (or chord) while you count out loud.

Step 7: Play the notes or chords of the song on your guitar while saying the names of the notes or chords out loud.

Step 8: Play the notes or chords of the song on your guitar while counting out loud and focusing on the correct rhythms.

Step 9: Play the song by yourself.

Step 10: Play along with the recorded version of the song.

Be sure repeat steps 6–10 using a pick and then without a pick for the melodies. Also, repeat steps 6–10 to be able to play the chords of the song as well.

When you play melodies without a pick, *plant* your thumb (P) on the fourth string and use your index finger (I) to pluck the third string, your middle finger (M) to pluck the second string and your ring finger (A) to pluck the first string. You should use free strokes.

Lesson 3

"G to B — Changing Strings" (Song)

Lesson Concepts
- "G to B Changing — Strings" (Song)

Note: You can lightly rest your middle, ring and little fingers on the top of the guitar when you use a pick to steady your right hand. When using a pick, play the eight notes "down-up."

G TO B — CHANGING STRINGS

(Brian K. Rivers)

Play & Do... Video examples at *www.bestmusicpublications.com*

- Practice picking the 2nd and 3rd strings alternating between each string. Lightly rest your middle, ring and little fingers on the top of the guitar when you use a pick to steady your right hand.
- Go through the 10-step process for learning the melody to the song "G to B Changing Strings." Use a variety of right-hand techniques including: pick, standard finger assignment, alternating index and middle fingers, and thumb.
- Go through steps 6–10 of the 10-step process for the song "G to B Changing Strings" playing the chords *using a pick*. Choose any strum pattern in 4/4 time.

LESSON 4

"G to A — Keeping Your Left-Hand Fingers Ready" (Song)

Lesson Concepts
- G to A — Keeping Your Left-Hand Fingers Ready" (Song)

When you play this song, you should practice it both with and without a pick. To start, set your left-hand playing the A note. Remember the three P's of tone production from Unit 2 / Lesson 1. Always keep your second finger hovering over the second fret of the third string ready to fret the A note. When you are playing the G note, set your thumb position while fretting the A note, because your thumb should never move when changing from the A note to the G note.

When using a pick, play the eight notes "down-up."

G TO A — KEEPING YOUR LEFT-HAND FINGERS READY
(Brian Rivers)

Play & Do... Video examples at *www.bestmusicpublications.com*

- Go through the 10-step process for learning the melody to the song "G to A — Keeping Your Fingers Ready." Use a variety of right-hand techniques including: pick, standard finger assignment, alternating index and middle fingers, and thumb.
- Go through steps 6–10 of the 10-step process for the song (no pick), playing the chords *using a pick*. Choose any strum pattern in 4/4 time.

LESSON 5

"Hot Crossed Buns" with Melody (Song)

Lesson Concepts
- "Hot Cross Buns" with Melody (Song)

HOT CROSS BUNS
WITH MELODY

(Traditional)

Hot cross buns! Hot cross buns! One a pen-ny, two a pen-ny, hot cross buns!

Play & Do... Video examples at *www.bestmusicpublications.com*

- Go through the 10-step process for learning the melody to the song "Hot Cross Buns with Melody." Use a variety of right-hand techniques including: pick, standard finger assignment, alternating index and middle fingers, and thumb.
- Go through steps 6–10 of the 10-step process for the song "Hot Cross Buns with Melody," playing the chords *using a pick*. Choose any strum pattern in 4/4 time.

LESSON 6

More Notes — C and D

> *Lesson Concepts*
> - The Notes C and D on the Second String
> - Left-Hand Position

The Notes C and D on the Second String

The next two notes, C and D, are *fretted notes* on the second string.

Notes

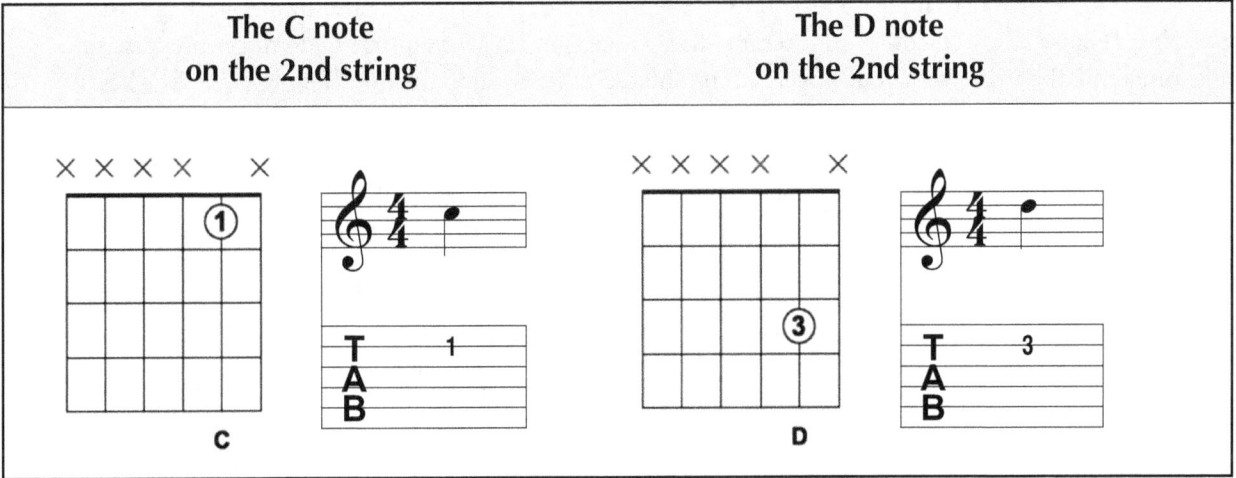

Left-Hand Position

Remember to keep your unused left-hand fingers "ready" to play any other notes.

Play & Do... Video examples at *www.bestmusicpublications.com*

- Play the C note and pluck it using a variety of right-hand techniques including; pick, standard finger assignment, alternating index and middle fingers and thumb. Say or sing the note name as you play it. Look at the standard notation for the C note as you do this exercise.
- Now, repeat the first two steps with the D note.
- Randomly play the notes G, A, B, C, and D in any order using a variety of right-hand techniques including; pick, standard finger assignment, alternating index and middle fingers and thumb. You can repeat notes and say the names as you play them! Be sure to use the correct finger for fretted notes!

51

LESSON 7

"Aura Lee" (Song)

> **Lesson Concepts**
> - Rests
> - "Aura Lee" (Song)

Rests

The song "Aura Lee" has a half note rest in measures 4 and 8. A rest means silence, so you must stop (mute) the C note from sounding. One way to mute the C note is to use the side of your right-hand thumb to rest against the second string. (Figure 3.7.1) The other way to mute the C note is to release your left-hand finger pressure so you are still contacting the string with your finger, but not holding the string to the fret. (Figure 3.7.2) The best way to mute the C note is to combine both techniques.

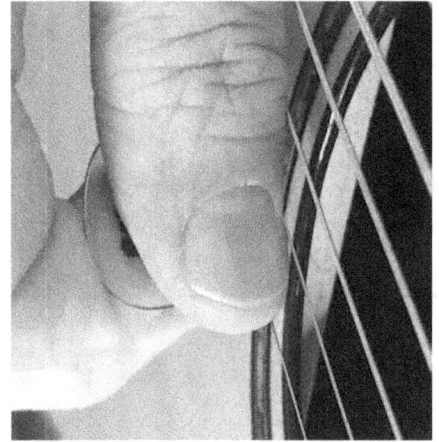

Figure 3.7.1

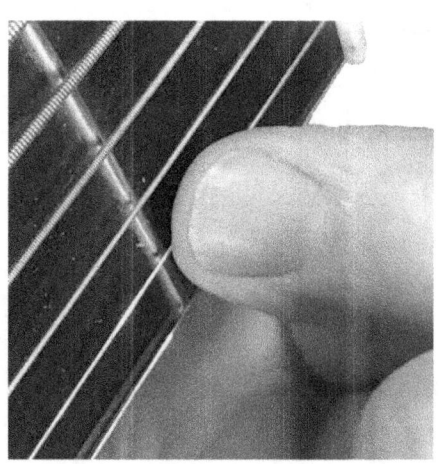

Figure 3.7.2

AURA LEE

(American Civil War Song*)

* *If this melody sounds familiar, it is, indeed, the melody used for Elvis Presley's "Love Me Tender."*

UNIT THREE • LESSON 7

Play & Do... Video examples at *www.bestmusicpublications.com*

- Practice muting the C note with each muting technique, and then combining the techniques.
- Go through the 10-step process for learning the melody to the song "Aura Lee." Use a variety of right-hand techniques including: pick, standard finger assignment, alternating index and middle fingers, and thumb.
- Go through steps 6–10 of the 10-step process for the song "Aura Lee," playing the chords *using a pick*. Choose any strum pattern in 4/4 time.

LESSON 8

"German Waltz" (Song)

> **Lesson Concepts**
> - "German Waltz" (Song)

GERMAN WALTZ

(Theobald Boehm)

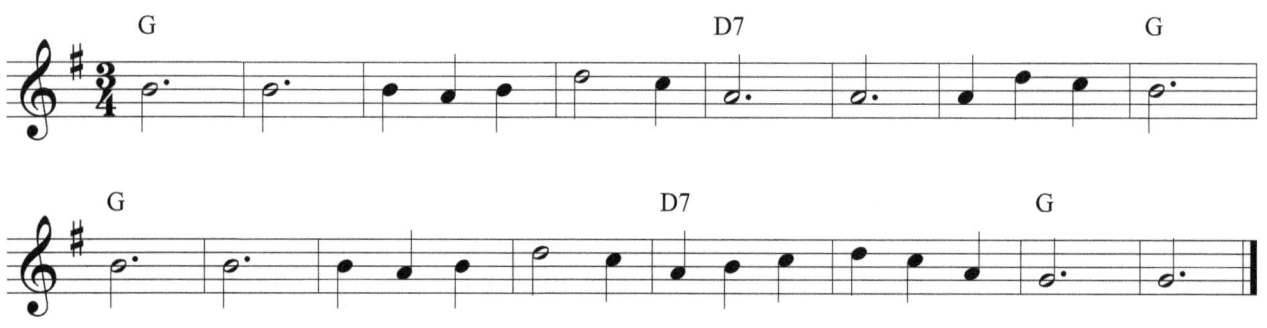

Play & Do... Video examples at *www.bestmusicpublications.com*

- Go through the 10-step process for learning the melody to the song "German Waltz." Use a variety of right-hand techniques including: pick, standard finger assignment, alternating index and middle fingers, and thumb.
- Go through steps 6–10 of the 10-step process for the song "German Waltz," playing the chords *using a pick*. Choose any strum pattern in 4/4 time.

LESSON 9

More Notes — E, F♯, and G

> **Lesson Concepts**
> - Notes: E, F♯, and G
> - Left-Hand Positiion

Notes

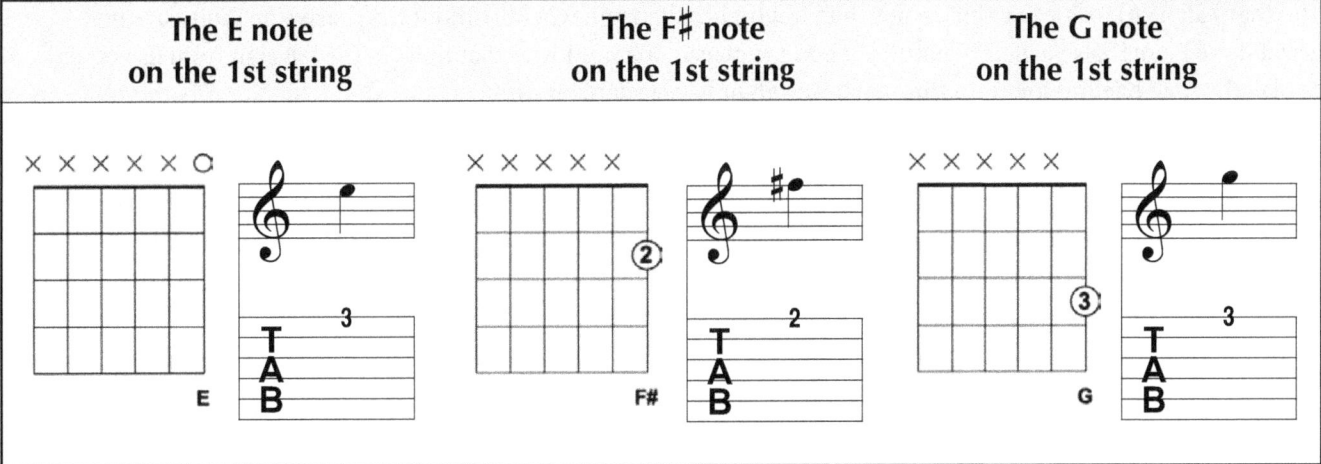

Left-Hand Position

Remember to keep your unused left-hand fingers "ready" to play any other notes.

Play & Do... Video examples at *www.bestmusicpublications.com*

- Play and pluck each of the three notes using a variety of right-hand techniques including: pick, standard finger assignment, alternating index and middle fingers, and thumb. Say or sing the note name as you play it. Look at the standard notation for each note as you do this exercise.
- Randomly play the notes G, A, B, C, D, E, F♯, and G in any order using a variety of right-hand techniques including: pick, standard finger assignment, alternating index and middle fingers, and thumb. You can repeat notes and say the names as you play them. Be sure to use the correct finger for fretted notes!

55

LESSON 10

G Major Scale and Key Signatures

> **Lesson Concepts**
> - Sharp and Flat Signs
> - Key Signature
> - G Major Scale

Sharp and Flat Signs

The sharp sign (♯) tells you to play a note one fret higher than you would without the sharp sign. You have not learned the F note (also called "F natural"), but it is played one fret lower that the F♯. The flat sign (♭) tells you to play the note one fret lower. In this book, we will only use sharp signs.

Key Signatures

In this example, a key signature is used to indicate the key at the beginning of the piece of music. It indicates that *all the F notes should be played as F♯*. The key signature appears directly to the right of the treble clef, and the sharp sign (♯) is located on the F line. The F♯ indicates that all F notes are sharp even if they appear elsewhere on the staff, not just on the top line.

G Major Scale

When you play the *G major scale*, remember to play all down strokes.

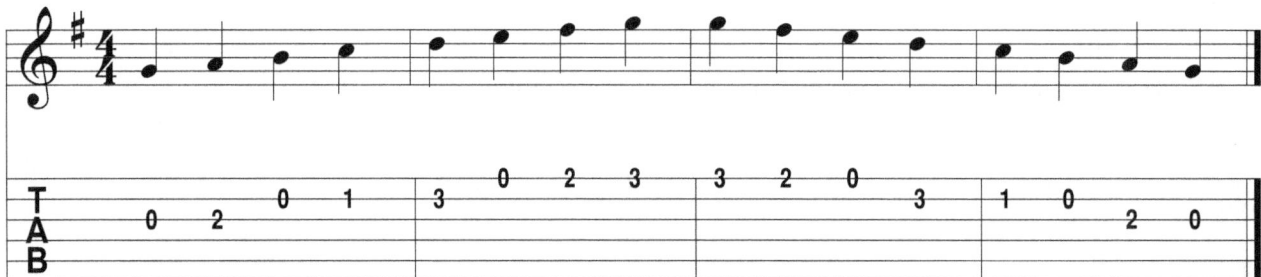

Play & Do... Video examples at *www.bestmusicpublications.com*

- Play the G major scale using a variety of right-hand techniques including; pick, standard finger assignment, alternating index and middle fingers, and thumb. Repeat ten times. Be sure to use the correct finger for fretted notes!

LESSON 11

Dotted Quarter Note Rhythm

Lesson Concepts
- Dotted Quarter Note
- Musical Math

Dotted Quarter Note

When a dot is added directly after a quarter note (or rest), it is known as a dotted quarter note. The dot adds half the value to the note or rest that the dot follows. A quarter note or rest is equal to one beat while a dotted quarter note or rest is worth 1 + ½ beats, or 1½ beats total.

Musical Math

Think of a dotted quarter note as *musical math*:

$$\quarter\text{.} = \quarter + \eighth$$

A dotted quarter note is the same as a quarter note tied to an eighth note:

$$\quarter \;\tie\; \eighth = \quarter\text{.}$$

The next lesson has an example of a song that includes the dotted quarter note rhythms, and how to count them.

Lesson 12

"Merrily We Roll Along" (Song)

Lesson Concepts
- "Merrily We Roll Along" (Song) with Melody and Counts and Picking Notation
- "Merrily We Roll Along" (Song) with Melody and Lyrics

"MERRILY WE ROLL ALONG" – MELODY WITH COUNTS AND PICKING NOTATION

(Traditional)

"MERRILY WE ROLL ALONG" WITH MELODY AND LYRICS

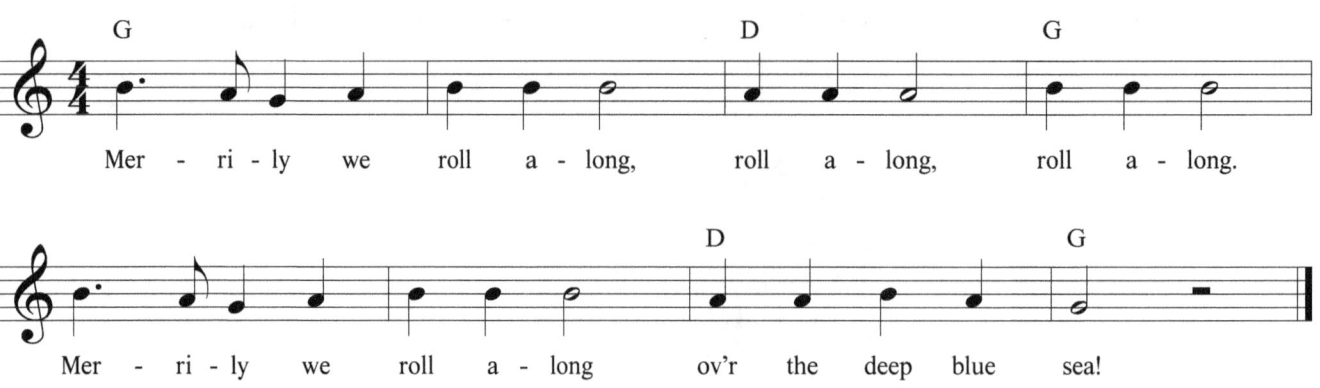

Play & Do... Video examples at www.bestmusicpublications.com

- Play the melody of "Merrily We Roll Along" using a variety of right-hand techniques including: pick, standard finger assignment, alternating index and middle fingers, and thumb. Be sure to use the correct fingers for fretted notes!
- Play the chords of "Merrily We Roll Along" *using a pick*. Choose any strum pattern in 4/4 time.
- Repeat the first two steps while playing along with the recorded music.

58

Lesson 13

Dynamics and Dynamic Markings

Lesson Concepts
- Dynamics
- Dynamic Markings
- Crescendo and Decrescendo/Diminuendo Markings

Dynamics

The term *dynamics* is used to describe the loudness or softness of the music. A change in volume adds a new dimension to music by adding additional drama and impact.

Dynamic Markings

Dynamics are divided into eight levels, from quietest to loudest.

Dynamic Marking	Italian Word	English Meaning
ppp	Pianississimo	Very very quiet
pp	Pianissimo	Very quiet
p	Piano	Quiet
mp	Mezzo Piano	Medium quiet
mf	Mezzo Forte	Medium loud
f	Forte	Loud
ff	Fortissimo	Very loud
fff	Fortississimo	Very very loud

Crescendo, Decrescendo, and Diminuendo Markings

Crescendo, *decrescendo*, and *diminuendo* marks are other forms of *dynamic* markings that indicate a gradual change in volume instead of a sudden change in volume.

Dynamic Marking	Abbreviation	Italian Word	English Meaning
⟨	*cresc.*	Crescendo	Gradually becoming louder
⟩	*decreas.*	Decrescendo	Gradually becoming softer
	dim.	Diminuendo	Gradually becoming softer

Play & Do... Video examples at *www.bestmusicpublications.com*

- Play the G major scale (Unit 3 / Lesson 10) and start insert *p* (quietly) and crescendo to insert *f* (loud) as you ascend the scale from the low G to the high G. Then decrescendo from insert *f* to *p* as you descend from the high G to the low G.
- Repeat the above steps from *pp* to *ff*.
- Choose one note and play repeating eighth notes using a pick. Then, alternating fingering with the right hand, play from *pp* to *ff* while keeping the eighth notes at a steady tempo.
  Tip: When using a pick, use a relaxed pick grip to play quieter and a firm pick grip to play louder.

LESSON 14

"Ode to Joy" (Song)

Lesson Concepts
- "Ode to Joy" (Song) Guitar 1
- "Ode to Joy" (Song) Guitar 2

ODE TO JOY
From Symphony #9

(Ludwig van Beethoven)

Guitar 1

Guitar 2

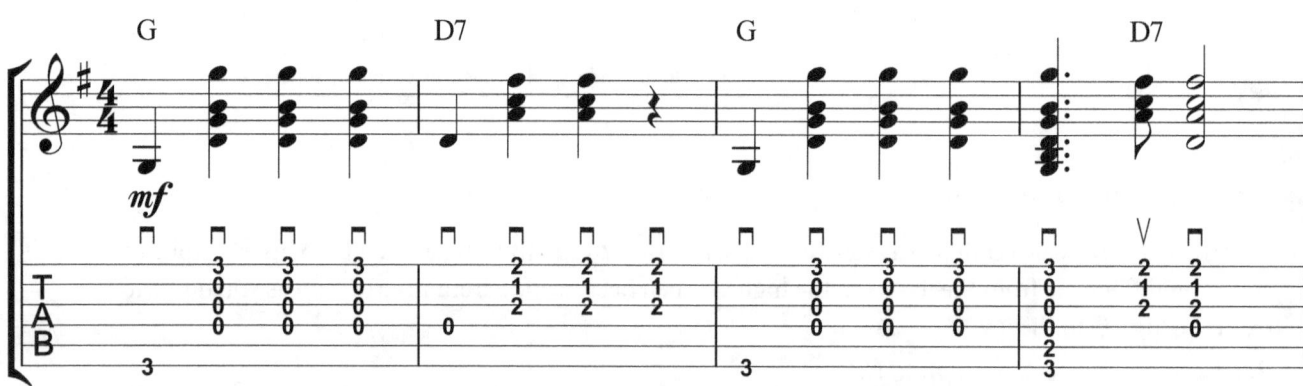

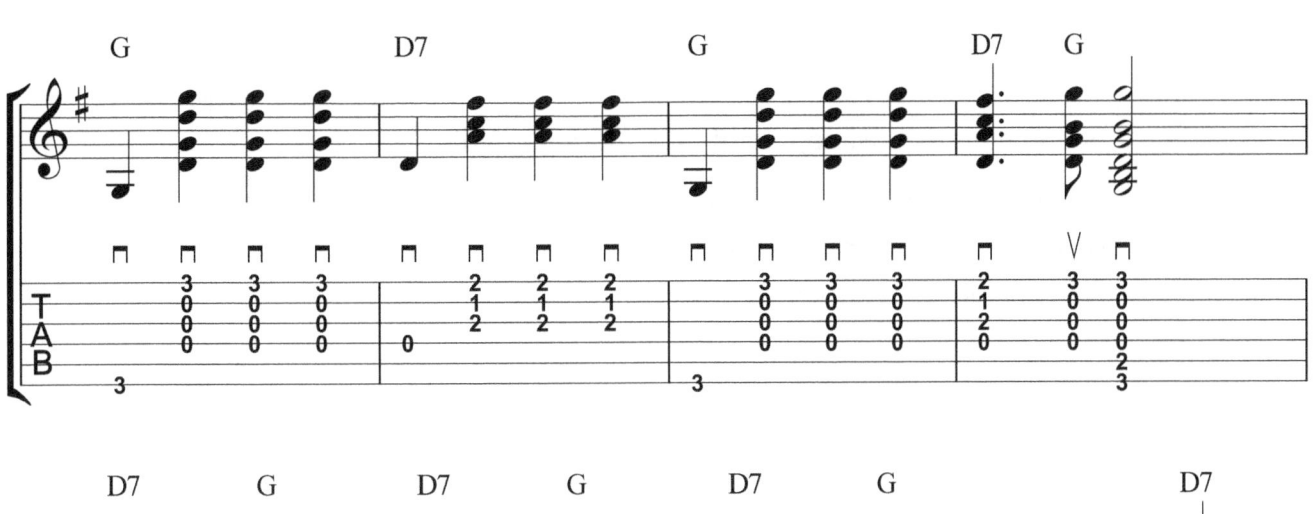

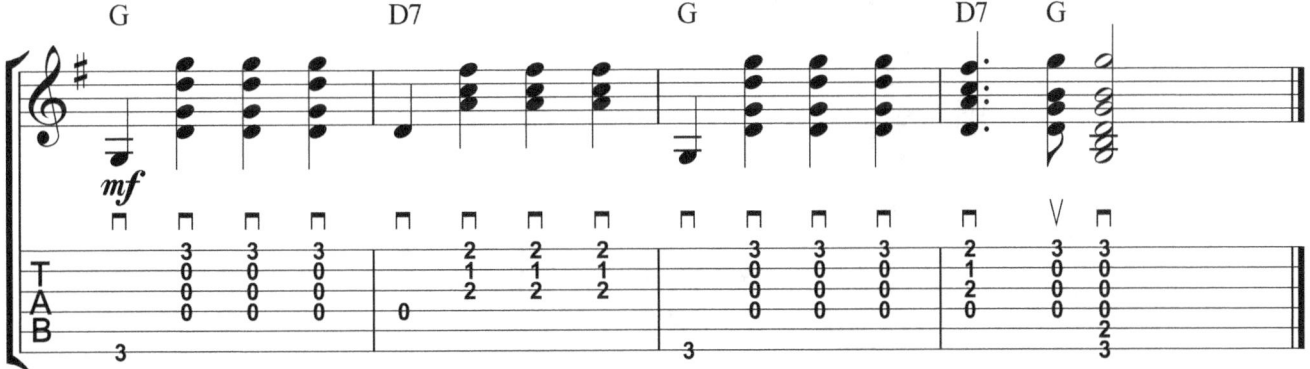

 **Play & Do…** Video examples at *www.bestmusicpublications.com*

- Play the melody to "Ode to Joy" using a variety of right-hand techniques including: pick, standard finger assignment, alternating index and middle fingers, and thumb. Be sure to use the correct fingers for fretted notes!
- Play the chord accompaniment to "Ode to Joy" playing the chords *using a pick*.
- Play the chord accompaniment to "Ode to Joy" playing the chords *using your right-hand fingers*. Only play the highest three strings with your fingers [assigned fingering], except when there are six notes in the chord, in which case you strum all six strings with your thumb.
- Repeat the first three steps while playing along with the recorded music.

Review and Summary

You should be able to demonstrate and identify the following skills:

- Play and read the notes G, A, B, C, D, E, F♯, and G
- Play eighth, quarter, dotted quarter, half, dotted half and whole note rhythms
- Play a G major scale (one octave) from memory
- Read TAB Notation
- Play Dynamics at six levels from *pp* to *ff*
- Play any part in any song from Unit 3 with the recordings

Unit 4

Secondary Chords in the Key of G

Am, Bm and Em (ii–iii–vi)

LESSON 1

Secondary Chords in the Key of G — Am, Bm, and Em (ii, iii, vi)

> *Lesson Concepts*
> - Secondary Chords in the Key of G — Am, Bm, and Em (ii, iii, vi)
> - Standard Fingerings for the Secondary Chords in the Key of G — Am, Bm, and Em (ii, iii, vi)
> - Simplified and Challenge Chords Fingerings

Secondary Chords in the Key of G — Am, Bm, and Em (ii, iii, vi)

The secondary chords in any major key are always *minor* chords. In the key of G, they are Am (ii), Bm (iii) and Em (vi). *Lower case Roman numerals represent minor chords.* Minor chords are represented with the letter name of the chord followed by either an "m" or a "min" and occasionally a "—" symbol. Therefore, Am, Amin or A— are the same—all indicating "A minor."

Standard Fingerings for the Secondary Chords in the Key of G — Am, Bm, and Em (ii, iii, vi)

Am or ii	Bm or iii	Em or vi

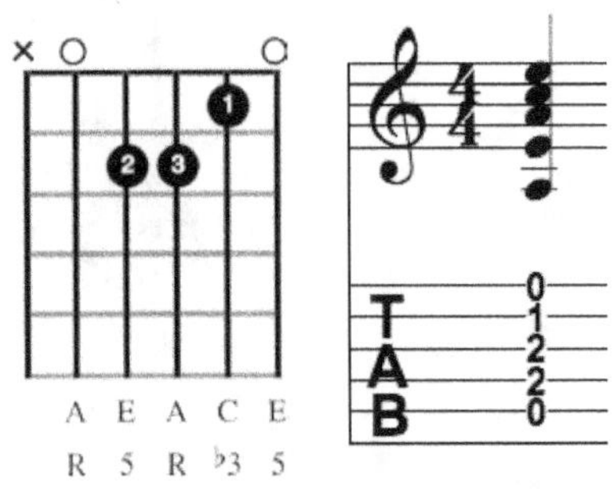

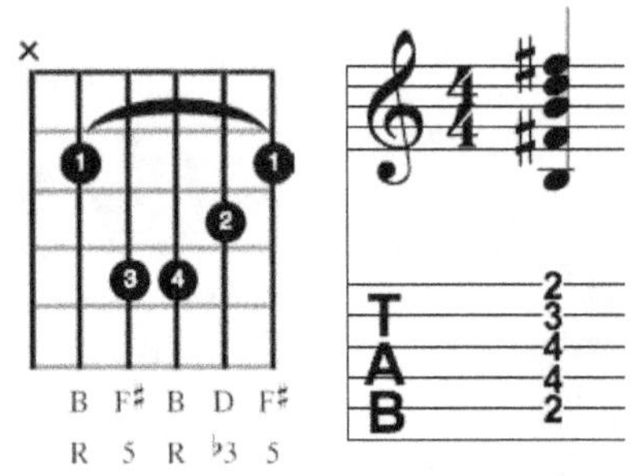

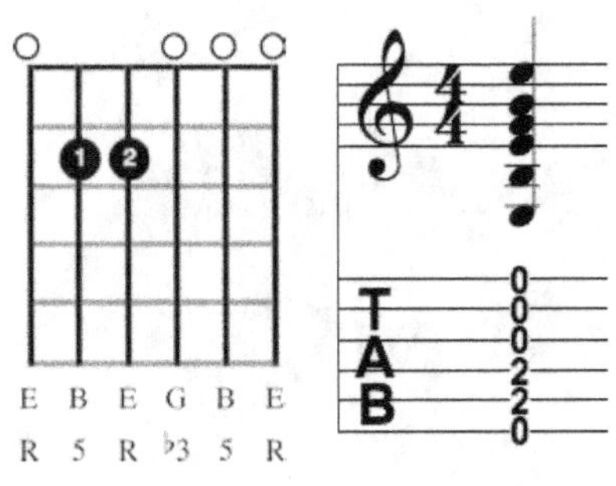

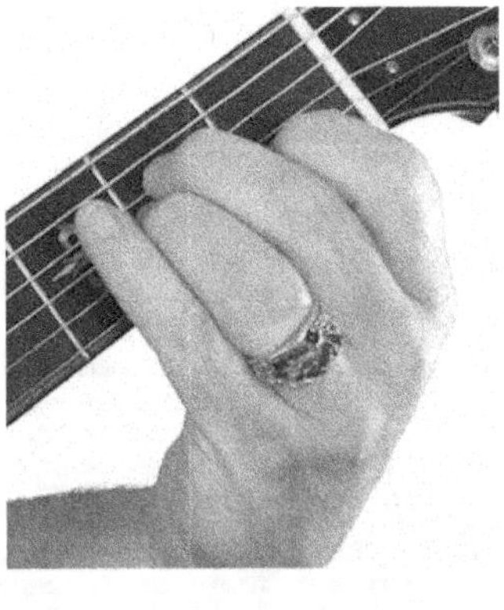

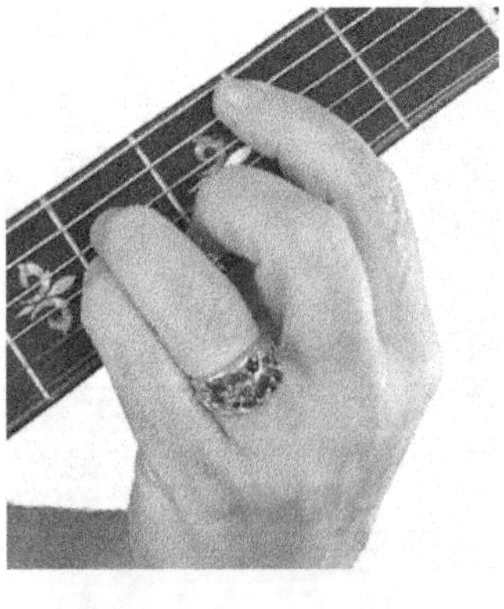

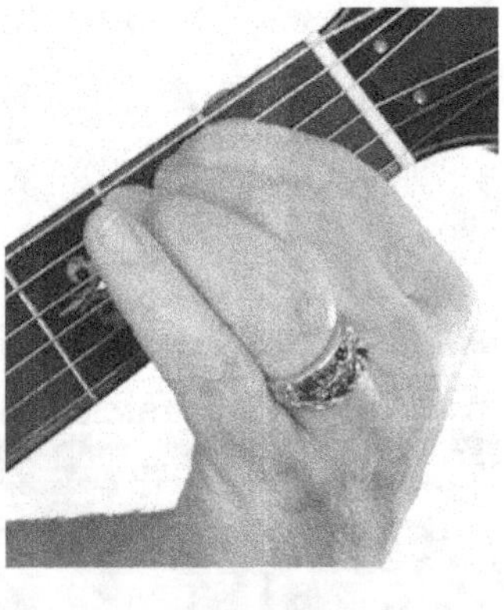

Simplified and Challenge Chords Fingerings

Simplified and challenge chords fingerings for all the chords in this book can be found at *www.bestmusicpublications.com*

Play & Do... Video examples at *www.bestmusicpublications.com*

- Finger (play) each chord and be mindful of the three P's of tone production, picking each string of the chord to be sure each string is making a pleasant sound. Make sure to say the name of the chord as you play it!
- "Catch and release" each chord 25 times. Strum the chord as you apply pressure and then check that each string is still sounding good. If it's not, go back and check the three P's of tone production.
- Recite the specific names and universal names for the secondary chords in the key of G. Say: "The secondary chords in the key of G are: A minor — also known as the ii chord, B minor — also known as the iii chord, and E minor — also known as the vi chord."
- Fill in the universal primary and secondary chord names for the key of G in the spaces below:

I = _____   ii = _____   iii = _____   IV = _____   V = _____   vi = _____

LESSON 2

"On Second Thought" (Song)

Lesson Concepts
- "On Second Thought" (Song) Guitar 1
- "On Second Thought" (Song) Guitar 2

This song brings together many of the skills you have learned so far.

ON SECOND THOUGHT

(Brian K. Rivers)

Guitar 1– Melody

Guitar 2 – Accompaniment

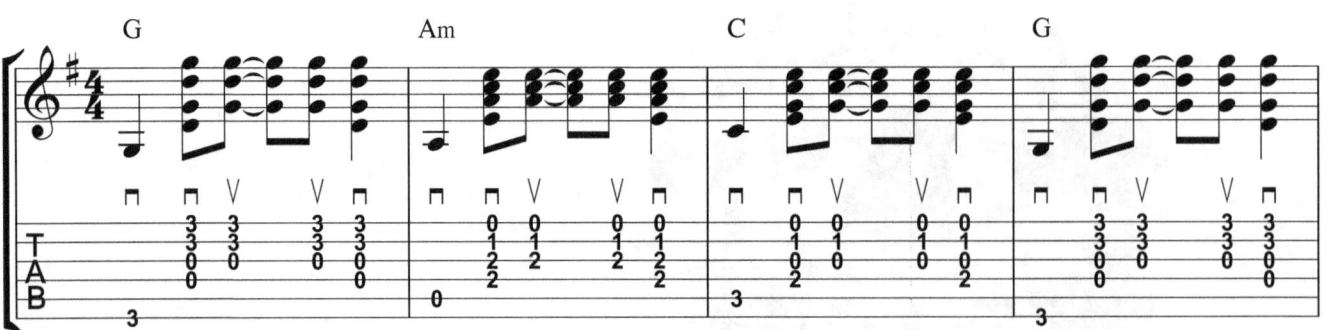

UNIT FOUR • LESSON 2

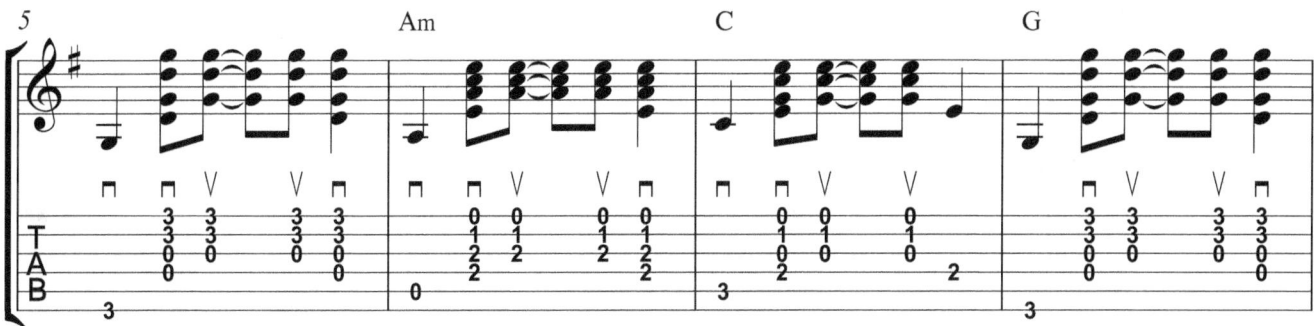

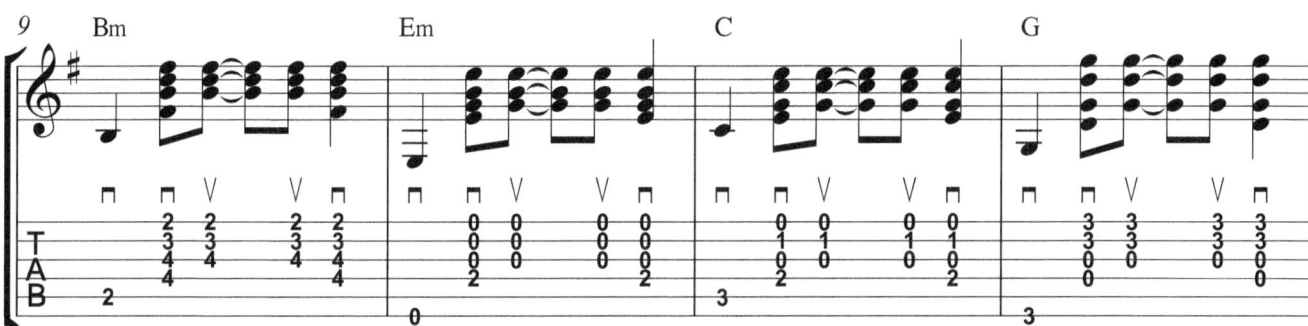

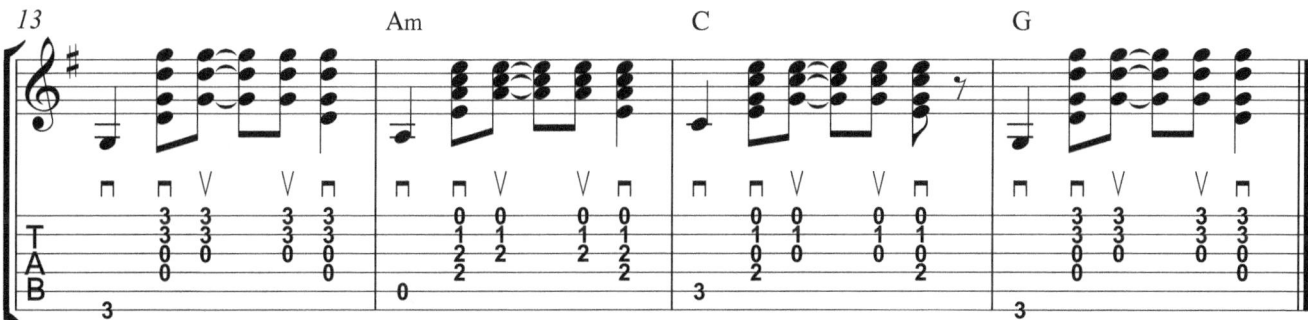

Play & Do... Video examples at *www.bestmusicpublications.com*

- Play the melody to "On Second Thought," using a variety of right-hand techniques including: pick, standard finger assignment, alternating index and middle fingers and thumb. Be sure to use the correct fingers for fretted notes!
- Play the chord accompaniment to "On Second Thought," *using a pick*.
- Play the chord accompaniment to "On Second Thought," *using your right-hand fingers*.
- Repeat the first three steps while playing along with the recorded music.
- Fill in the universal chord names for the key of G in the spaces below:

    G = _____   Am = _____   Bm = _____   C = _____   D = _____   Em = _____

67

LESSON 3

"Minor Inconvenience" (Song)

Lesson Concepts
- "Minor Inconvenience" (Song) Guitar 1
- "Minor Inconvenience" (Song) Guitar 2

This song brings together many of the skills you have learned so far.

MINOR INCONVENIENCE

(Brian K. Rivers)

Guitar 1– Melody

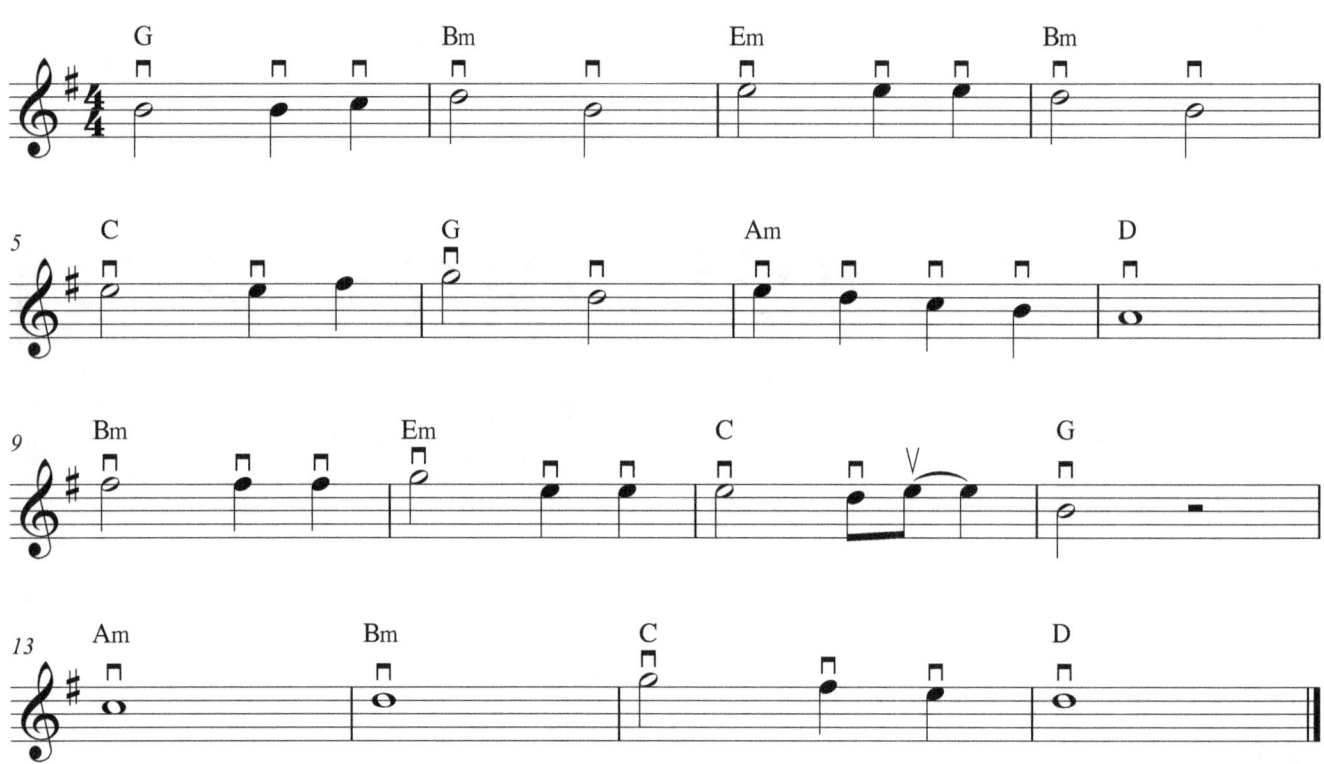

Guitar 2 – Accompaniment

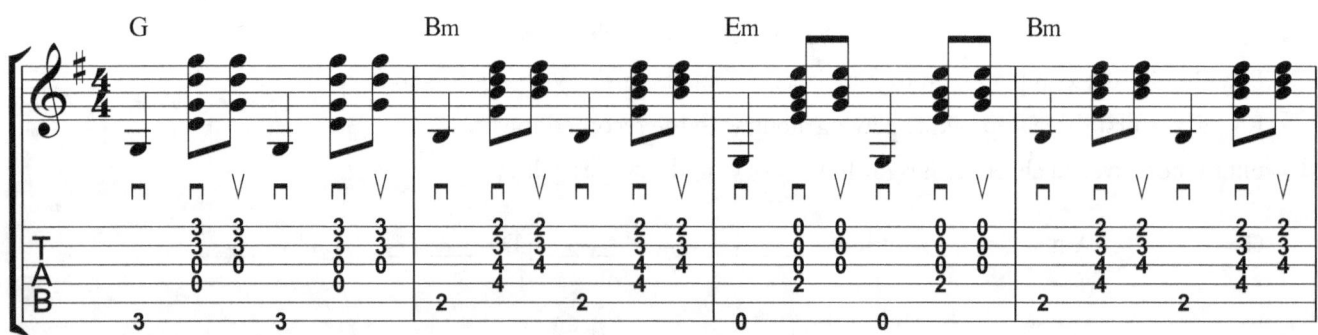

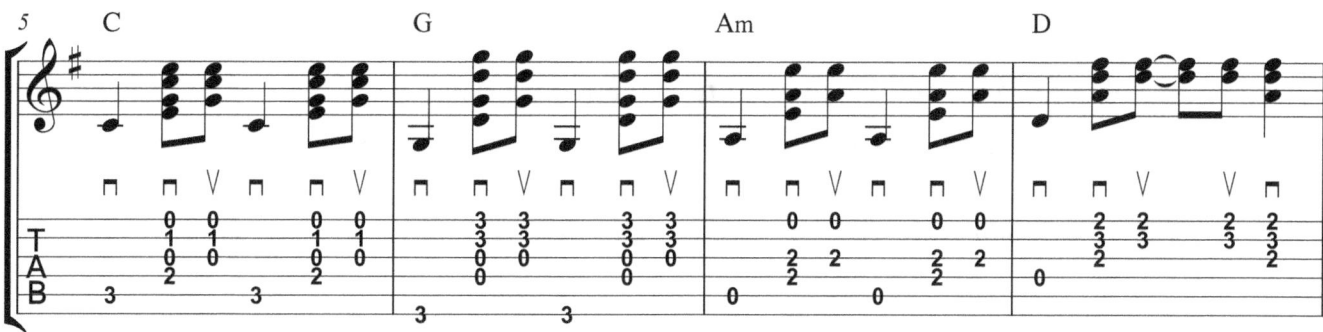

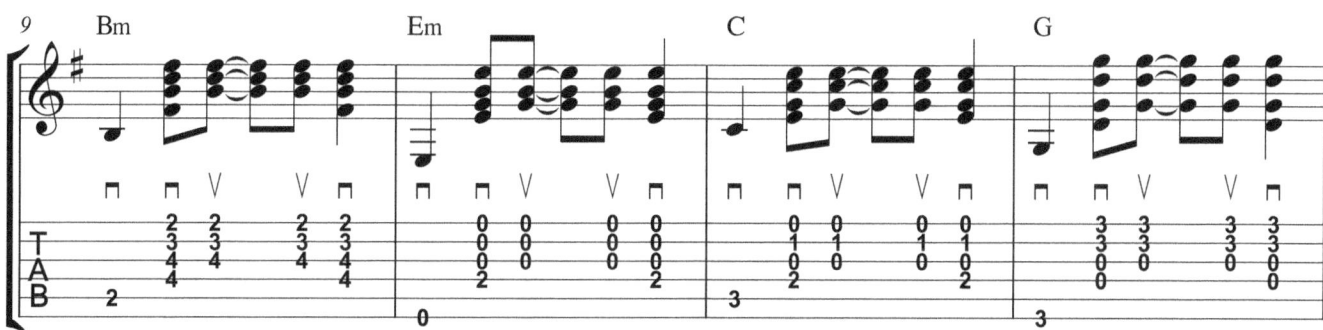

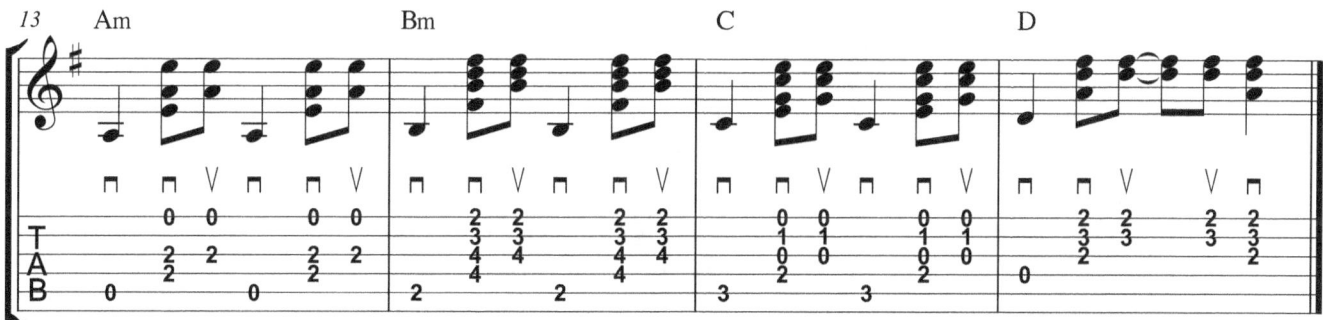

 **Play & Do...** Video examples at *www.bestmusicpublications.com*

- Play the melody to "Minor Inconvenience," using a variety of right-hand techniques including: pick, standard finger assignment, alternating index and middle fingers and thumb. Be sure to use the correct fingers for fretted notes!
- Play the chord accompaniment to "Minor Inconvenience," *using a pick.*
- Play the chord accompaniment to "Minor Inconvenience," *using your right-hand fingers.*
- Repeat the first three steps while playing along with the recorded music.

Review and Summary

You should be able to demonstrate and identify the following skills:

- Identify and play the secondary minor chords in the key of G with their Roman numeral equivalents
- Play any part in any song from Unit 4 with the recordings
- Fill in the universal primary and secondary chord names for the key of G in the spaces below:

I = _____   ii = _____   iii = _____   IV = _____   V = _____   vi = _____

UNIT 5

Notes in the Key of G on the Lowest Three Strings

Lesson 1

More Notes — D, E and F♯ (Fourth String)

Lesson Concepts

- Notes: D, E, F♯ (Fourth String)

Notes: D, E, F♯ (Fourth String)

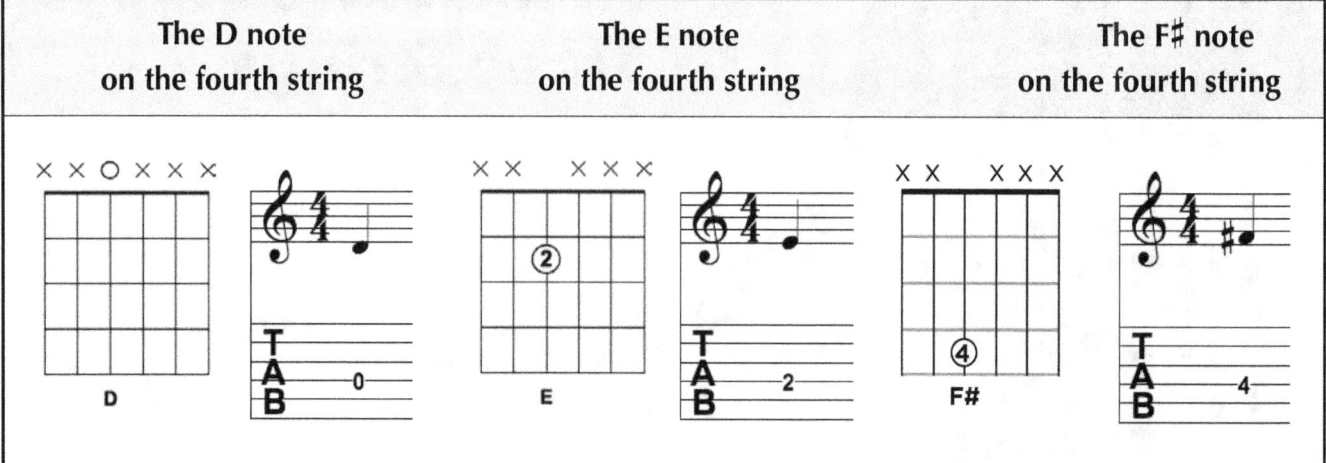

Play & Do... Video examples at *www.bestmusicpublications.com*

- Play and pluck each of the three new notes using a variety of right-hand techniques including: pick; standard finger assignment; and alternating index and middle fingers and thumb. Look at the standard notation for the notes as you do this exercise.
- Randomly play all the notes you know in any order using a variety of right-hand techniques including: pick, standard finger assignment, and alternating index and middle fingers, and thumb. You can repeat notes and say the names as you play them. Be sure to use the correct finger for fretted notes!

LESSON 2

First and Second Endings

Lesson Concepts
- Endings
- How to Play Endings

Endings

Endings are used in conjunction with repeat signs to make the song fit on fewer pages. Endings also help you see what material is repeated and what material is different.

First endings are marked with a bracket with the number 1 and almost always have a repeat sign at the end. An ending can be one or more measures long. The start of the first ending is marked by the bracket and the number 1, and the end is marked with the repeat sign. First endings look like this:

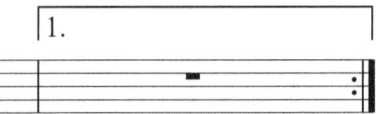

Second endings vary more than first endings. Second endings start with a bracket and have a number 2 and usually lead to the next sections of music. Again, the length of the ending can be one or more measures. Examples of second endings look like this:

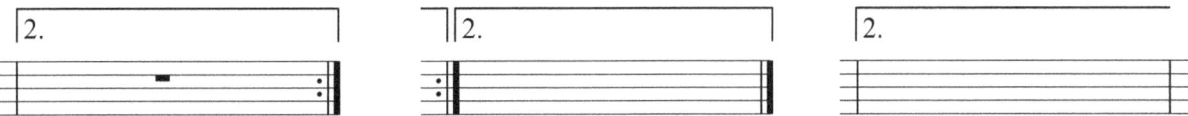

How to Play Endings

Play from the beginning through the first ending up to the repeat sign. Then go back to the previous forward repeat sign (or the beginning of the music if there is no previous forward repeat sign). Now you are repeating previously played music for the second time. When you arrive at the first ending, skip it and go directly to the music in the second ending *instead*. Often in more complicated arrangements, the repeats may be numbered higher than two, but the same principles apply.

Lesson 3

"Old MacDonald" (Song)

Lesson Concepts
- "Old Mac Donald" (Song) Primary Chords

Note: It is assumed that you will play unmarked notes as a down stroke. The recorded version of this song plays the entire song once as written with repeats!

OLD MACDONALD

(Traditional Folk Song)

Play & Do... Video examples at www.bestmusicpublications.com

- Play the melody to "Old MacDonald" using a variety of right-hand techniques including: pick; standard finger assignment; and alternating index and middle fingers and thumb. Be sure to use the correct fingers for fretted notes!
- Play the chord accompaniment to "Old MacDonald" *using a pick*. Try to figure out the strum pattern by ear.
- Play the chord accompaniment to "Old MacDonald" *using your right-hand fingers*.
- Repeat the first three steps while playing along with the recorded music.

LESSON 4

The Pickup Measure

> **Lesson Concepts**
> - Song Form
> - Aligned Melody
> - Displaced Melody
> - Incomplete Measure

Song Form
"Old MacDonald" has a 16-bar (measure) song form.

Aligned Melody
"Old MacDonald" has an *aligned melody* meaning the melody starts when the form starts, on beat 1 of the first measure.

Displaced Melody
Some songs have a displaced melody. A *displaced melody* is a melody that starts somewhere other than beat one of the first measure of the song form. In "Old MacDonald," the first ending has a single low D note at the end that is the start of a displaced melody meaning the melody starts before the song form.

Incomplete Measure
If the melody is displaced *before* the beginning of the song form, it requires a *pickup measure*, which is an incomplete measure before the beginning of the song form. If the melody is displaced *after* the song form starts, no pickup measure is needed.

The next song, "The Streets of Laredo," is an example of a song with a melody displaced by one beat. The pickup measure of 1 beat in length allows the melody to be notated in advance of the song form. A pickup measure is always an *incomplete measure* and will only have the needed rhythms and notes notated. The notated notes are at the end of the incomplete measure, so there are no rests in advance of the melody to create a complete measure.

Lesson 5

"Streets of Laredo" (Song)

Lesson Concepts
- "The Streets of Laredo" (Song)

Note: It is assumed that you will play unmarked notes as a down stroke.

STREETS OF LAREDO

(Traditional Cowboy Song)

Play & Do... Video examples at www.bestmusicpublications.com

- Play the melody of "The Streets of Laredo" using a variety of right-hand techniques including: pick, standard finger assignment, and alternating index and middle fingers, and thumb. Say the note names as you play them. Be sure to use the correct fingers for fretted notes!
- Play the chord accompaniment of "The Streets of Laredo," playing the chords *using a pick*. Try to figure out the strum pattern by ear.
- Play the chord accompaniment of "The Streets of Laredo," playing the chords *using standard finger assignment*.
- Repeat the first three steps while playing along with the recorded music.

LESSON 6

"Brother John" (Song)

> **Lesson Concepts**
> - "Brother John" (Song)

Note: It is assumed that you will play unmarked notes as a down stroke.

BROTHER JOHN

(Traditional)

   **Play & Do...** Video examples at *www.bestmusicpublications.com*

- Play the melody to "Brother John," using a variety of right-hand techniques including: pick, standard finger assignment, and alternating index and middle fingers, and thumb. Say the names as you play them. Be sure to use the correct fingers for fretted notes!
- Play the chord accompaniment to "Brother John" *using a pick.* Try to figure out the strum pattern by ear.
- Play the chord accompaniment to "Brother John" u*sing standard finger assignment.*
- Repeat the first three steps while playing along with the recorded music.

77

LESSON 7

Syncopation

Lesson Concepts
- Syncopated Rhythms

Syncopated Rhythms

A melody or rhythm is *syncopated* when the rhythms fall on a beat other than the strong numbered beats. You will learn standard eighth note syncopations. When playing syncopated rhythms, keep your *quarter note frame* motion steady. If you do this, you will naturally play the syncopated rhythms with an upstroke of your pick. You will first learn the rhythms as strum patterns.

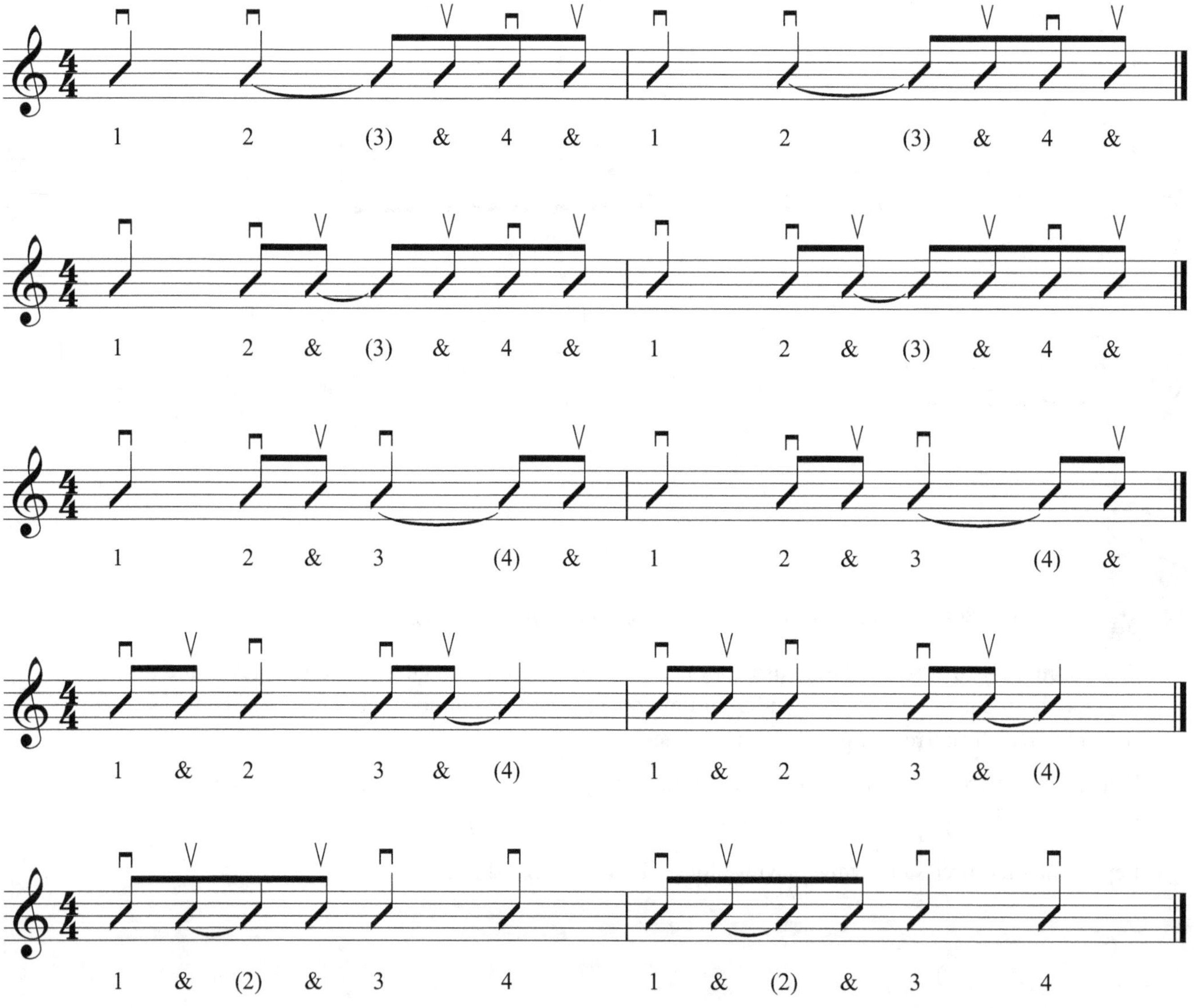

UNIT FIVE • LESSON 7

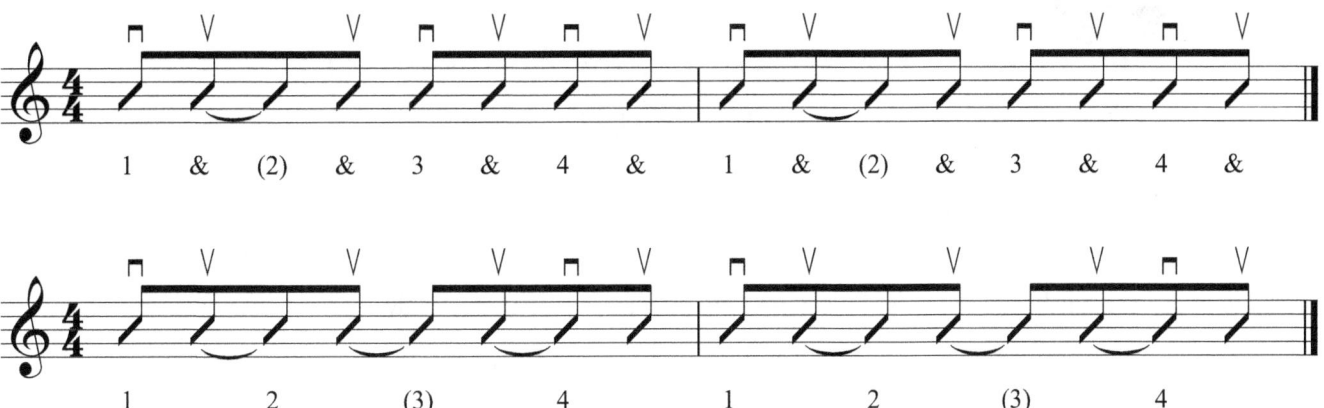

 **Play & Do...** Video examples at *www.bestmusicpublications.com*

- Play the Syncopated Rhythms with the chord of your choice. Use a variety of right-hand techniques including: pick, standard finger assignment, and thumb. Say the note names as you play them. Be sure to use the correct fingers for fretted notes!
- Repeat step one with a G chord while playing along with the recorded music.

Lesson 8

"This Little Light of Mine" (Song)

Lesson Concepts
- "This Little Light of Mine" (Song)

The melody of "This Little Light of Mine" is a good example of a syncopated melody.

THIS LITTLE LIGHT OF MINE

(Traditional)

Play & Do… Video examples at *www.bestmusicpublications.com*

- Play the melody of "This Little Light of Mine" using a variety of right-hand techniques including: pick, standard finger assignment, and alternating index and middle fingers, and thumb. Be sure to use the correct fingers for fretted notes!
- Play the chord accompaniment of "This Little Light of Mine" playing the chords *using a pick.* Try to figure out the strum pattern by ear.
- Play the chord accompaniment of "This Little Light of Mine" playing the chords *using standard finger assignment.*
- Repeat the first three steps while playing along with the recorded music.

Lesson 9

"Amazing Grace" (Song)

Lesson Concepts
- "Amazing Grace" (Song)

AMAZING GRACE

(Traditional)

Play & Do... Video examples at www.bestmusicpublications.com

- Play the melody of "Amazing Grace" using a variety of right-hand techniques including: pick, standard finger assignment, and alternating index and middle fingers, and thumb. Be sure to use the correct fingers for fretted notes!
- Play the chord accompaniment of "Amazing Grace" playing the chords *using a pick*. Try to figure out the strum pattern by ear.
- Play the chord accompaniment of "Amazing Grace" playing the chords *using standard finger assignment*.
- Repeat the first three steps while playing along with the recorded music.

Lesson 10

"Oh My Darling, Clementine" (Song)

Lesson Concepts
- "Oh My Darling, Clementine" (Song)

Note: The picking directions have been intentionally left out; if you have a question, refer to Unit 3/Lesson 11.

OH MY DARLING, CLEMENTINE
WITH MELODY

(Percy Montrose)

In a cav-ern, in a can-yon ex-ca-vat-ing for a

mine, dwelt a min-er for-ty-nin-er and his daugh-ter Cle-men-

tine. Oh my dar-ling, oh my dar-ling, oh my dar-ling, Cle-men-

tine, you are lost and gone for-ev-er, oh my dar-ling, Cle-men-tine.

Play & Do... Video examples at www.bestmusicpublications.com

- Play the melody to "Oh My Darling, Clementine" using a variety of right-hand techniques including: pick, standard finger assignment, and alternating index and middle fingers, and thumb. Be sure to use the correct fingers for fretted notes!

- Play the chord accompaniment to "Oh My Darling, Clementine" playing the chords *using a pick.* Try to figure out the strum pattern by ear.

- Play the chord accompaniment to "Oh My Darling, Clementine" playing the chords *using standard finger assignment.*

LESSON 11

More Notes — A, B, and C (Fifth String)

> **Lesson Concepts**
> - Notes: A, B, C (Fifth String)

Notes: A, B, C (Fifth String)

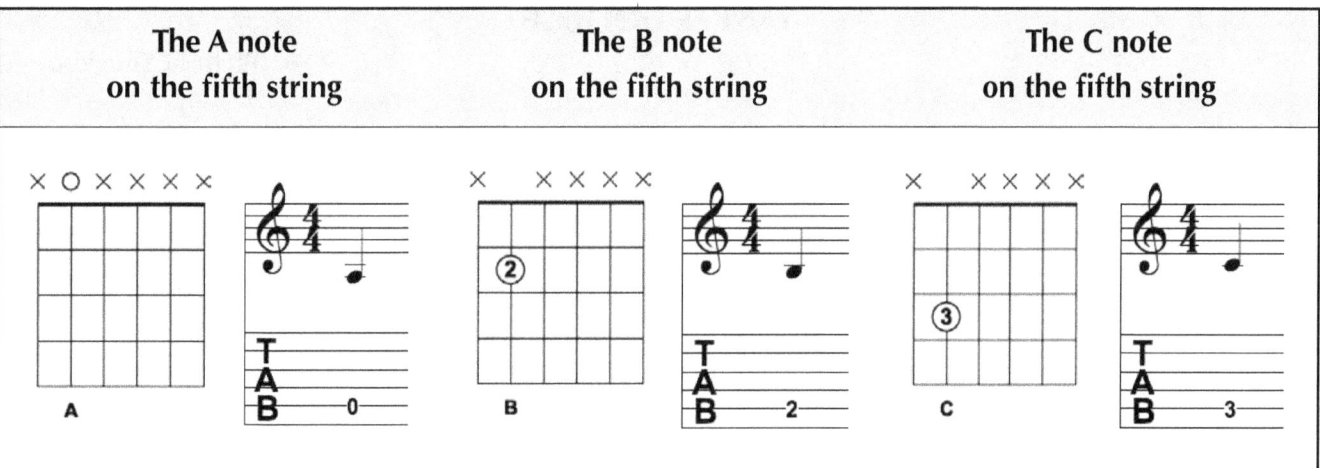

Play & Do... Video examples at *www.bestmusicpublications.com*

- Play and pluck each of the three new notes using a variety of right-hand techniques including: pick, standard finger assignment, and alternating index and middle fingers, and thumb. Say or sing the note name as you play. Look at the standard notation for the notes as you do this exercise.

- Randomly play the notes all you know in any order using a variety of right-hand techniques including: pick, standard finger assignment, and alternating index and middle fingers, and thumb. You can repeat notes and say the names as you play them. Be sure to use the correct fingers for fretted notes and the correct right-hand fingers to pluck the strings!

Lesson 12

"Yankee Doodle" (Song)

Lesson Concepts
- "Yankee Doodle" (Song)

Note: The picking directions have been intentionally left out; if you have a question, refer to Unit 3/Lesson 11.

YANKEE DOODLE

(Richard Shuckburgh)

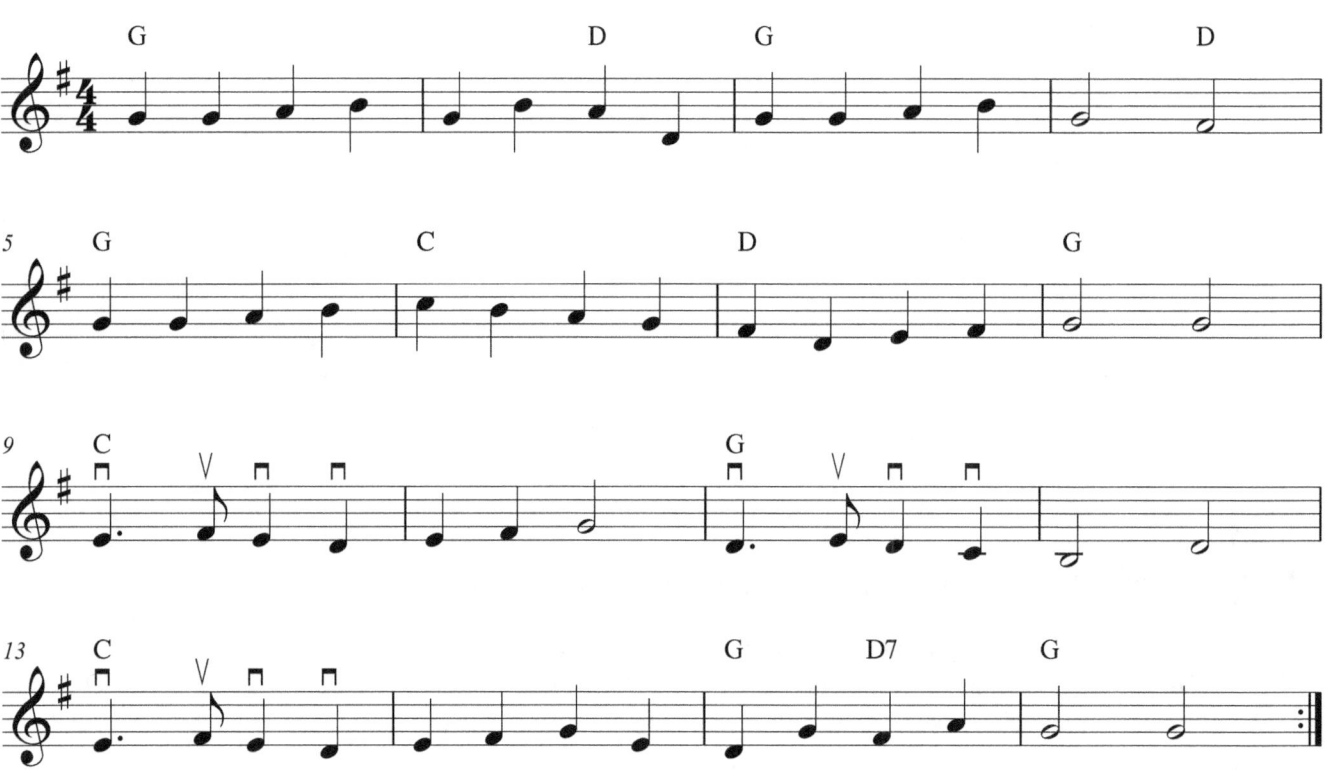

Play & Do... Video examples at *www.bestmusicpublications.com*

- Play the melody to "Yankee Doodle" using a variety of right-hand techniques including: pick, standard finger assignment, and alternating index and middle fingers, and thumb. Be sure to use the correct fingers for fretted notes!

- Play the chord accompaniment to "Yankee Doodle" playing the chords *using a pick*. Try to figure out the strum pattern by ear.

- Play the chord accompaniment to "Yankee Doodle" playing the chords *using standard finger assignment*.

- Repeat the first three steps while playing along with the recorded music.

84

LESSON 13

Accidentals and Fermatas

Lesson Concepts
- Accidentals
- Fermatas

Accidentals

Accidentals are notes that are not in the key of the song. When accidentals occur, they are indicated with either the flat (♭), sharp (♯) or natural sign in front of the note. The flat symbol means play the note one fret lower. The sharp symbol means play the note one fret higher. The natural (♮) symbol cancels a previous sharp or flat in the measure or key signature. It is important to understand that once an accidental appears in a measure, *it is in effect for the entire measure unless it is canceled by a natural sign*. The next song "Santa Lucia" has a few accidentals.

Fermata

The *fermata* symbol looks like this: 𝄐 The fermata tells us to *hold* the note longer than its normal value. It feels like the steady beat freezes for a moment and then returns. How long you hold the note is up to the performer or conductor. The next song "Santa Lucia" has a fermata in the second to the last measure.

Play & Do... Video examples at *www.bestmusicpublications.com*

- Locate the *fermata* in the next song "Santa Lucia" in Unit 5 / Lesson 14.
- Locate the *accidentals* in the next song "Santa Lucia" in Unit 5 / Lesson 14.

LESSON 14

"Santa Lucia" (Song)

Lesson Concepts
- "Santa Lucia" (Song) Guitar 1
- "Santa Lucia" (Song) Guitar 2

SANTA LUCIA

(Traditional Neapolitan Song
Transcribed by Teodoro Cottrau)

Guitar 1

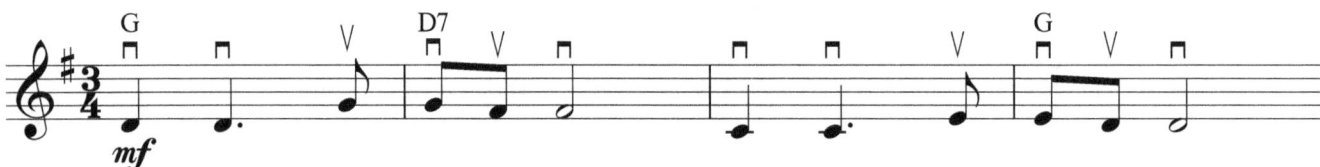

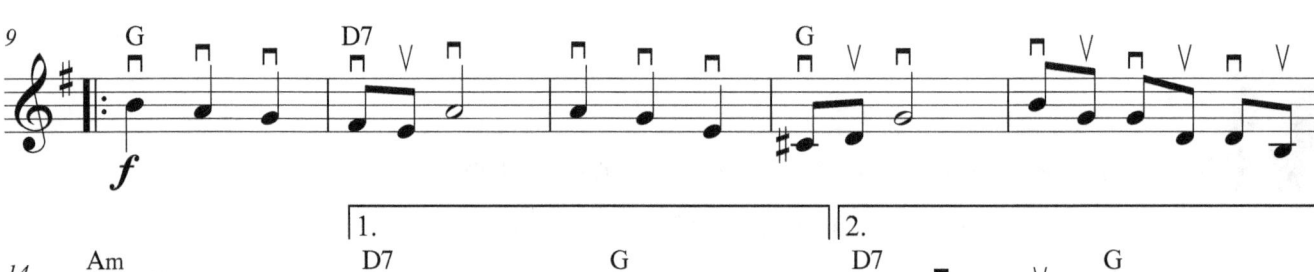

Guitar 2

UNIT FIVE • LESSON 14

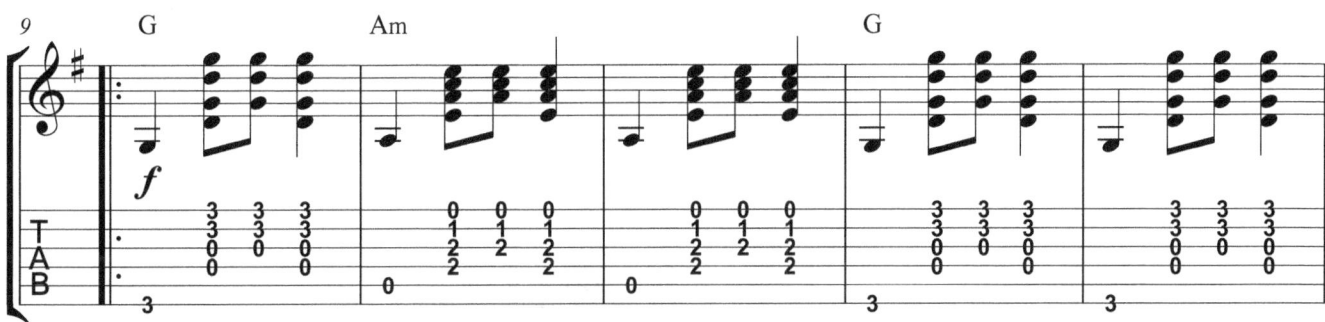

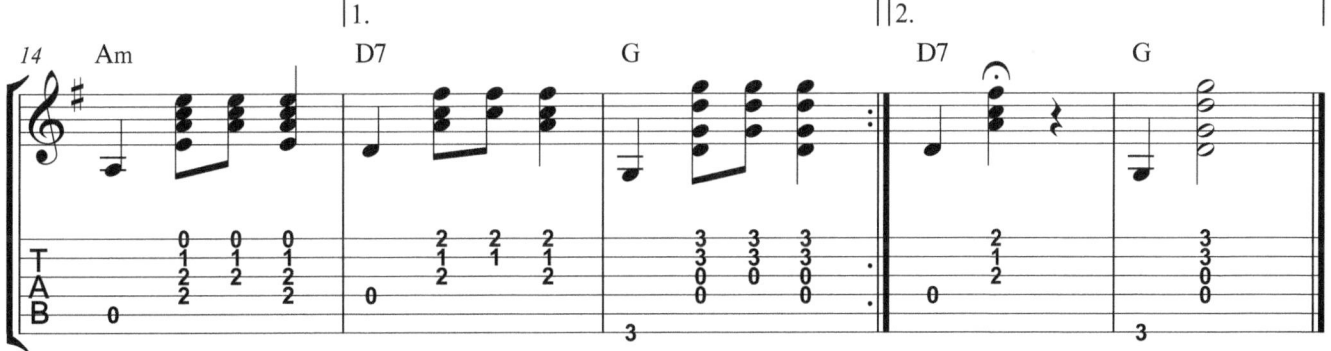

 **Play & Do…** Video examples at *www.bestmusicpublications.com*

- Play the melody to "Santa Lucia" using a variety of right-hand techniques including: pick, standard finger assignment, and alternating index and middle fingers, and thumb. Be sure to use the correct fingers for fretted notes!
- Play the chord accompaniment to "Santa Lucia" playing the chords *using a pick*.
- Play the chord accompaniment to "Santa Lucia" playing the chords *using standard finger assignment*.
- Repeat the first three steps while playing along with the recorded music.

LESSON 15

More Notes — G (Sixth String)

Lesson Concepts
- Low G Note (Sixth String)

Low G Note (Sixth String)

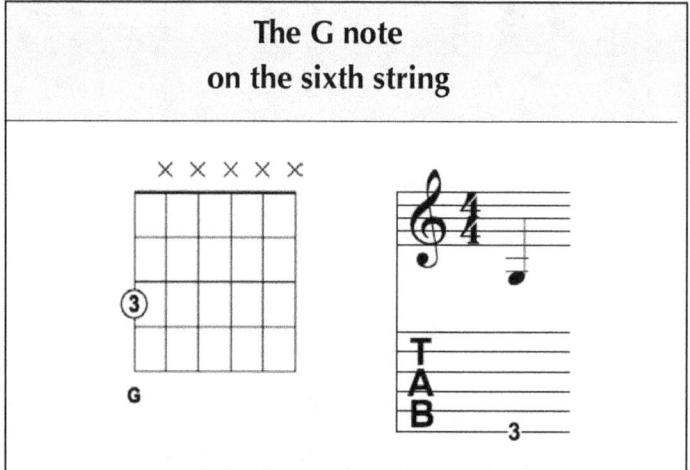

Play & Do... Video examples at *www.bestmusicpublications.com*

- Play and pluck the new note using a variety of right-hand techniques including: pick, standard finger assignment, and alternating index and middle fingers, and thumb. Say or sing the note name as you play it. You should be looking at the standard notation for the note as you do this exercise.

- Randomly play all the notes you know in any order using a variety of right-hand techniques including: pick, standard finger assignment, and alternating index and middle fingers, and thumb. You can repeat notes and say the names as you play them. Be sure to use the correct finger for fretted notes!

Lesson 16

G Major Scale — Two Octave

Lesson Concepts
- G Major Scale (Two Octave)

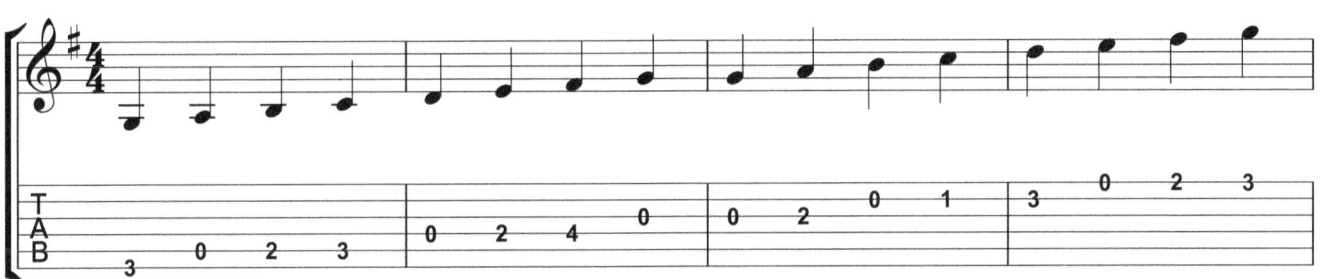

Play & Do... Video examples at *www.bestmusicpublications.com*

- Play the two Octave G major scale and start *p* (quietly) and crescendo to *f* (loud) as you ascend the scale from the low G to the high G, then decrescendo from *f* to *p* as you descend from the high G to the low G.
- Repeat the above step from *pp* to *ff*.
- Memorize the Two Octave G major scale.

LESSON 17

G Major — No Training Wheels

Lesson Concepts
- G Major — No Training Wheels (No Tablature)

G MAJOR – NO TRAINING WHEELS

UNIT FIVE • LESSON 17

 **Play & Do...** Video examples at *www.bestmusicpublications.com*

- Point to each note and say the note name.
- Go through the song and count the rhythms keeping a steady beat.
- Play G major (No training wheels...) using a variety of right-hand techniques including: pick, standard finger assignment, and alternating index and middle fingers, and thumb.
- Play along with the recording with each picking style.

LESSON 18

"On Second Thought" (Song)

Lesson Concepts
- "On Second Thought" (Song)

ON SECOND THOUGHT

(Brian K. Rivers)

GUITAR 1

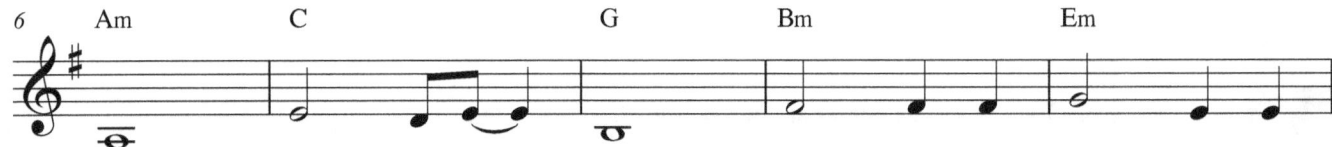

Guitar 2

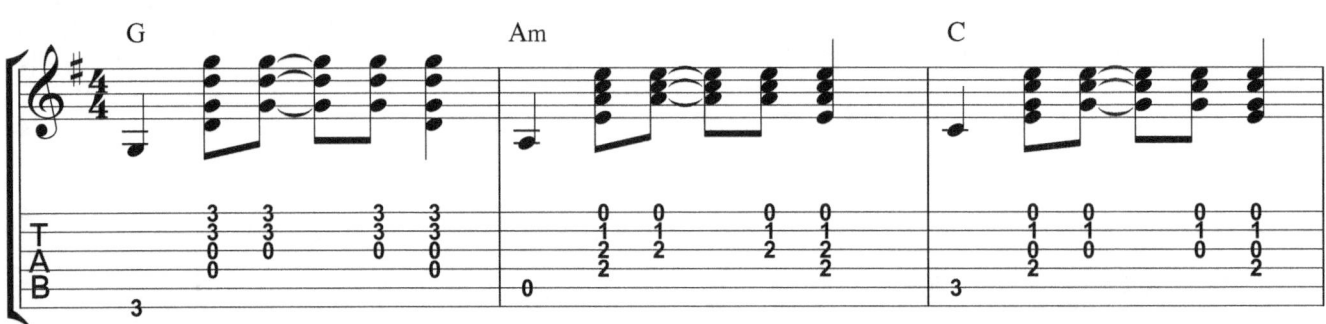

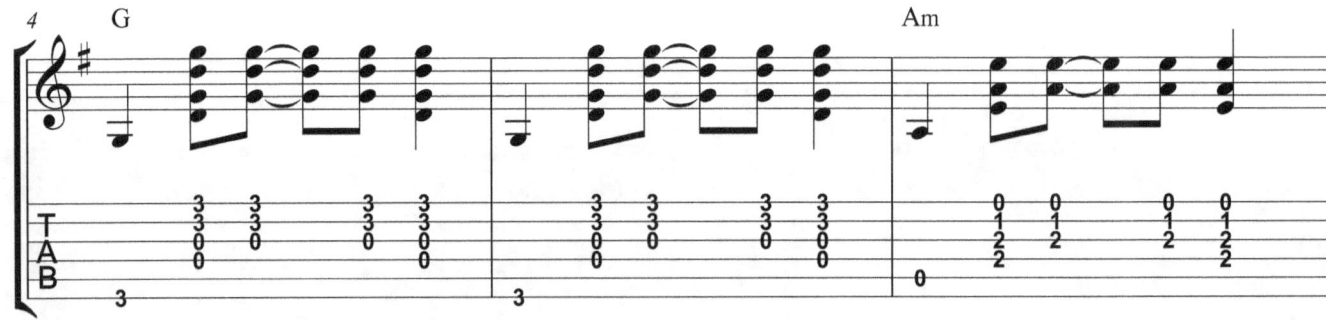

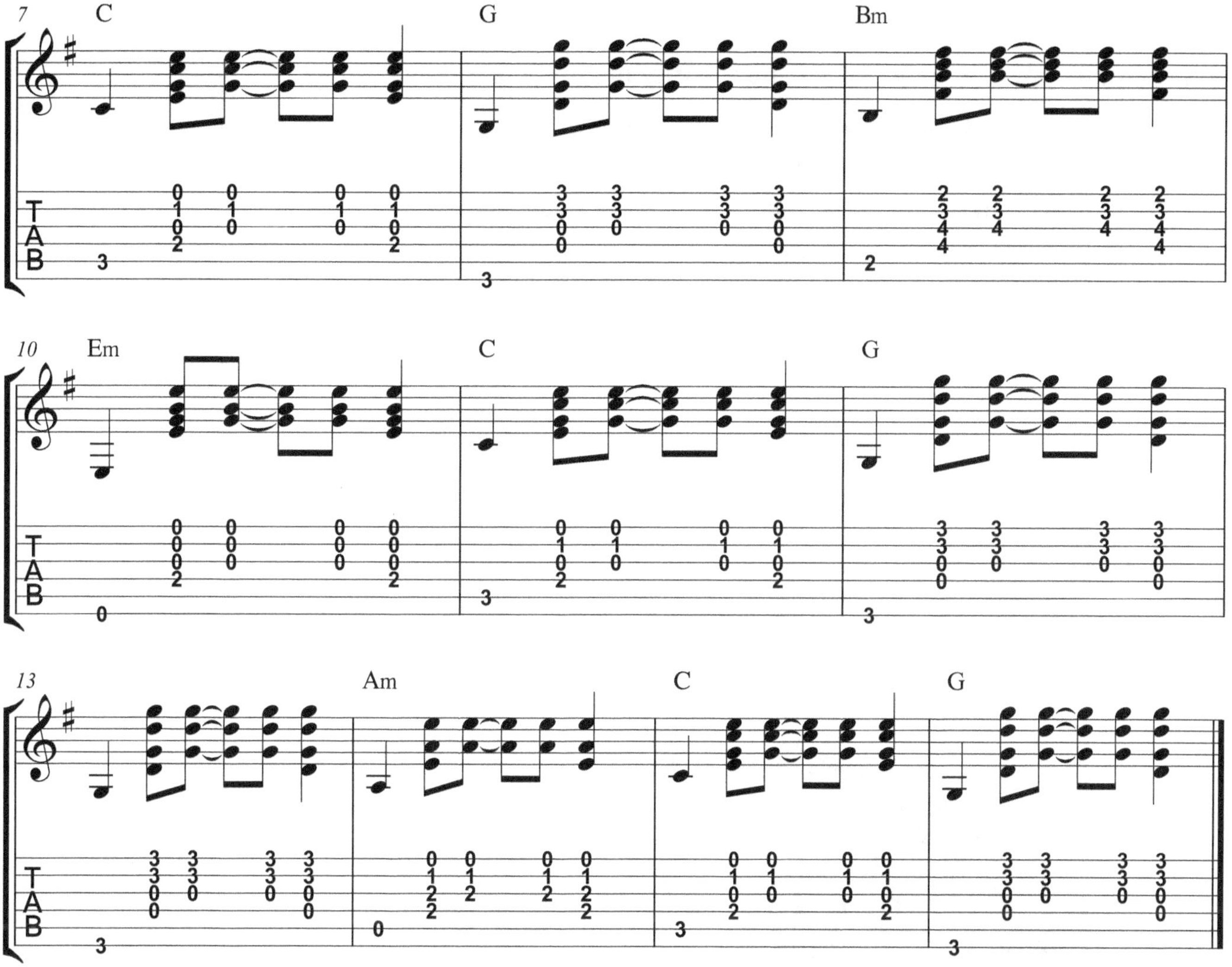

UNIT FIVE • LESSON 18

Play & Do... Video examples at *www.bestmusicpublications.com*

- Play the melody to "On Second Thought" using a variety of right-hand techniques including: pick, standard finger assignment, and alternating index and middle fingers, and thumb. Be sure to use the correct fingers for fretted notes!
- Play the chord accompaniment to "On Second Thought" playing the chords *using a pick.*
- Play the chord accompaniment to "On Second Thought" playing the chords *using your right-hand fingers.*
- Repeat the first three steps while playing along with the recorded music.
- Find two other guitar players, and each plays a different part using the version of this song from Unit 4 / Lesson 2.

THE BEST GUITAR METHOD

Review and Summary

You should be able to demonstrate and identify the following skills:

- Play and identify the notes in the Key of G on all six strings
- Play a two octave G major scale from memory
- Play any part of any song from Unit 5 with the full speed recordings
- Reading endings, repeats, pick-up measures
- Syncopated eighth note rhythms
- Accidentals
- Fermatas

Unit 6

The Key of E Minor

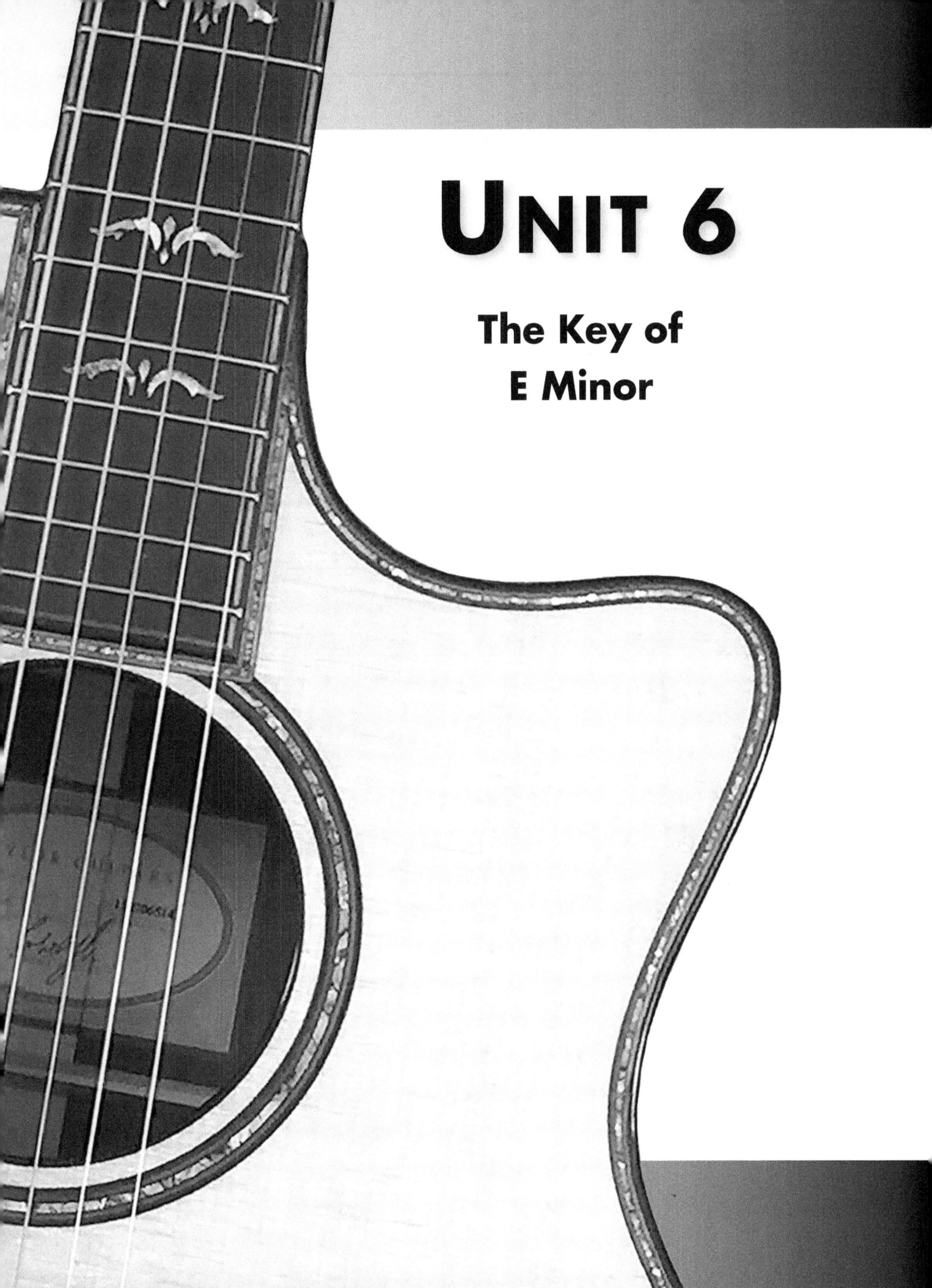

LESSON 1

Relative Minor Keys

Lesson Concepts
- Relative Major and Minor Keys
- Natural Minor Scale

Relative Major and Minor Keys

You already know most of the chords and notes in the key of E minor because E minor and G major have the same notes! The seven notes in the key of G major are: G, A, B, C, D, E, F♯. The seven notes in the key of E minor are: E, F♯, G, A, B, C, D. The order in which the notes are arranged determines if they are a G major scale of an E minor scale. When playing a G major scale, the notes are ordered: G, A, B, C, D, E, F♯; when playing an *E natural minor* scale, the notes are ordered: E, F♯, G, A, B, C, D. (Figure 6.1.1)

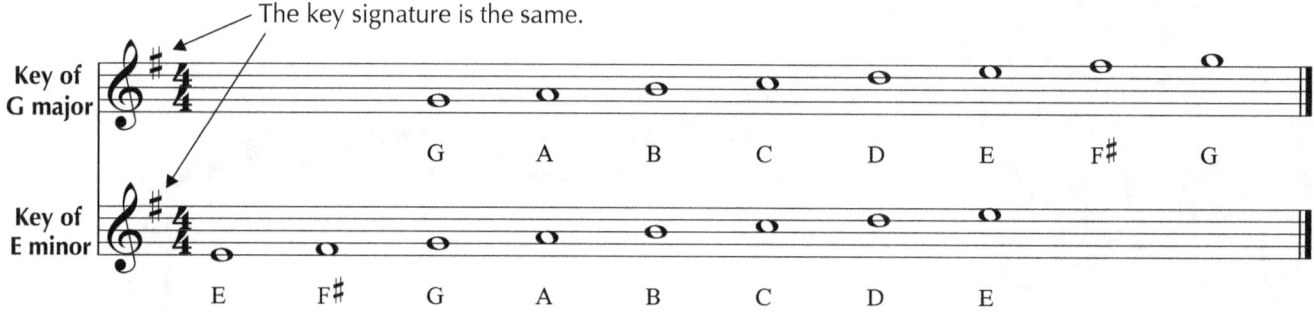

Figure 6.1.1

Play & Do... Video examples at *www.bestmusicpublications.com*

- Play the G major scale and then play the E natural minor scale.

LESSON 2

Primary Chords in the Key of E Minor — Em, Am, Bm and B7 (i, iv, v, V7)

> **Lesson Concepts**
> - Primary Chords in the Key of E Minor
> - Standard Fingerings for the Primary Chords in the Key of E Minor — Em, Am, Bm, and B7 (i, iv, v, V7)
> - Catch and Release
> - Simplified and Challenge Primary Chords in the Key of E Minor

Primary Chords in the Key of E Minor — Em, Am, Bm and B7 (i, iv, v, V7)

There are four primary chords in any minor key. Three of the primary chords are minor chords, and one is a dominant 7 chord. In the key of E minor, the primary chords are Em (i), Am (iv), Bm (v) and B7 (V7). You already know Em, Am, and Bm, so the only new chord is B7.

Standard Fingerings for the Primary Chords in the Key of E Minor — Em, Am, Bm, and B7 (i, iv, v, V7)

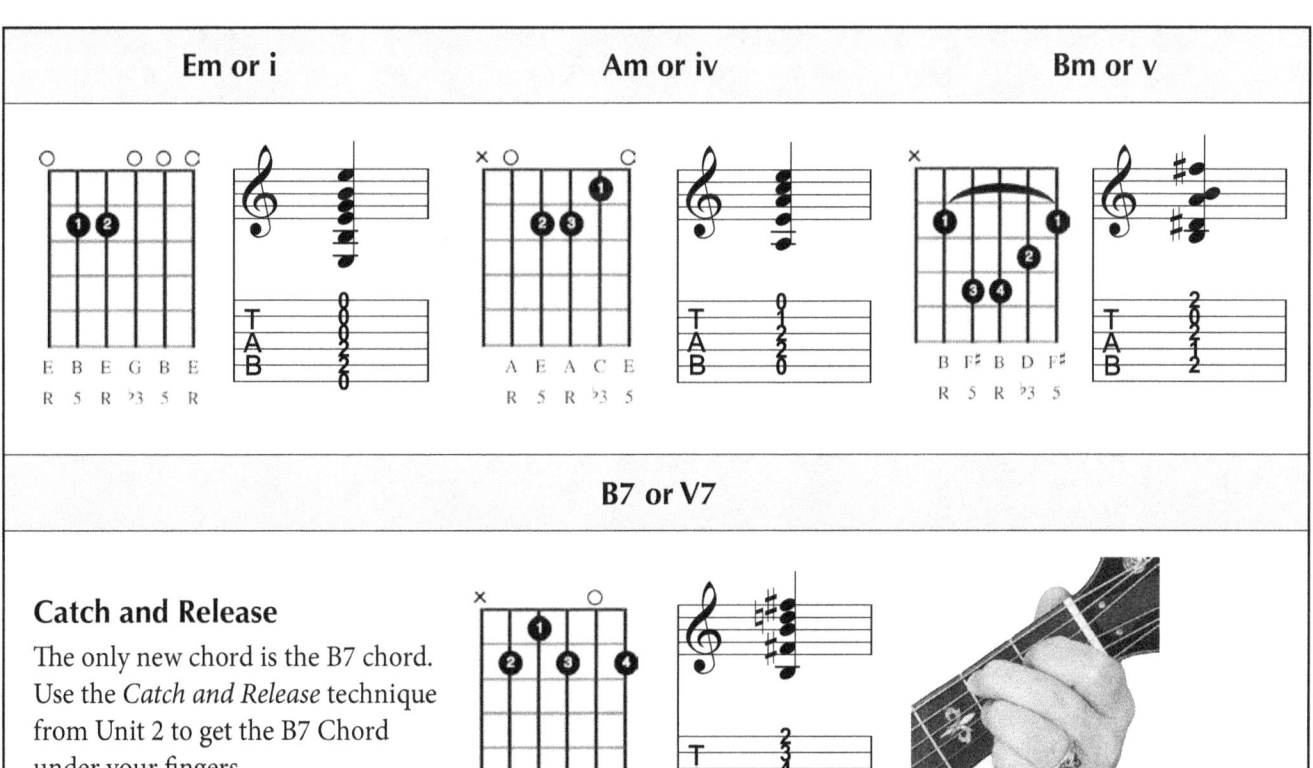

Catch and Release

The only new chord is the B7 chord. Use the *Catch and Release* technique from Unit 2 to get the B7 Chord under your fingers.

97

Simplified and Challenge Chords Fingerings

Simplified and challenge chords fingerings for all the chords in this book can be found at *www.bestmusicpublications.com*.

 **Play & Do…** Video examples at *www.bestmusicpublications.com*

- Finger (play) each chord and make sure you are mindful of the three P's of tone production and pick each string of the chord to be sure each string is making a good sound.
- "Catch and release" each chord, strum the chord as you apply pressure and then check that each string is still sounding good. If it's not sounding good, go back and check the three P's of tone production.
- As you play the chord, say the specific names and universal names for the primary chords in the key of E minor. Say: "Em — also known as the i chord, Am — also known as the iv chord and Bm — also known as the v chord, and B7 also known as the V7 chord."
- Memorize the specific names and universal names for the primary chords in the key of E minor.
- Fill in the universal primary chord names for the key of E minor in the spaces below:

i = _____   iv = _____   v = _____   V7 = _____

LESSON 3

Resolution

> **Lesson Concepts**
> - Major and Minor Keys and Chords
> - Resolution to Determine Major and Minor Keys
> - Resolution of a Chord Progression

Major and Minor Keys and Chords

Most people associate a minor tonality with a "sad" emotion and a major tonality with a "happy" emotion. A good way to tell if a song is in a major or minor key is to look at the chord progression. If the chord progression starts or ends (or both) on a minor chord, it is likely in a minor key. Some songs will go in and out of major and minor keys, and then you can probably make the argument for a key change mid-song. Sometimes the verse will be in the minor key, with the verse chord progression starting/ending on a minor chord, and then the chorus moving to the relative major key by starting/ending with a major chord.

Resolution to Determine Major or Minor Keys

A common question is; "If the E minor and G major have the same seven notes and the same key signature, how do you know what key you are in?" The answer is the *point of resolution*. Earlier you learned about the idea of resolution when you learned suspended chords. *Resolution is the point where the music seems to come to rest*, the point when you aren't waiting for the next musical event to happen. Most songs end at a point of resolution. The point of resolution is what determines if the music is in a major or minor key.

Resolution of a Chord Progression

The most common resolution of a chord progression is the V7 chord leading to either the I or the i depending on if the chord progression is in a major or minor key. In minor keys, you can also have the v chord resolving to the i chord at the end of the chord progression. The reason you want to look at the first and last chord of a progression is that sometimes the V7, V or v chord happens just before the last measure and then the *last chord is the resolution (I or i)*. Other times, the V7, V or v chord is the very last chord of the progression and then resolves when it gets back to the *beginning of the progression*. Every one of the songs you have learned in G major ends on either the I or the V or the V7 chord. If the song ended on the V or V7, it started on the I chord. The songs you will learn in the minor keys will follow the same pattern.

Play & Do... Video examples at *www.bestmusicpublications.com*

- Go back through the songs you have learned in Units 1-5 and circle the V or V7 that proceeds the I chord just before the end or at the end of the song.
- Mark the I chord following the circled V or V7 chord "point of resolution."
- Mark the v chord to the i chord in the next song, "Minor Problem" as you did for your previous songs.

99

LESSON 4

"Minor Problem" (Song)

Lesson Concepts
- "Minor Problem" (Song) Guitar 1
- "Minor Problem" (Song) Guitar 2

MINOR PROBLEM

(Brian K. Rivers)

Guitar 1

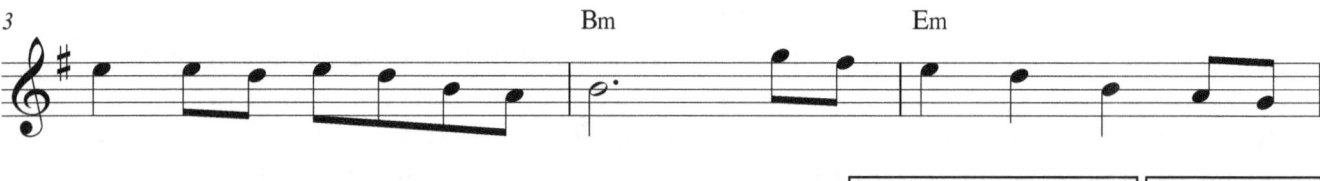

Guitar 2

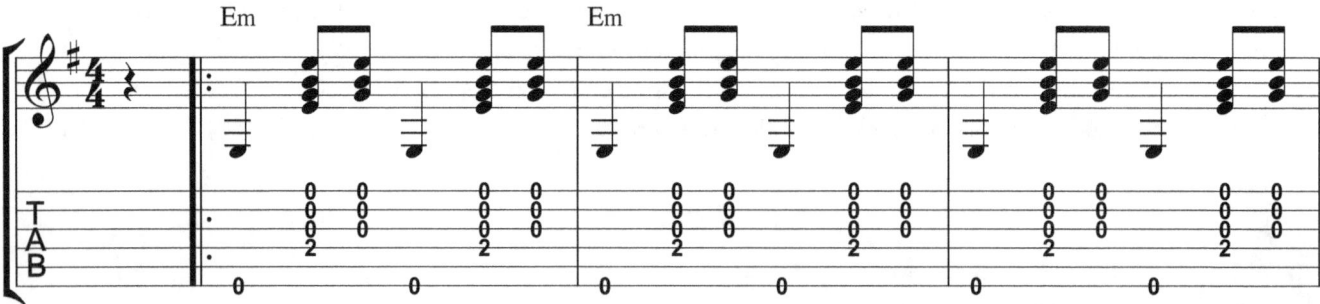

100

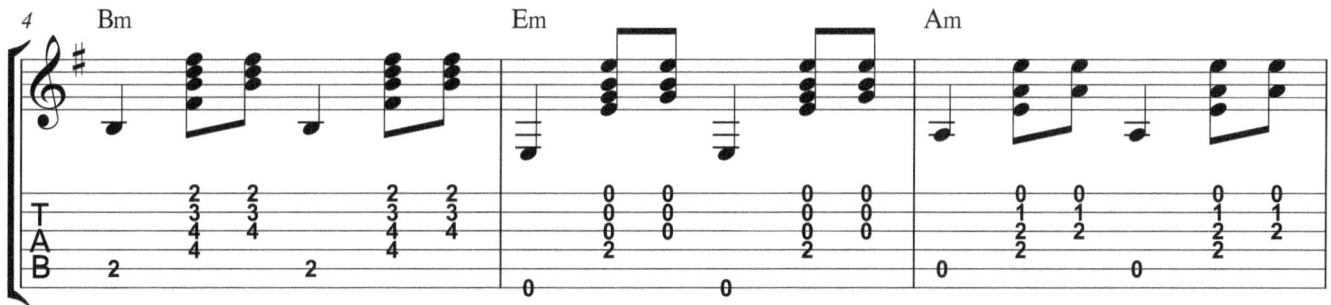

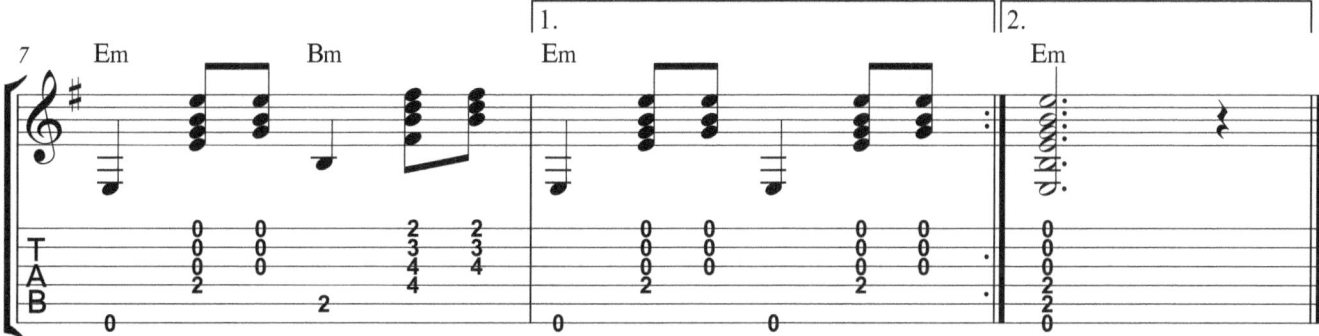

 **Play & Do...** Video examples at *www.bestmusicpublications.com*

- Play the melody to "A Minor Problem" using a variety of right-hand techniques including: pick, standard finger assignment, and alternating index and middle fingers, and thumb. Be sure to use the correct fingers for fretted notes!
- Play the chord accompaniment to "A Minor Problem" playing the chords *using a pick*.
- Play the chord accompaniment to "A Minor Problem" playing the chords *using standard finger assignment*.
- Repeat the first three steps while playing along with the recorded music.
- Fill in the universal chord names for the primary chords in the key of E minor in the spaces below:

Em = _____   Am = _____   Bm = _____

LESSON 5

Secondary Chords in the Key of E Minor — G, C, and D (III, VI, VII)

Lesson Concepts
- Secondary Chords in the Key of Em — G, C, and D (III, VI, VII)
- Standard Fingerings for the Secondary Chords in the Key of Em — G, C, and D (III, VI, VII)
- Simplified and Challenge Chords Fingerings

Secondary Chords in the Key of Em — G, C, and D (III, VI, VII)

The secondary chords in any minor key are always *major* chords. In the key of E minor, secondary chords are G (III), C (VI) and D (VII). You will notice that the secondary chords in a minor key are the same as the primary three major chords in the related major key (G major in this case).

Standard Fingerings for the Secondary Chords in the Key of Em — G, C, and D (III, VI, VII)

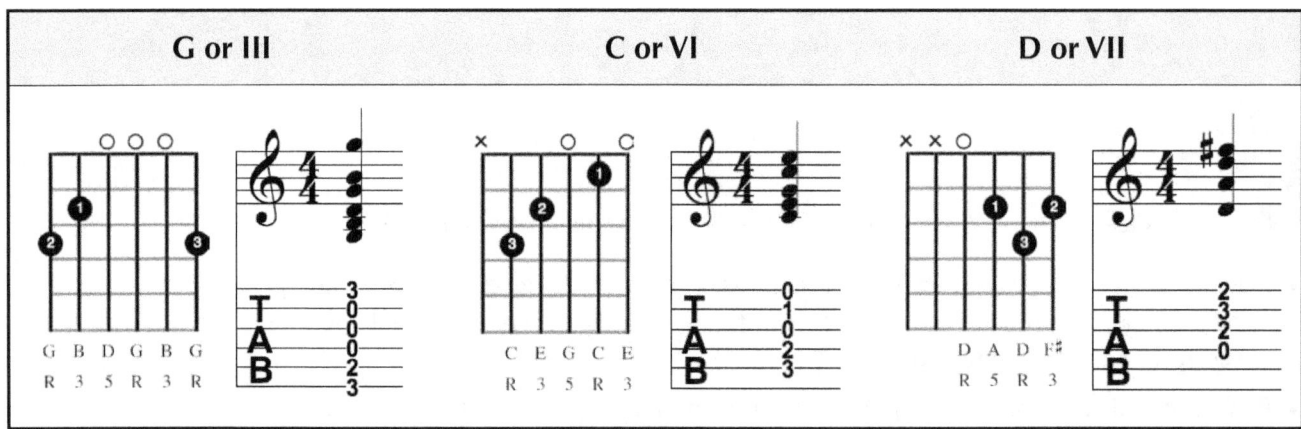

Simplified and Challenge Chords Fingerings

Simplified and challenge chords fingerings for all the chords in this book can be found at *www.bestmusicpublications.com*.

Play & Do... Video examples at *www.bestmusicpublications.com*

- As you play the chord, say the specific names and universal names for the secondary chords in the key of E minor. Say: "G — also known as the III chord, C — also known as the VI chord and D — also known as the VII chord."
- Memorize the specific names and universal names for the primary chords in the key of E minor.
- Fill in the universal chord names for the primary and secondary chords in the key of E minor in the spaces below:

Em = _____   G = _____   Am = _____   Bm = _____   C = _____   D = _____

102

LESSON 6

"St. James Infirmary" (Song)

Lesson Concepts
- "St. James Infirmary" (Song) Guitar 1
- "St. James Infirmary" (Song) Guitar 2

ST. JAMES INFIRMARY

(Traditional)

Guitar 1

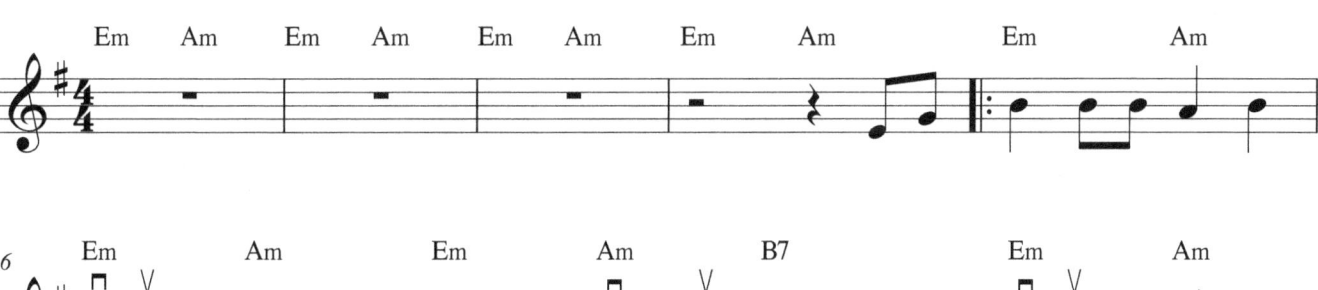

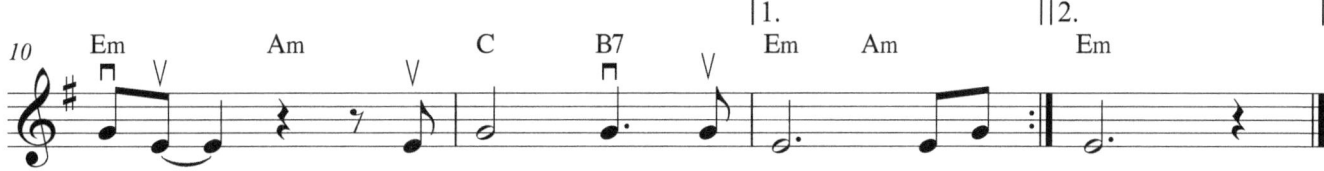

THE BEST GUITAR METHOD

Guitar 2

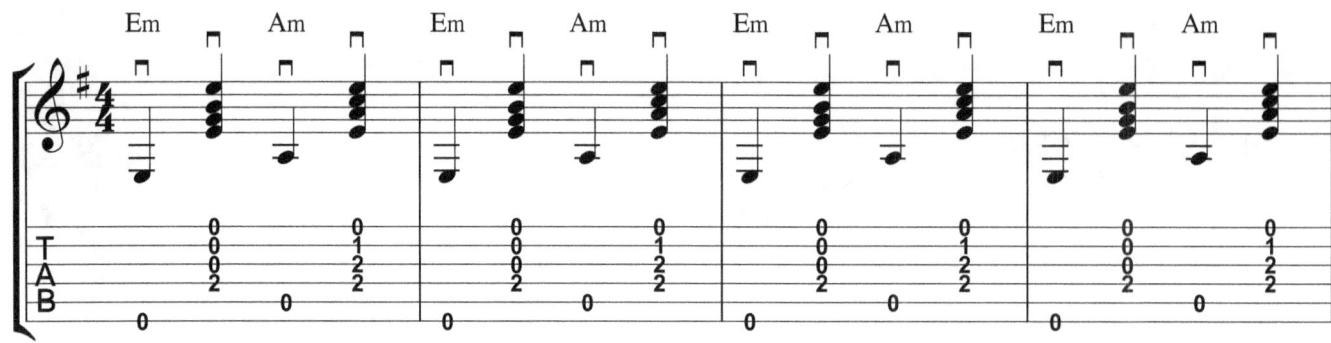

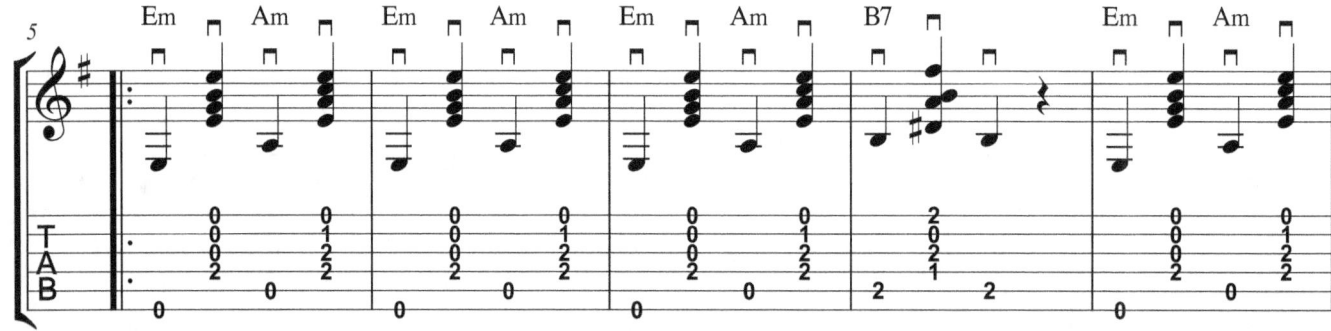

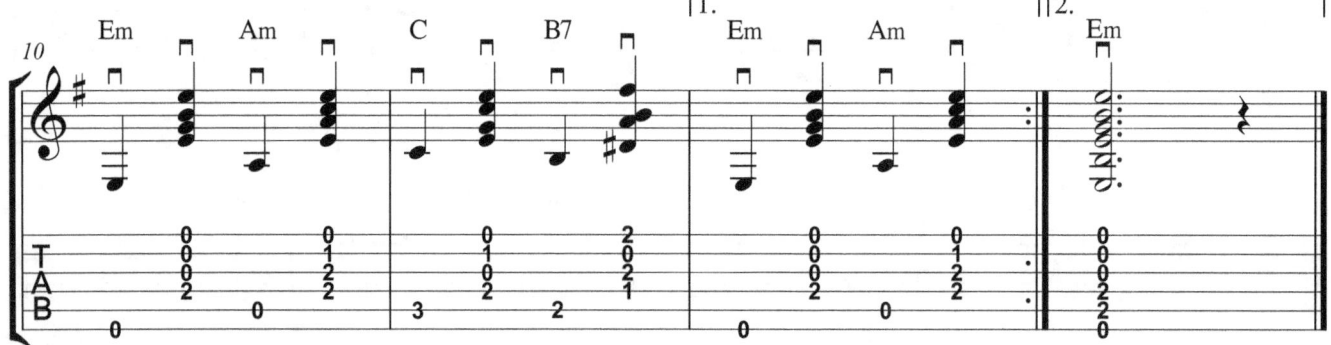

Play & Do... Video examples at *www.bestmusicpublications.com*

- Play the melody to "St. James Infirmary" using a variety of right-hand techniques including: pick, standard finger assignment, and alternating index and middle fingers, and thumb. Be sure to use the correct fingers for fretted notes!
- Play the chord accompaniment to "St. James Infirmary" playing the chords *using a pick*.
- Play the chord accompaniment to "St. James Infirmary" playing the chords *using standard finger assignment*.
- Repeat the first three steps while playing along with the recorded music.
- Fill in the chord names for the key of E minor in the spaces below:

i = _____   III = _____   iv = _____   v = _____   V7 = _____   VI = _____   VII = _____

104

LESSON 7

New Notes — D♯ and C♯

Lesson Concepts
- Notes: D♯ and C♯ on the Fourth and Second Strings
- Half Steps and the ♯ Sign

The D♯ note on the fourth string	The D♯ note on the second string	The C♯ note on the fifth string

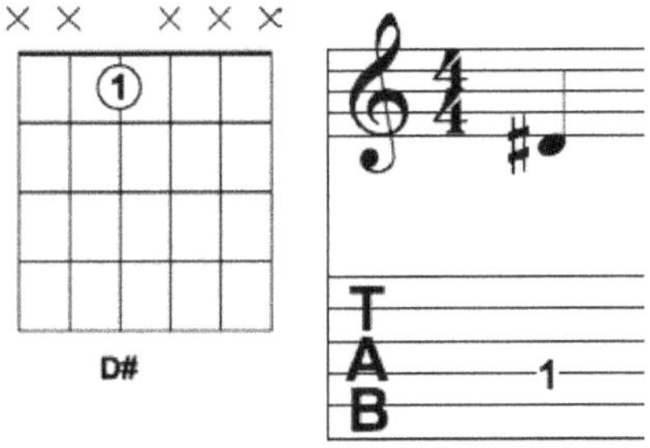

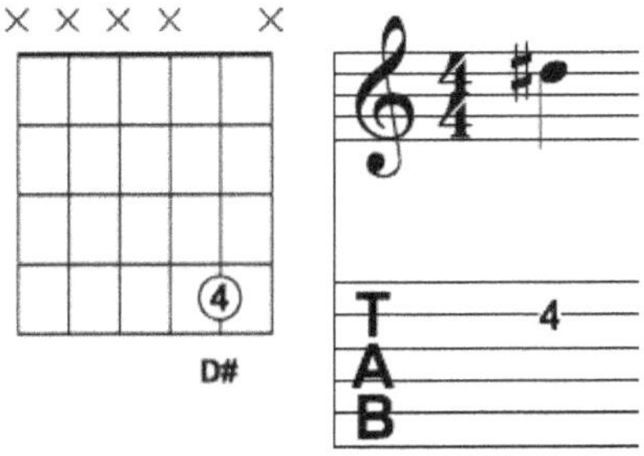

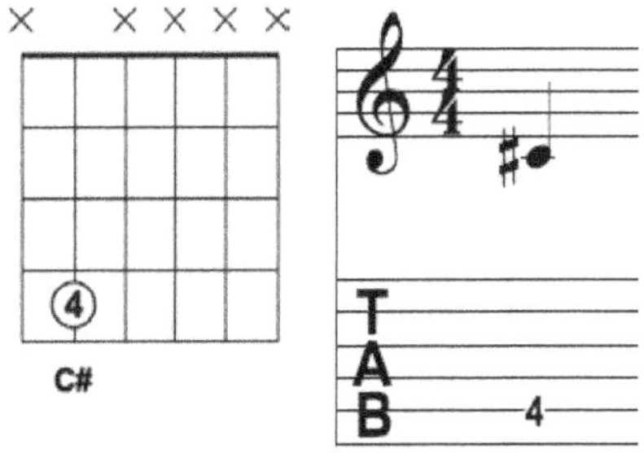

The C♯ note on the second string

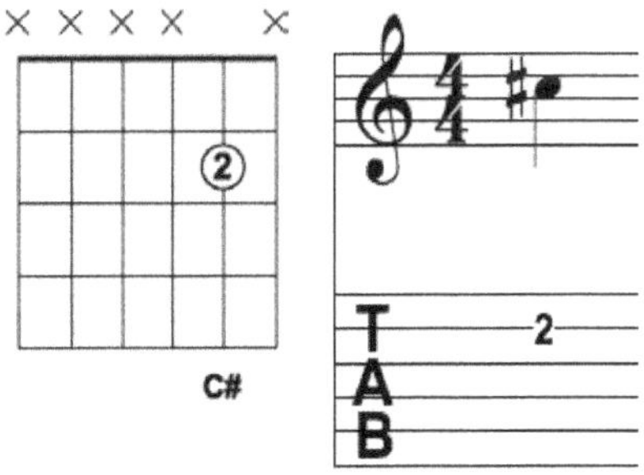

Half Steps and the ♯ Sign

You will notice that each of these notes are simply one fret higher than the C and D notes you already know. The other term you use in music to mean one fret higher is *half-step*. For example, the note C♯ is a half-step higher than the C note. Another way of thinking about this is whenever you see a sharp sign (♯) it means a half-step higher than it would be without the sharp sign.

Play & Do... Video examples at *www.bestmusicpublications.com*

- Play and pluck each new note using a variety of right-hand techniques including: pick, standard finger assignment, and alternating index and middle fingers, and thumb. Say or sing the note name as you play it. Look at the standard notation for the note as you do this exercise.

- Randomly play all the notes you know in any order using a variety of right-hand techniques including: pick; standard finger assignment; and alternating index and middle fingers and thumb. You can repeat notes and say the names as you play them. Be sure to use the correct finger for fretted notes!

LESSON 8

Minor Scales — Natural, Pentatonic, Harmonic, Dorian and Melodic

> **Lesson Concepts**
> - Minor Scale Types
> - Natural Minor
> - Minor Pentatonic
> - Dorian Minor
> - Harmonic Minor
> - Melodic Minor

Minor Scale Types

Minor scales are harder to understand than major scales because there is more than *one type of minor scale*. The tradition is to use the standard natural minor key signature no matter what variation of the minor scale you are using. Here are the five most common minor scale types:

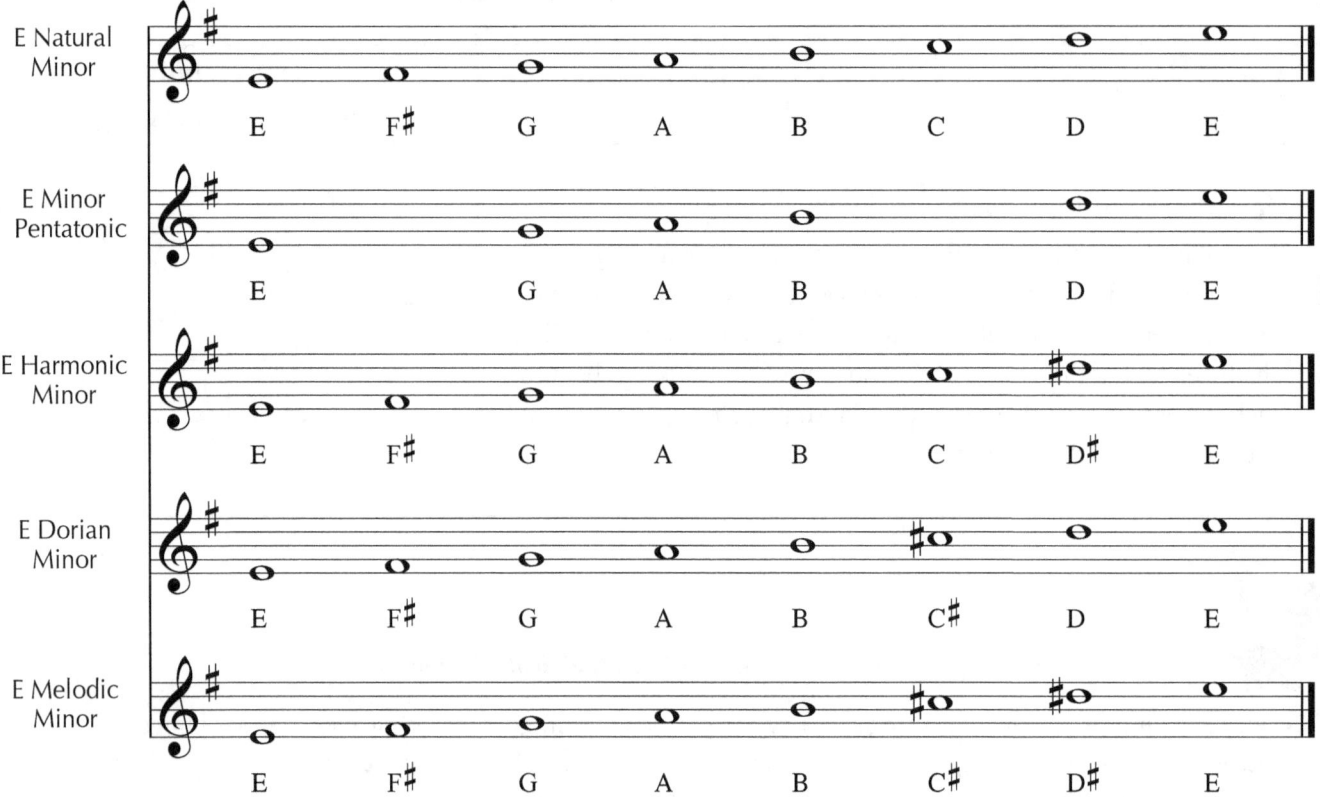

Natural Minor

You have already learned that E natural minor has the same notes as the G major scale. You will notice that all of these scales are written with the same key signature, the key signature for E minor.

Minor Pentatonic

Pentatonic scales are five-note scales, and the *E minor pentatonic scale* is simply the E natural minor scale missing the second and sixth note. The minor pentatonic scale is the most common minor scale for improvising and is, therefore, the scale to practice and memorize.

Dorian Minor

The melodic minor (also called the melodic mode) is just like the natural minor scale only the sixth note has been raised a half-step from C to C♯.

Harmonic Minor

The *harmonic minor* is just like the natural minor scale only the seventh note has been raised a half-step from D to D♯.

Melodic Minor

The *melodic minor* scale is just like the natural minor scale only the sixth, and seventh notes have been raised a half-step from C to C♯ and D to D♯.

Note: Traditionally this is only an ascending scale when you descend you play natural minor. While this is the traditional definition, modern Jazz players regularly use the ascending scale as the descending scale as well.

Here is a two octave E natural minor scale for reference:

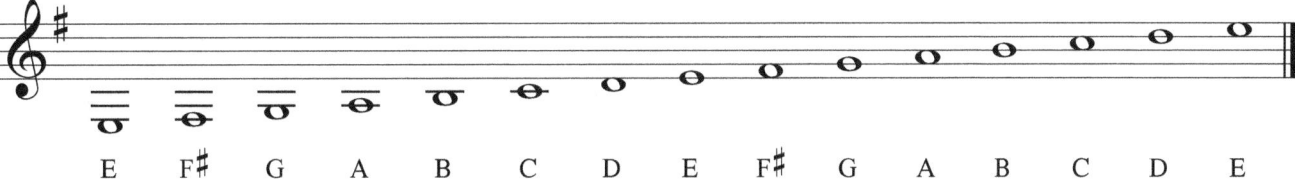

E   F♯   G   A   B   C   D   E   F♯   G   A   B   C   D   E

Play & Do… Video examples at *www.bestmusicpublications.com*

- Play the two octave E natural minor scale as written ascending and descending. Notice how the E natural minor scale shares the same notes with the G major scale.
- Memorize the two octave E natural minor scale as written ascending and descending.
- Play a two octave E minor pentatonic scale by skipping the F♯ and C notes of the written E natural minor scale. Play the E minor pentatonic scale ascending and descending.
- Memorize the two octave E minor pentatonic scale you just practiced.
- Starting on the note E:

    1. Write the note names for E natural minor scale: _____ _____ _____ _____ _____ _____ _____

    2. Write the five note names for E minor pentatonic scale: _____ _____ _____ _____ _____

LESSON 9

Other Chord Variations that are Common in the Key of E Minor

Lesson Concepts
- Minor 7 Chords

Minor 7th Chords

It is very common to *substitute a minor 7 chord* in place of a simple *minor chord.* In some instances, the *minor 7 chord* can be an easier chord to play as well as adding some flavor to the sound of the chord. This idea of substituting a minor 7 chord for a minor chord works for both the *minor secondary chords in the major keys and the minor primary chords in the minor keys.*

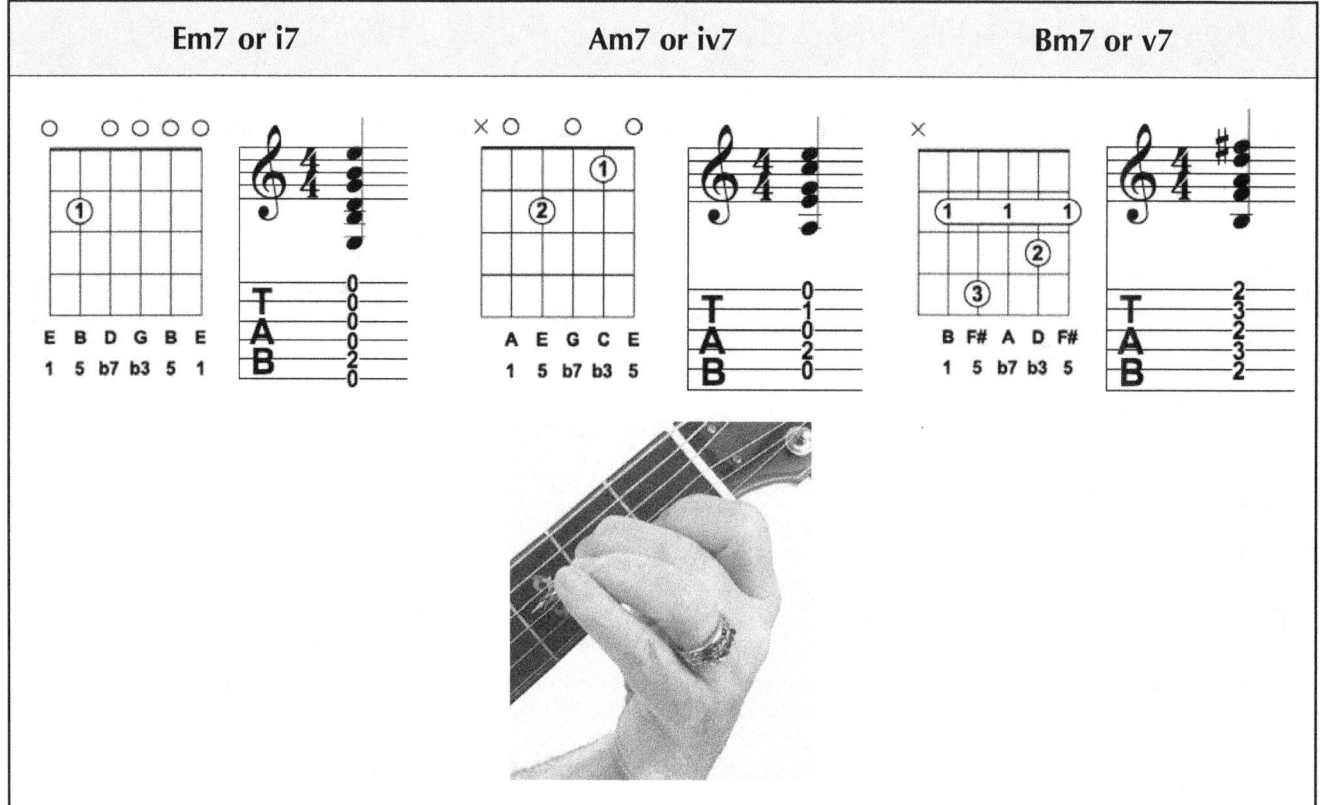

Play & Do... Video examples at *www.bestmusicpublications.com*

- Play any of the previous songs in this book that use minor chords and try substituting the minor 7 chord for the minor chords as you play the accompaniments.

LESSON 10

Single Note Slur Techniques — Hammer-On, Pull-Off, and Slide

> **Lesson Concepts**
> - Slurs
> - Hammer-On
> - Pull-Off
> - Hammer-On/Pull-Off
> - Pull-Off/Hammer-On

Slurs

A slur is to smoothly transition from one note to the next by minimizing or eliminating the attack (start) of the slurred note. The musical symbol for a slur looks like a rhythmic tie, except the two notes are not the same. Slurs can be ascending, descending, or a combination of ascending and descending if there are three or more notes.

Hammer-On

To play an ascending slur on the guitar, you use a *hammer-on* technique by picking a lower note, and then on the same string, fret a higher note in such a way that the higher note sounds without picking it. To get the higher note to sound, be aware of the "3Ps" position, placement and pressure. Additionally, you need to have a fast finger speed when hammering-on the higher note. The finger speed is not the amount of time between notes, but the actual speed of the finger as it hammers the higher note. Figure 6.10.1 how a slur from the open D note on the fourth string to the E note on the fourth string is notated in standard notation and TAB notation.

Figure 6.10.1

In figure 6.10.1 you slurred from an open note. Figure 6.10.2 is an example of a slur from a fretted E note to a fretted F note on the fourth string. Be sure to *keep the pressure on the E note* as you hammer-on the F note.

Figure 6.10.2

Pull-Off

To play a descending slur on the guitar, you use a *pull-off* technique. To play a *pull-off to an open string,* you fret a higher fretted note and then pull off to get the open note to sound. When you remove your finger from the higher fingered note, pull it slightly sideways toward the floor. You are essentially picking the note with your left hand as you remove your finger. Figure 6.10.3 shows a slur from the fretted E note on the fourth string to the open D note on the fourth string in standard notation and TAB notation.

Figure 6.10.3

To play a pull-off from one fretted note to another the technique is the same except that you must be fingering both the lower and higher notes at the same time. If you are fretting the lower note, it will sound when you pull off the higher note. Figure 6.10.4 shows a slur from the fretted F note on the fourth string to the fretted E note on the fourth string in standard notation and TAB notation.

Figure 6.10.4

THE BEST GUITAR METHOD

Hammer-On/Pull-Off and Pull-Off/Hammer-On

You can combine the two techniques when the slur is more complex, but again, you will only pick the very first note! Figure 6.10.5 is an example of a hammer-on/pull-off. Figure 6.10.6 is an example of a pull-off/hammer-on.

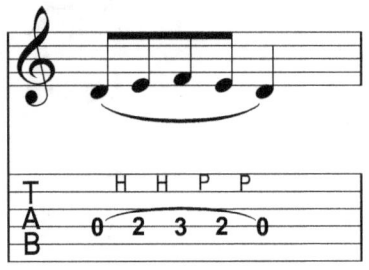

Figure 6.10.5

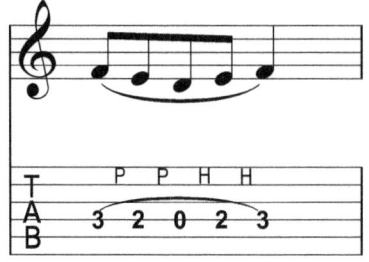

Figure 6.10.6

Slides

Another slur technique on the guitar is a *slide*. To *slide* between two notes, keep the finger pressure constant and slide the finger either up or down on the string. Figure 6.10.7 shows an example of an up slide and down slur.

Figure 6.10.6

Play & Do... Video examples at *www.bestmusicpublications.com*

- Practice string hammer-ons (start with an open string note). Use each finger, i.e., open to the first finger, open to the second finger, open to the third finger, open to the fourth finger.
- Practice pull-offs to open strings and fretted notes. Use different fingers and finger combinations so you can pull off with any finger.
- Practice hammer-ons from open strings and fretted notes. Use different fingers and finger combinations so you can hammer-on with any finger.
- Practice sliding up and down between two notes with each finger.

LESSON 11

Hammer-On (Slur) and Pull-Off (Slur) Chord Technique

Lesson Concepts
- Applying the Hammer-On and Pull-Off Technique to Chords

Applying the Hammer-On and Pull-Off Technique to Chords

The technique is the same for the right-hand except that you form a chord with one or more fingers lifted (open), and strum followed by the lifted finger(s) hammering-on to complete the chord. You can also do the opposite and strum the chord with all the fingers down and then pull-off a finger to an open string. This technique is quite a bit harder than single note slurs but is a very common technique and adds interest to your accompaniments.

Play & Do... Video examples at *www.bestmusicpublications.com*

- Strum the open strings and then finger an Am chord by hammering-on all the notes.
- Strum the open strings and then finger an Em chord by hammering-on all the notes.
- Strum the open strings and then finger an B7 chord by hammering-on all the notes.
- Strum a C chord without putting your second finger down, and then hammer-on your second finger to complete the C chord.

LESSON 12

"Western Slurry" (Song)

Lesson Concepts
- "Western Slurry" (Song) Guitar 1
- "Western Slurry" (Song) Guitar 2

WESTERN SLURRY
(Brian K. Rivers)

Guitar 1

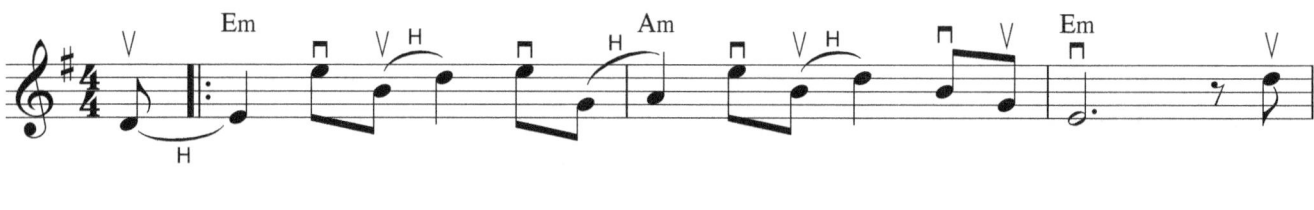

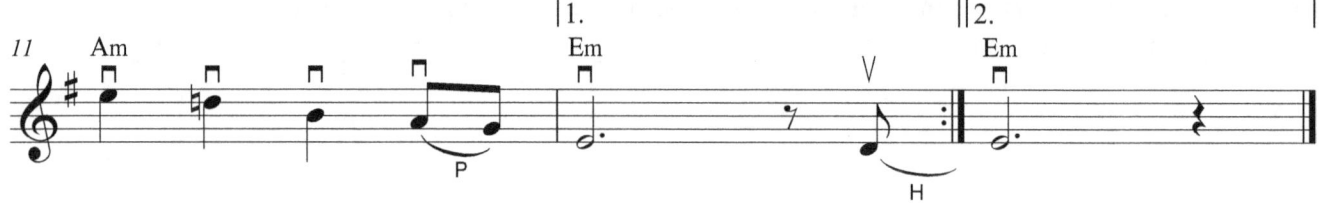

Guitar 2

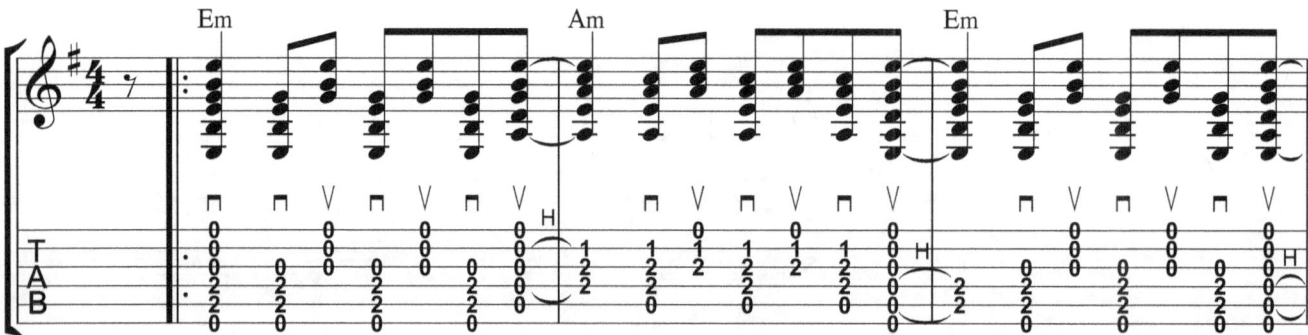

UNIT SIX • LESSON 12

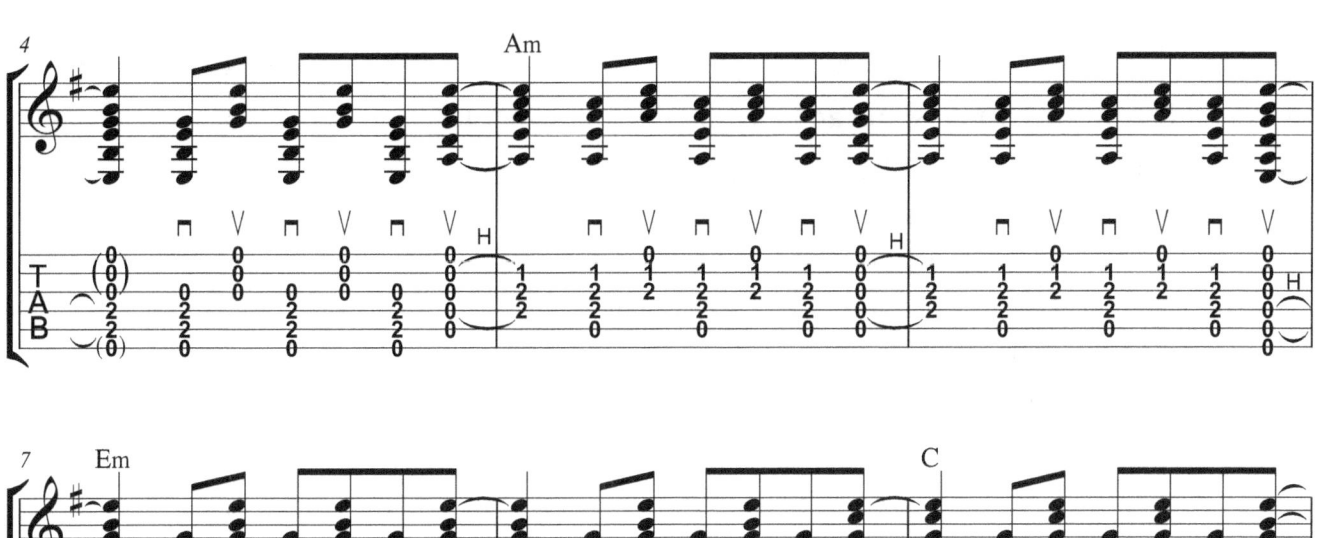

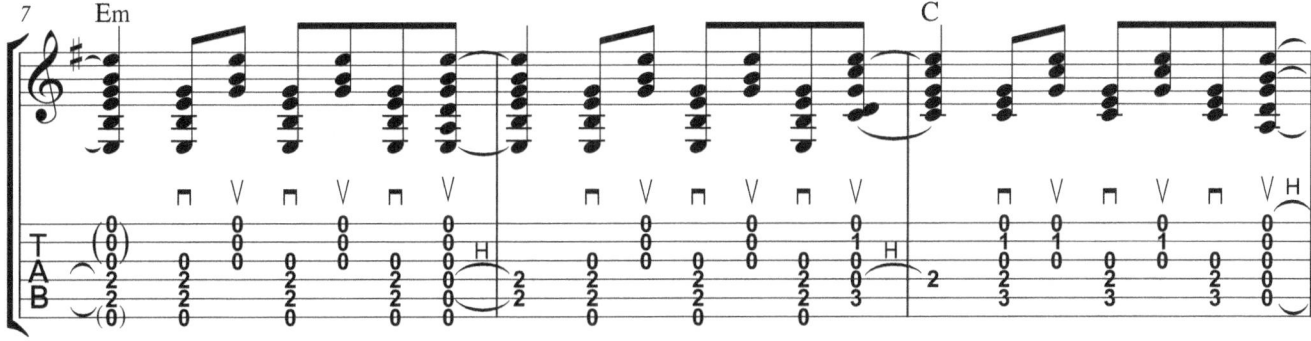

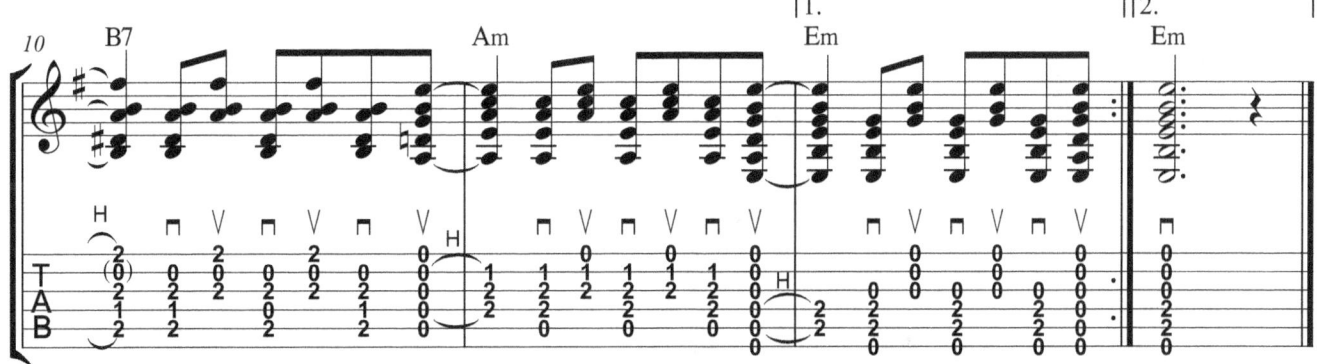

 **Play & Do...** Video examples at *www.bestmusicpublications.com*

- Identify the slur in the melody and practice each one.
- Play the melody to "Western Slurry" using a variety of right-hand techniques.
- Identify the slurs in the accompaniment and practice each one.
- Play the chord accompaniment to "Western Slurry" playing the chords *using a pick*.
- Play the chord accompaniment to "Western Slurry" playing the chords *using your right-hand fingers*.
- Repeat the steps two, four and five while playing along with the recorded music.

Review and Summary

You should be able to demonstrate and identify the following skills:

- Play and identify the primary and secondary chords in the Key of Em
- Play a two octave E natural minor scale from memory
- Play a two octave E minor pentatonic scale from memory
- Play Em7, Am7, and Bm7
- Play slurs with hammer-on, pull-off, and slide techniques
- Fill in the primary and secondary chord names for the key of E minor in the spaces below:

i = _____   III = _____   iv = _____   v = _____   V7 = _____   VI = _____   VII = _____

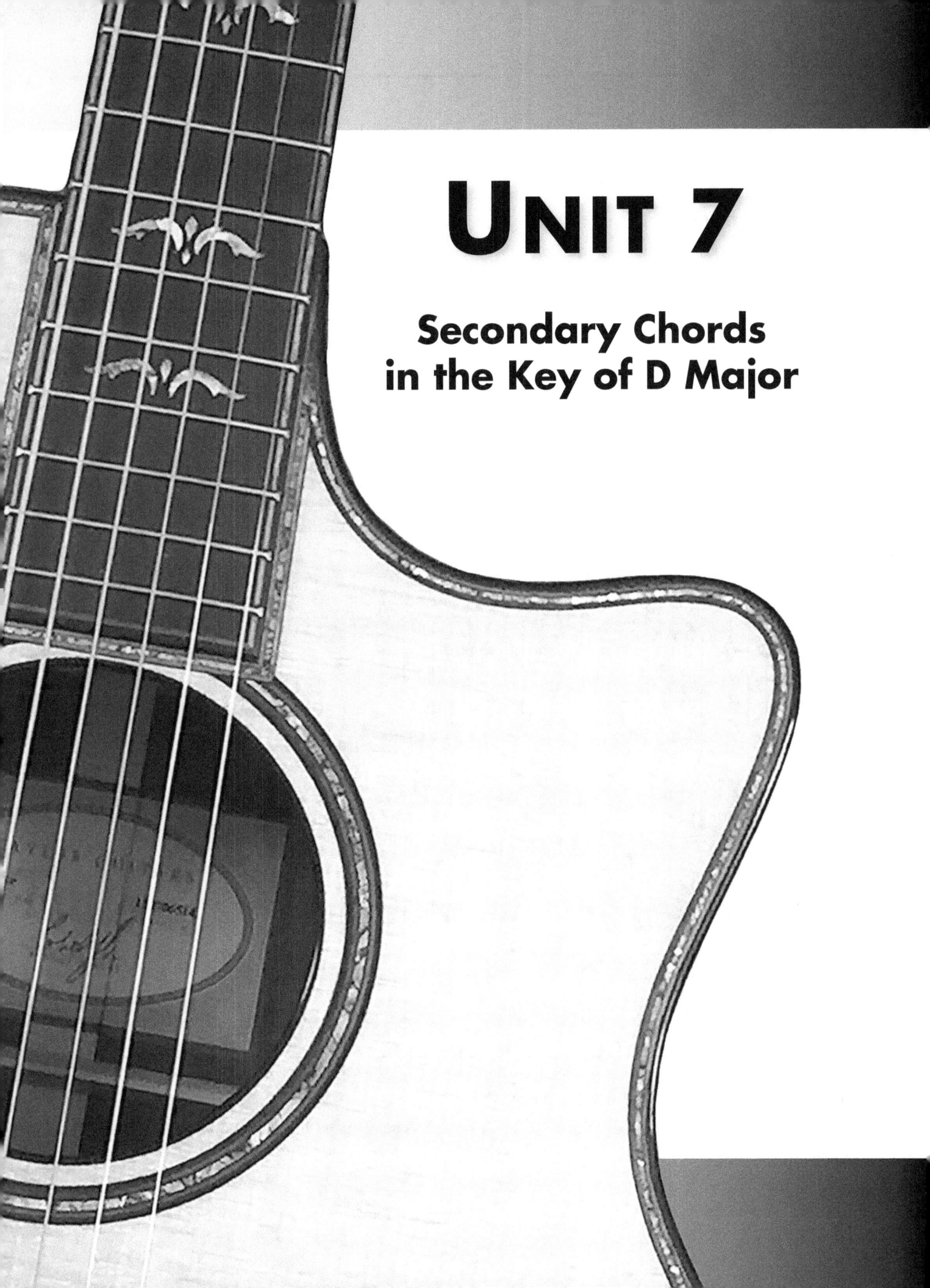

UNIT 7

Secondary Chords in the Key of D Major

Lesson 1

Primary Chords in the Key of D — D, G, A, and A7 (I, IV, V, V7)

> **Lesson Concepts**
> - Primary Chords in the Key of D — D, G, A and A7 (I, IV, V, V7)
> - Standard Fingerings for the Primary Chords in the Key of D — D, G, A and A7 (I, IV, V, V7)
> - Simplified and Challenge Chords Fingerings

Primary Chords in the Key of D — D, G, A and A7 (I, IV, V, V7)

You already know the D and G chord. Because you are in the key of D, the D chord = I and the G chord = IV. The new chords are A (V) and A7 (V7).

Standard Fingerings for the Primary Chords in the Key of D — D, G, A and A7 (I, IV, V, V7)

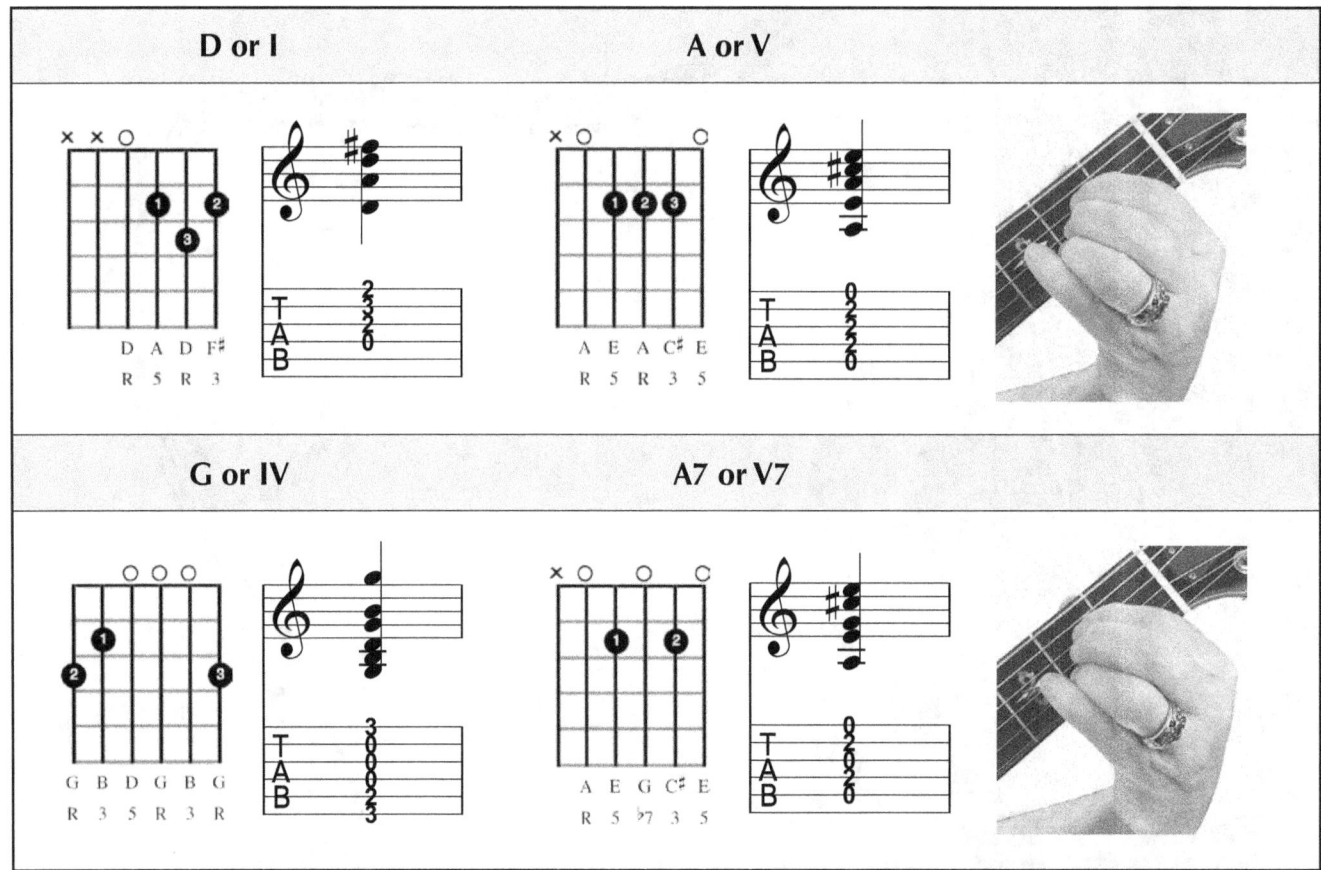

Simplified and Challenge Chords Fingerings

Simplified and challenge chords fingerings for all the chords in this book can be found at *www.bestmusicpublications.com*.

 **Play & Do...** Video examples at *www.bestmusicpublications.com*

- Finger (play) each new chord and make sure you are mindful of the three P's of tone production. Pick each string of the chord to be sure each string is making a good sound. As you play the chord, say the specific names and universal names for the primary chords in the key of D, say: "D — also known as the I chord, G — also known as the IV chord and A — also known as the V chord."

- "*Catch and release*" each chord, strum the chord as you apply pressure, and then check that each string is still sounding good. If it does not sound good, go back and check the three P's of tone production.

- Fill in the chord names for the primary chords in the key of D major in the spaces below:

    I = _____   IV= _____   V = _____   V7 = _____

- Memorize the specific names and universal names for the primary chords in the key of D.

LESSON 2

Transposing to a Different Key — The Same Only Different!

> **Lesson Concepts**
> - Roman Numerals – "Hot Cross Buns" – Universal Key
> - "Hot Cross Buns" – Key of G
> - Transposing: "Hot Cross Buns" – Key of D

Roman Numerals – "Hot Cross Buns" – Universal Key

The universal Roman numeral system is independent of the specific key. Figure 7.2.1 shows the chord progression to Hot Cross Buns in Universal Chord notation:

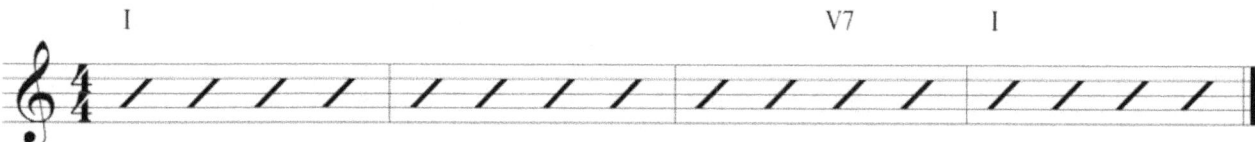

Figure 7.2.1

"Hot Cross Buns" – Key of G

Figure 7.2.2 shows Hot Cross Buns (with the melody) in the key of G.

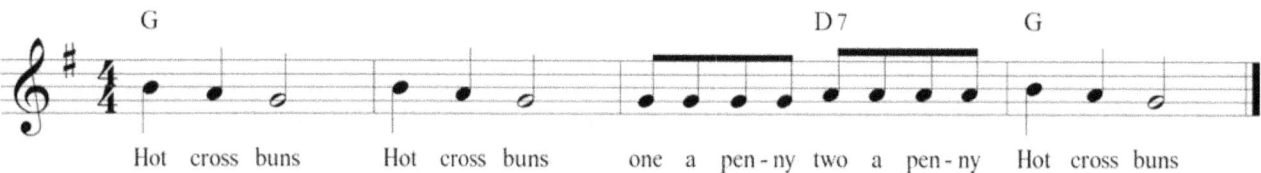

Figure 7.2.2

Transposing: "Hot Cross Buns" – Key of D

Transposing means to change the key of the song. When a song is transposed, you will still recognize the song, it just sounds higher of lower in pitch.

Figure 7.2.3 shows Hot Cross Buns (with the melody) in the key of D.

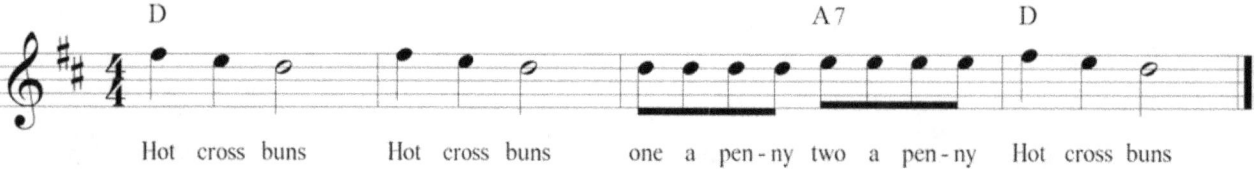

Figure 7.2.3

You can see in the keys of G (Figure 7.2.2) and D (Figure 7.2.3) that the chord progressions follow the same universal progression (Figure 7.2.1), but the key signatures (now F and C are both sharped), chord names and melody notes are different in each key. When a song is transposed to a different (changed to a different key), it is the same only different!

Play & Do... Video examples at *www.bestmusicpublications.com*

- Play the chords for "Hot Cross Buns" in the key of G with the recording.
- Play the chords for "Hot Cross Buns" in the key of D with the recording.
- Play the melody for "Hot Cross Buns" in the key of G with the recording.
- Play the melody for "Hot Cross Buns" in the key of D with the recording.

LESSON 3

"Amazing Grace" (Song)

Lesson Concepts
- "Amazing Grace" (Song) (Transposed to the Key of D) Guitar 1
- "Amazing Grace" (Song) (Transposed to the Key of D) Guitar 2

This song brings together many of the skills you have learned so far.

AMAZING GRACE

(Traditional)

Guitar 1

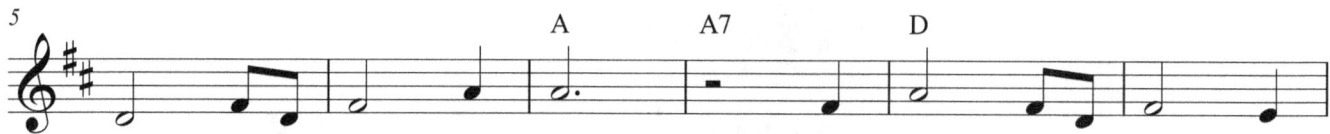

Guitar 2

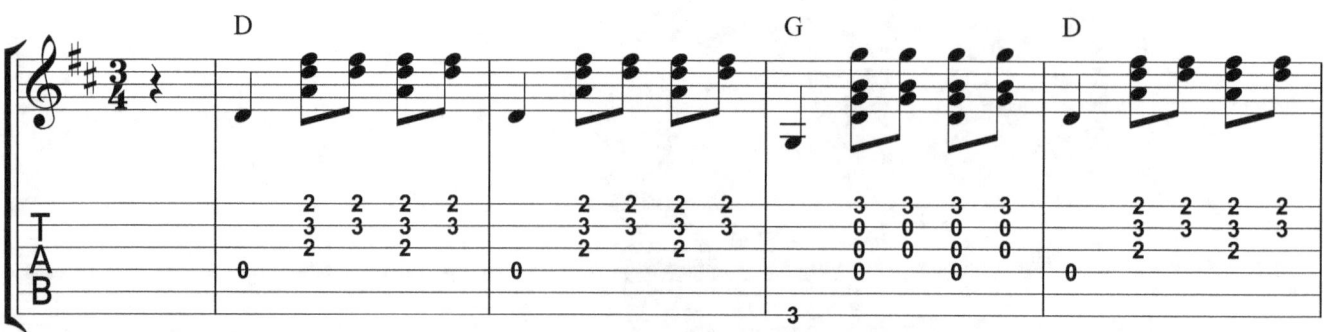

120

UNIT SEVEN • LESSON 3

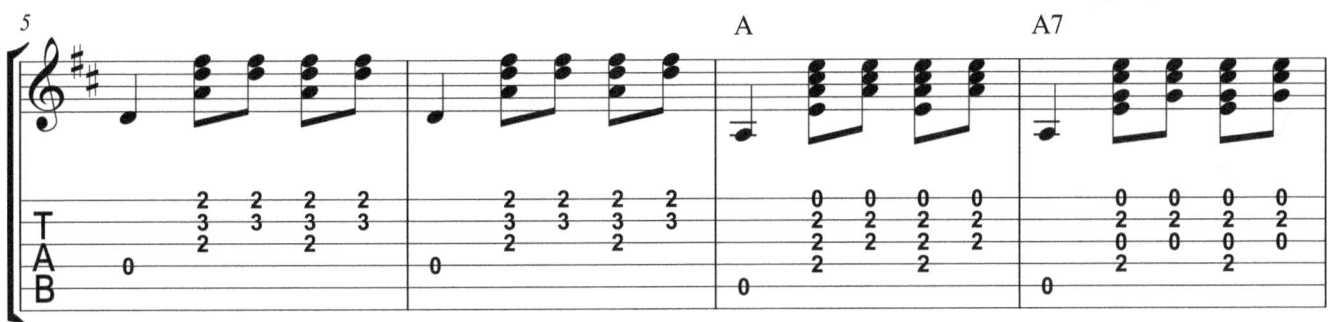

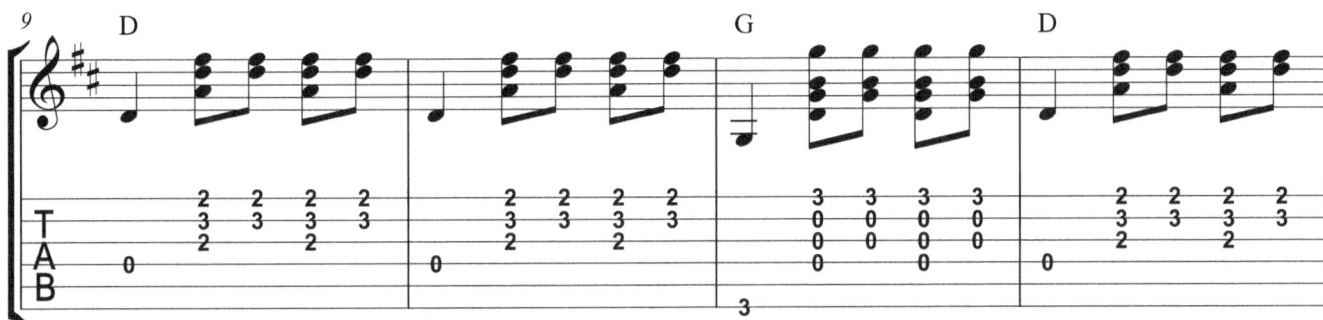

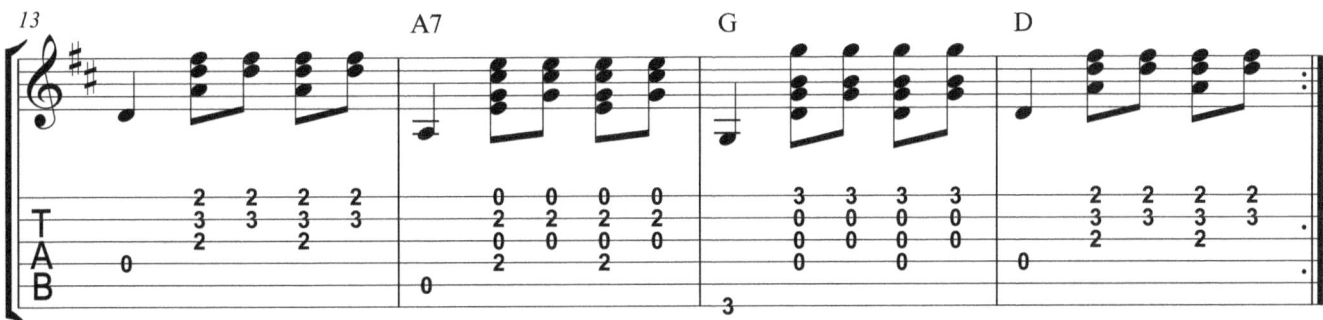

 **Play & Do...** Video examples at *www.bestmusicpublications.com*

- Play the melody to "Minor Inconvenience," using a variety of right-hand techniques including: pick, standard finger assignment, alternating index and middle fingers, and thumb. Be sure to use the correct fingers for fretted notes!
- Play the chord accompaniment to "Minor Inconvenience," *using a pick.*
- Play the chord accompaniment to "Minor Inconvenience," *using your right-hand fingers.*
- Repeat the first three steps while playing along with the recorded music.

LESSON 4

Secondary Chords in the Key of D — Em, F♯m, and Bm (ii, iii, vi)

> **Lesson Concepts**
> - Secondary Chords in the Key of D — Em, F♯m, and Bm (ii, iii, vi)
> - Standard Fingerings for the Secondary Chords in the Key of D — Em, F♯m, and Bm (ii, iii, vi)
> - Simplified and Challenge Chords Fingerings

Secondary Chords in the Key of D — Em, F♯m, and Bm (ii, iii, vi)

The secondary chords in any key are minor chords. In the key of D, the secondary chords are Em (ii), F♯m (iii) and Bm (vi). You already know how to play Em and Bm, so the only new chord is F♯m.

Standard Fingerings for the Secondary Chords in the Key of D — Em, F♯m, and Bm (ii, iii, vi)

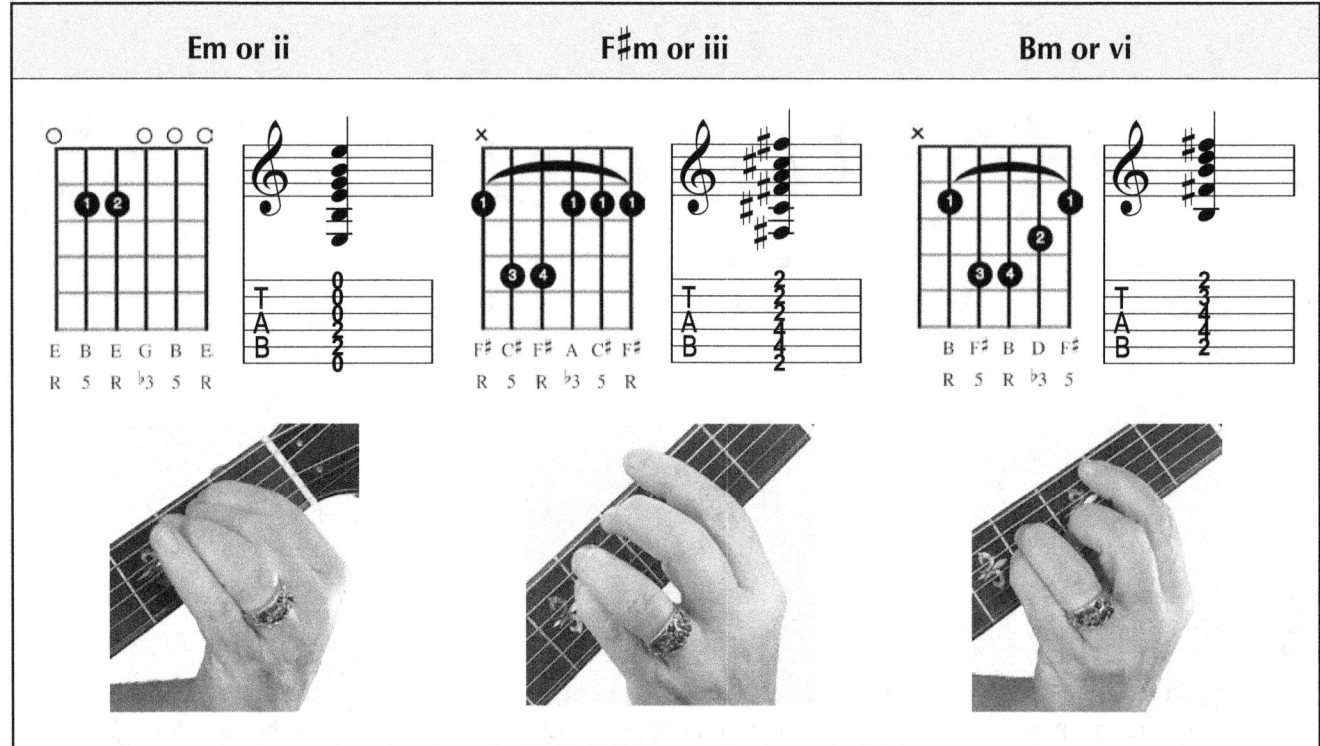

Simplified and Challenge Chords Fingerings

Simplified and challenge chords fingerings for all the chords in this book can be found at *www.bestmusicpublications.com*.

Play & Do... Video examples at *www.bestmusicpublications.com*

- Finger (play) each chord and make sure you are mindful of the three P's of tone production. Pick each string of the chord to be sure each string is making a good sound. "Catch and release" each chord, strum the chord as you apply pressure and then check that each string is still sounding good. If it's not, go back and check the three P's of tone production.

  Note: When you play the F♯m chord you may find that it is *very difficult* to get the third string to sound good. Make sure your first finger is flat and close to the second fret (placement), and there is flesh pushing on the third string (position). After that, make sure you are applying strong pressure with all your fingers, especially the first finger.)

- As you play the chord, say the specific names and universal names for the secondary chords in the key of D, say: "E minor, also known as the ii chord, F♯ minor, also known as the iii chord, and B minor, also known as the vi chord."

- Fill in the chord names for the secondary minor chords in the key of D major in the spaces below:

  ii = _____   iii = _____   vi = _____

- Memorize the specific names and universal names for the secondary chords in the key of D.
- Fill in the universal primary and secondary chord names for the key of D in the spaces below:

  I = _____   ii = _____   iii = _____   IV = _____   V = _____   vi = _____

Lesson 5

Notes—High A and Review of C#

> **Lesson Concepts**
> - C# Review and New Note A on The First String
> - Extended Position and Second Position

C# and Review and New Note A on the First String

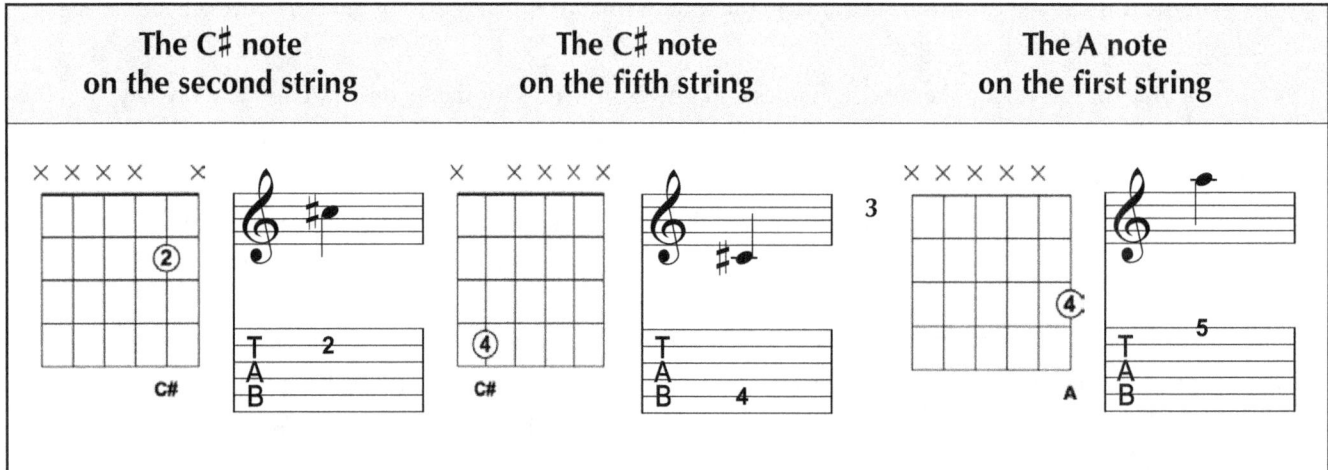

Extended Position and Second Position

Until now all the notes you have learned are in the first four frets on the guitar, and they are played in the *first position*. The high A note on the first string is played on the fifth fret, so you have two choices: either play it as an *extended first position* fingering or as a second position fingering. Either way, you use your fourth finger-- it's just a matter of whether you slide your hand (thumb) to the second position or simply leave your hand in the first position and stretch your hand (extended first position).

Play & Do... Video and audio examples at *www.bestmusicpublications.com*

- Finger the C# notes and say the name of the note while looking at the standard notation.
- Finger the A note as an extended first position fingering and say the name of the note while looking at the standard notation.
- Finger the A note a second position fingering and say the name of the note while looking at the standard notation.

LESSON 6

Sixteenth-Note Rhythms

> **Lesson Concepts**
> - Arm and Wrist Motion
> - Eighth-Note Frame and Single Notes
> - Eighth-Note Strumming Frame
> - Sixteenth Notes
> - Downbeats
> - Sixteenth-Note Rhythm Patterns

Arm and Wrist Motion

When strumming sixteenth note rhythms, your right arm motion originates from the wrist like you are turning a doorknob. You will create an accent by moving your arm from the elbow on the downbeats. Keep the arm motion to a minimum. Don't move very far beyond the highest string on the downbeat; play the next up stroke and the remaining three sixteenth notes with the wrist motion. As the tempos increases, the arm motion from the elbow becomes smaller.

Eighth-Note Frame and Single Notes

When picking sixteenth note rhythms with a single note, modify your pick grip to a single note grip. All the motions are much smaller than the strumming motion and happen within the space of a single string. The elbow will hardly move at all; almost all the motion is in the twisting of the arm and the wrist.

Eighth-Note Strumming Frame

You have only used a *quarter-note frame* when strumming for picking eighth note rhythms. To play sixteenth note rhythms, you need to use an eighth note frame. An *eighth-note frame* means moving your arm as if playing eighth notes with all down strokes. (Figure 7.6.1)

Figure 7.6.1

Sixteenth Notes

To play the sixteenth notes, you add the up strokes between the downs of the eighth note frame. (Figure 7.6.2)

Figure 7.6.2

125

THE BEST GUITAR METHOD

Downbeats

Downbeats should be accented, and since you are subdividing the beat into sixteenth notes, the accent will happen on the first of every group of four sixteenth notes. Use a motion from the elbow to play these downbeats. (Figure 7.6.3)

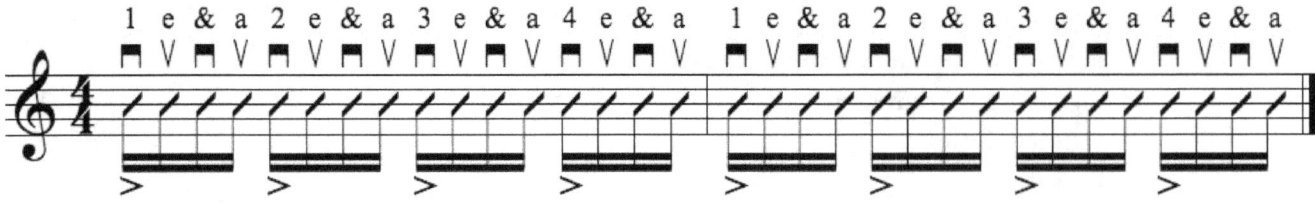

Figure 7.6.3

Sixteenth-Note Rhythm Patterns

UNIT SEVEN • LESSON 6

 **Play & Do…** Video examples at *www.bestmusicpublications.com*

- Step 1) Start with the eighth note frame and say *but don't play* the rhythm while continuing to move your right arm in a steady up and down manner as if you are strumming an eighth note frame. You can say either "down-down-down-down-down-down-down-down" or "1-and-2-and-3-and-4-and" as you move your arm in each downward motion.

- Step 2) Now *say it while you play it*. As you move in a downward motion strum the strings and say either "down-down-down-down-down-down-down-down" or "1-and-2-and-3-and-4-and" as you move your arm in each downward motion while strumming the strings. You can choose to play one of the chords you know, or you can simply strum open strings.

- Step 3) Now *play it, but don't say it*. That means strum the string, but instead of saying either "down-down-down-down-down-down-down-down" or "1-and-2-and-3-and-4-and" out loud, say it silently inside your head as you strum the strings.

To sum up the three-step sequence:

Say it don't play it while moving your arm using a quarter note frame.
Say it while you play it.
Play it while you say it silently inside of your head.

Repeat the three-step sequence for each of the sixteenth note rhythm patterns strumming strings.
Repeat the three-step sequence for each of the sixteenth note rhythm patterns playing a single note.
Repeat the three-step sequence for each of the sixteenth note rhythm patterns playing different single notes.

LESSON 7

Arpeggio Style Finger Picking

Lesson Concept
- Arpeggio Style Finger Picking

Arpeggio Style Finger Picking

Arpeggio style finger picking is common in both popular and classical guitar styles. The basic idea is to play the root note of a chord with your thumb and then use your index *(i)*, middle *(m)* and ring *(a)* fingers to individually pluck a *group of three strings.* Usually, you play either the first, second, and third strings as a group or second, third and fourth strings as a group, this is known as a string grouping. For now, you will only use eighth note patterns when finger picking. Remember to plant your fingers at the beginning of each four-note arpeggio, pulling them off one at a time. Figure 7.7.1 shows an example playing G, C, and D chords using string grouping 1, 2, 3:

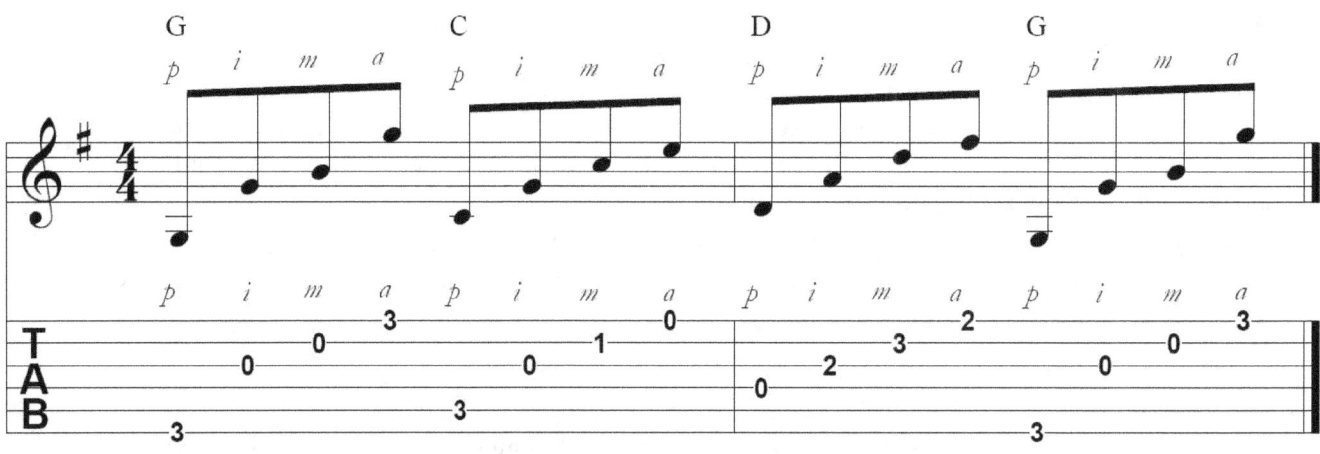

7.7.1

Figure 7.7.2 shows an example using string groupings 2, 3, 4. Notice that when you get to the D chord, you change string groupings to 1, 2, 3 because that is the only option for a D chord since it only has 4 strings.

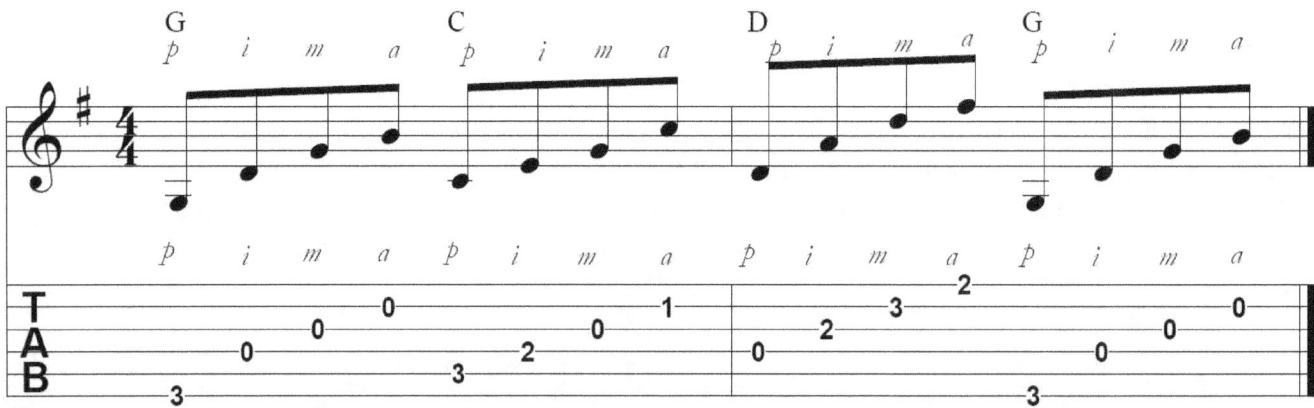

7.7.2

Figure 7.7.3 shows how the pattern would be repeated if the chord is held for longer than two beats.

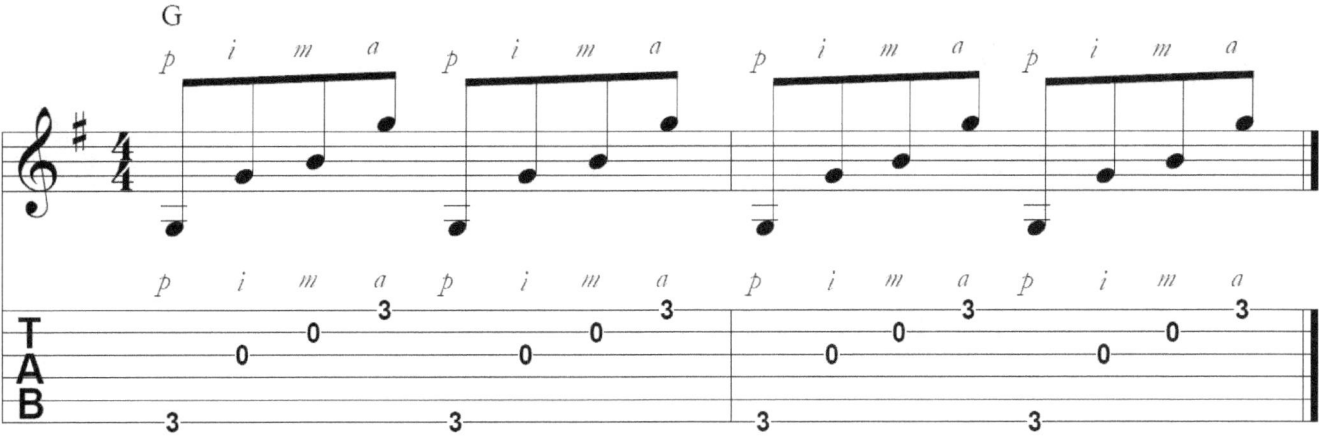

7.7.3

 **Play & Do...** Video examples at *www.bestmusicpublications.com*

- Practice each of the last three examples as written. Be sure to plant your three fingers as you pluck the root note.
- Practice the simple eighth note arpeggios for every chord you know using string grouping 1, 2, 3 using the correct root note.
- Practice the simple eighth note arpeggios for every chord you know using string grouping 2, 3, 4 (note: it won't work for the D chord, not enough strings) using the correct root note.

LESSON 8

"Canon in D" (Song)

Lesson Concepts
- "Canon in D" (Song)
- Multiple Parts for Ensemble Playing and Arrangement
- Something to Think About

"Canon In D" – Johann Pachelbel

"Canon in D" written by Johann Pachelbel is one of the most familiar classical pieces ever written. This "arrangement" brings together most of the skills and chords from your Unit 8 lessons. An *arrangement* is when an arranger takes the basic melodies and harmonies of a particular song and either assigns them to various instruments or embellishes the basic melodic, harmonic or rhythmic structures.

Multiple Parts for Ensemble Playing and Arrangement

Interestingly, the main chord progression in "Canon in D" is only four measures long, with different *themes and variations* that are layered and passed around an ensemble. Because of this, there are thousands of different "arrangements" of this song. Look up versions of this song online, and you will find things like "the one-hour version" or "the two-hour version." Have fun using the parts provided in the book to make your arrangement! Start with one, and then either switch to a different part or have a second guitar play a different part. Think of it as Pachelbel planted some flowers which have been picked, and now you get to make your arrangement. Have fun!

Play & Do... Video examples at *www.bestmusicpublications.com*

- Practice each of the melodic parts #1-5 for "Canon in D."
- Practice the Arpeggio Style Fingerpicking accompaniment for "Canon in D."
- Practice the strummed accompaniment for "Canon in D."
- Use the provided parts to make-up a solo arrangement.
- Make-up an ensemble arrangement by choosing the order of the parts played by you with others. Remember, any two parts or more parts sound good together!
- Consider adding dynamics to your arrangement. Traditionally it starts very quietly and then grows in volume as more parts are added.

Something to Think About

Much of modern music is now composed on computers using electronic "loops," many of which are only four bars long. Many musicians find this disturbing because it seems too repetitive and harmonically limited. Interestingly, Pachelbel limited himself to a four-bar harmonic structure way back around 1680AD. Is a simple chord progression a limitation on creativity or an opportunity? What do you think?

UNIT SEVEN • LESSON 8

CANON IN D

(Johann Pachelbel)

131

THE BEST GUITAR METHOD

132

LESSON 9

D Major Scale

> **Lesson Concept**
> - D Major Scale

D Major Scale

 **Play & Do...** Video examples at *www.bestmusicpublications.com*

- Practice the D major scale with your pick. Use alternate picking.
- Practice the D major scale playing the notes finger style (fourth string – *p*, third string –*I*, second string – *m*).
- Practice the D major scale playing the notes alternate finger style (*i – m – i – m*).
- Memorize the D major scale left-hand fingering and note names.

LESSON 10

The Key of D Major — No Training Wheels

Lesson Concept
- The Key of D Major — No Training Wheels (No Tablature)

D MAJOR – NO TRAINING WHEELS

Play & Do… Video examples at *www.bestmusicpublications.com*

- Play D major (No training wheels…) using a variety of right-hand techniques including: pick- standard finger assignment, alternating index and middle fingers, and thumb.
- Play along with the recording using each right-hand picking technique.

LESSON 11

Alternate Bass

> **Lesson Concepts**
> - Alternate Bass
> - Alternate Bass Note for an A and D Chord
> - Alternate Bass Note For a C Chord
> - Alternate Bass Note For an E Chord
> - Alternate Bass Note For a G Chord

Alternate Bass

Alternate bass is similar to playing the root note on beat one but adds an *alternate bass* note on beat 3 in a measure. An alternate bass note is a *chord tone* other than the root of the chord. Usually, the fifth of the chord is the alternate bass note, but you occasionally will use the third of the chord. The alternate bass note is often on the adjacent string below the root string, on the same fret as the root. If the alternate bass note is on the *adjacent string* above the root string, it is two frets above the root note fret. One notable exception is the open G chord where the root note is on the sixth string third fret, and the alternate bass note is on the open fourth string.

Alternate Bass Note for an A and D Chord

The A and D chords are examples of chords that have the alternate bass note on the adjacent string below the open root note, located on the same fret.

The alternate bass note for an A chord. (Figure 7.11.1)

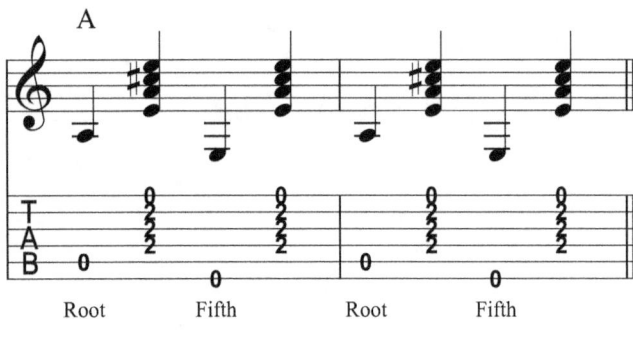

Figure 7.11.1

The alternate bass note for an A chord. (Figure 7.11.1)

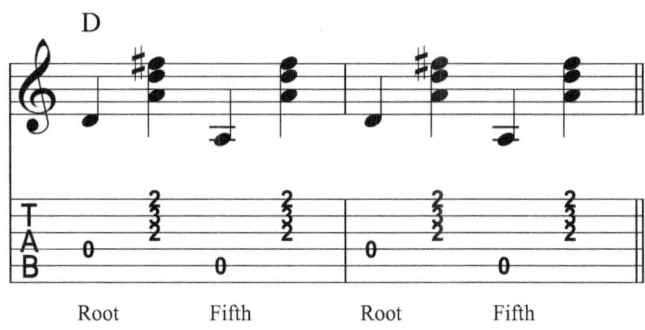

Figure 7.11.2

Alternate Bass Note for a C Chord

The C chord is an example of a chord that has the alternate bass note on the adjacent string *below* the *fretted* root note, located on the same fret. To play the fretted alternate bass note, move your third finger from the fifth string to the sixth string.

The alternate bass note for a C chord. (Figure 7.11.3)

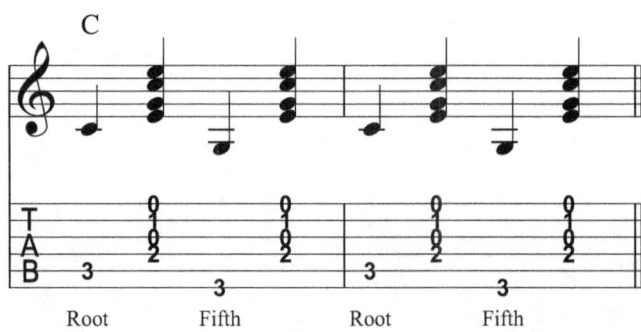

Figure 7.11.3

136

Alternate Bass Note for an E Chord

The E chord is an example of a chord that has the alternate bass note on the adjacent string *above* the *open* root note, located two frets higher than the open root note.

The alternate bass note for an E chord*. (Figure 7.11.4)

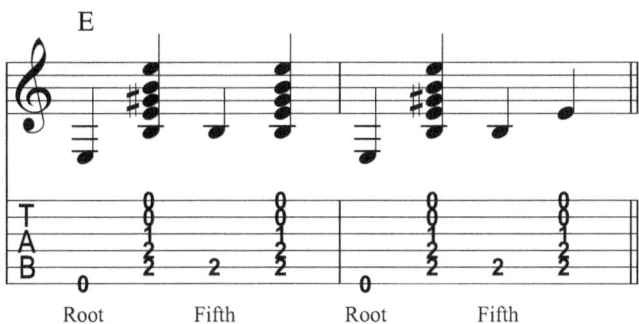

Figure 7.11.4

* Note: You have not learned this chord yet, but you can find the fingering in Unit 8 / Lesson 1.

Alternate Bass Note for a G Chord

The G chord is unique; the alternate bass note is *not on an adjacent string*. The alternate bass note for a G chord is on the fourth string (two strings above the fretted root note).

The alternate bass note for a G chord. (Figure 7.11.5)

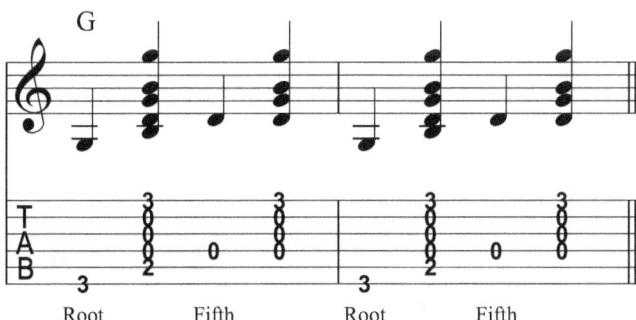

Figure 7.11.5

 **Play & Do…** Video examples at *www.bestmusicpublications.com*

- Play each chord you know and identify the fifth of the chord for each chord.
- Practice strumming quarter notes in 4/4 time playing the root note on beat 1 and the alternate bass note (fifth) of the chord on beat 3 and strum the high strings of the chord on beats 2 and 4. Do this for every chord you know and try to memorize the fifth of the chord.

LESSON 12

"Yankee Doodle" (Song)

Lesson Concepts
- "Yankee Doodle" (Song) Guitar 1
- "Yankee Doodle" (Song) Guitar 2

YANKEE DOODLE

(Richard Shuckburgh)

GUITAR 1

GUITAR 2

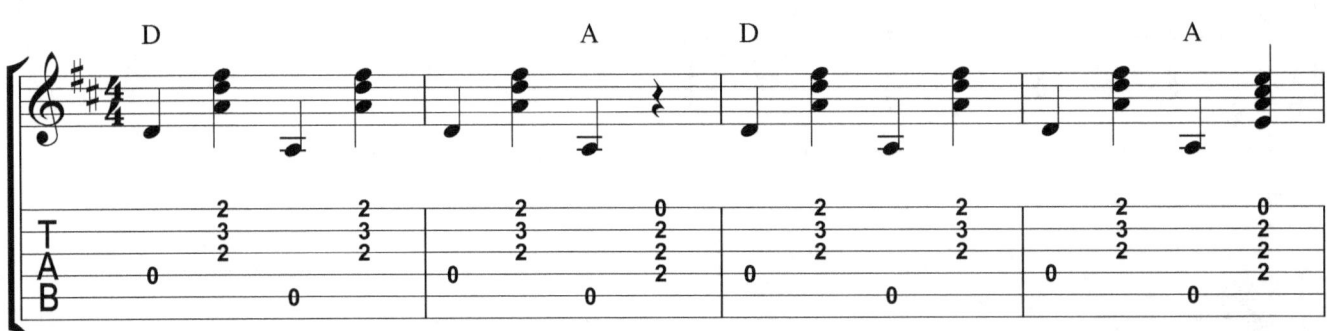
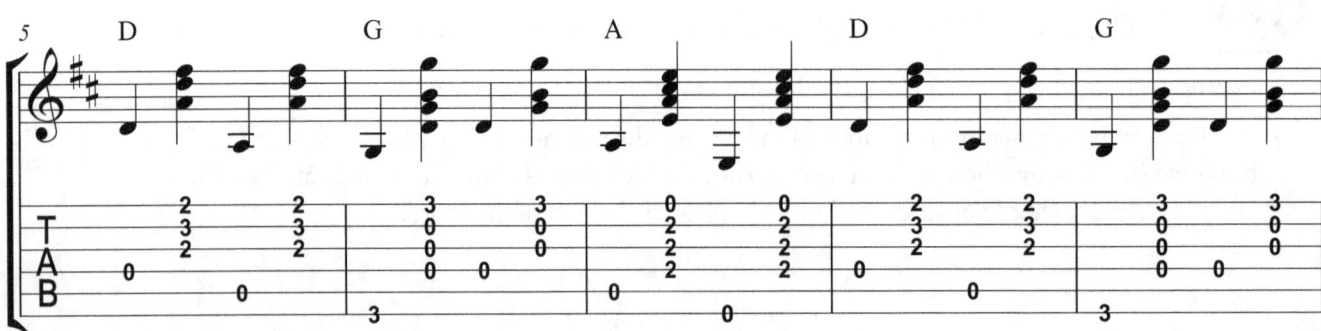

UNIT SEVEN • LESSON 12

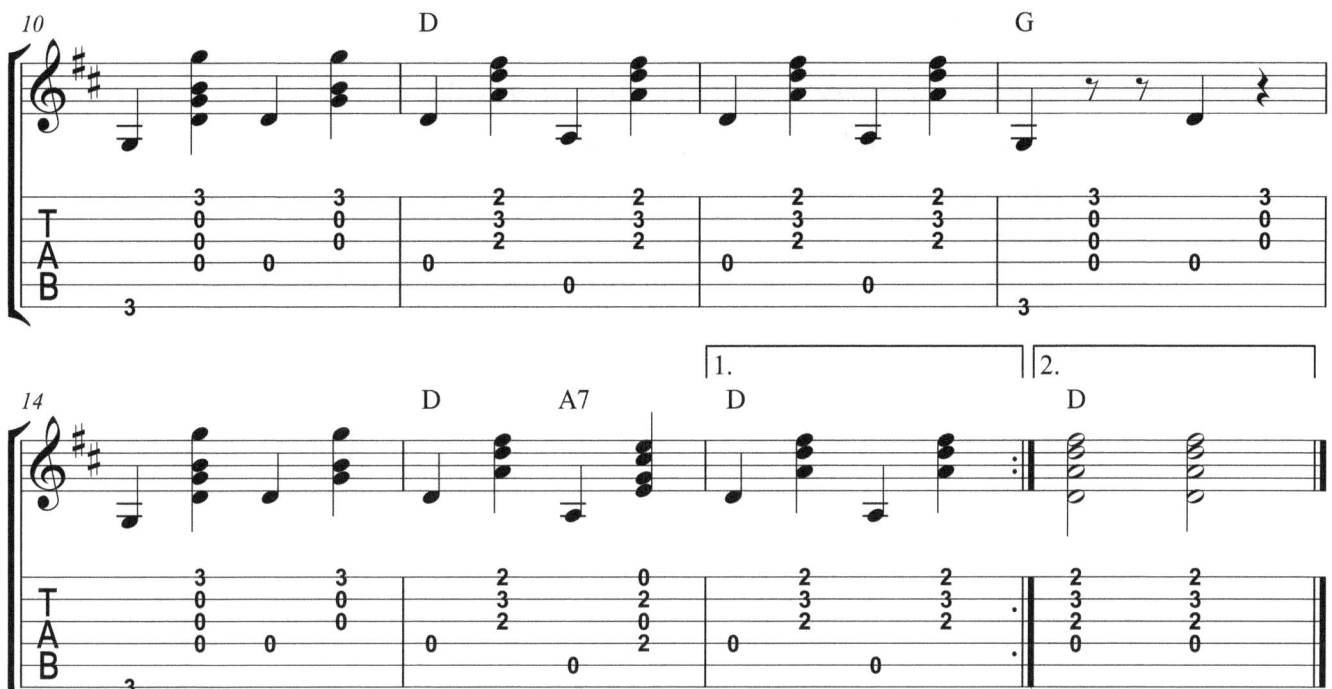

Play & Do… Video examples at *www.bestmusicpublications.com*

- Play the melody to "Yankee Doodle" using a variety of right-hand techniques including: pick, standard finger assignment, alternating index and middle fingers, and thumb. Be sure to use the correct fingers for fretted notes!
- Play the chord accompaniment to "Yankee Doodle" playing the chords *using a pick*.
- Play the chord accompaniment to "Yankee Doodle" playing the chords *using your right-hand fingers*.
- Repeat the first three steps while playing along with the recorded music.
- Memorize the alternate bass notes for the chords D, G, A and C chords.

THE BEST GUITAR METHOD

Review and Summary

You should be able to demonstrate and identify the following skills:

- Play and identify the primary and secondary chords in the key of D
- Play a one-octave D major scale from memory
- Play basic sixteen note rhythms
- Identify the root note and alternate bass notes for the primary chords in the key of D and C
- Play all songs in Unit 7 with the full speed recordings
- Fill in the primary and secondary chord names for the key of D major in the spaces below:

I = _____ ii = _____ iii = _____ IV = _____ V = _____ V7 = _____ vi = _____

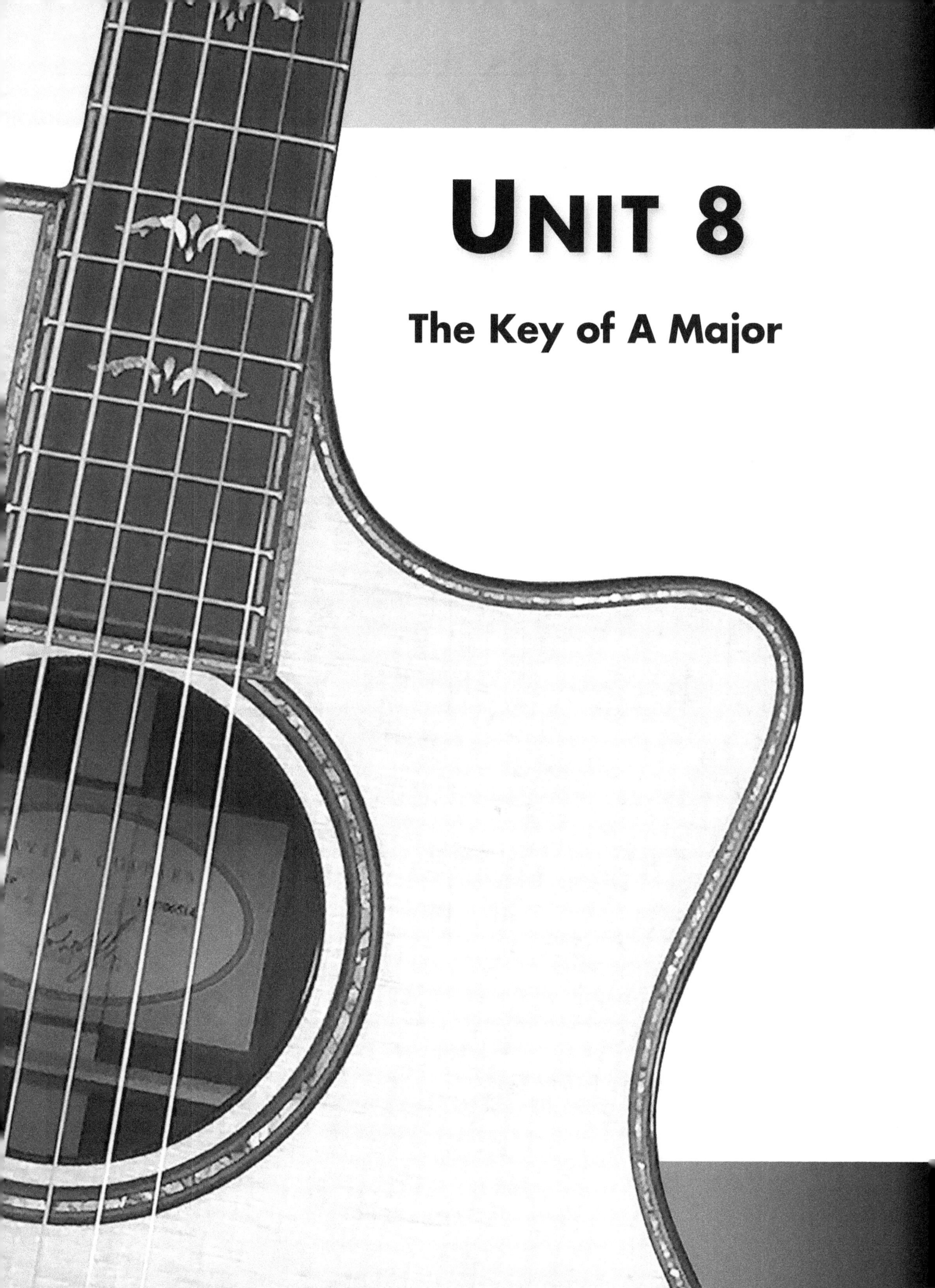

UNIT 8

The Key of A Major

LESSON 1

Primary Chords in the Key of A — A, D, E and E7 (I, IV, V, V7)

> **Lesson Concepts**
> - Primary Chords in the Key of A — A, D, E and E7 (I, IV, V, V7)
> - Standard Fingerings for the Primary Chords in the Key of A — A, D, E and E7 (I, IV, V, V7)
> - Simplified and Challenge Chords Fingerings

Primary Chords in the Key of A — A, D, E and E7 (I, IV, V, V7)

You already know the A and D chords. The new chords are E and E7.

Standard Fingerings for the Primary Chords in the Key of A — A, D, E and E7 (I, IV, V, V7)

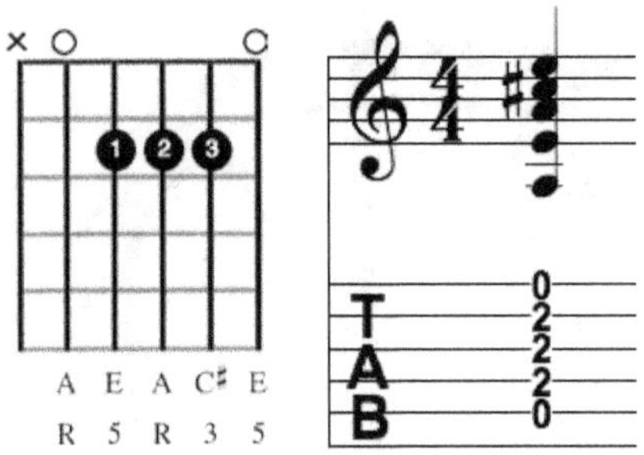

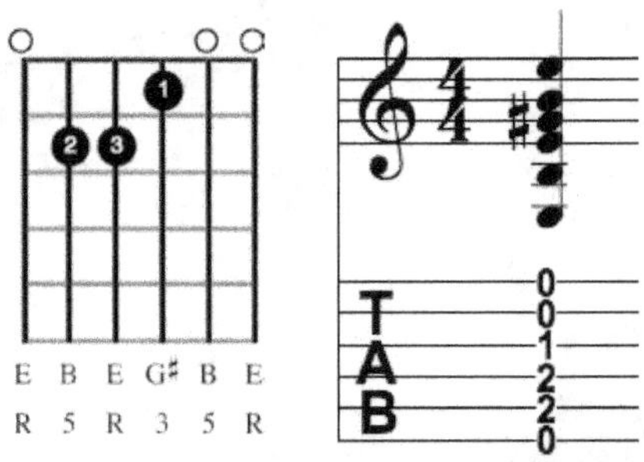

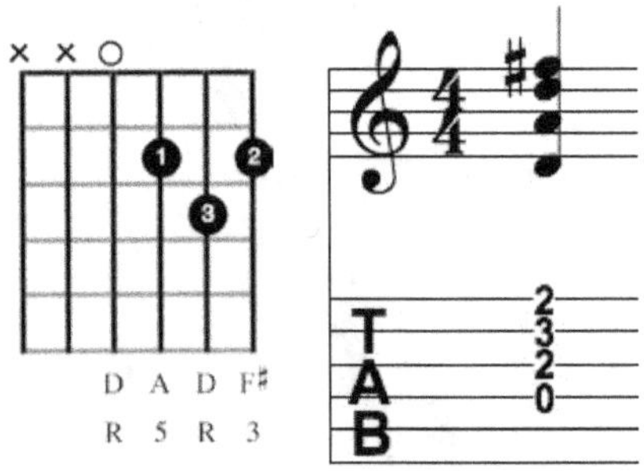

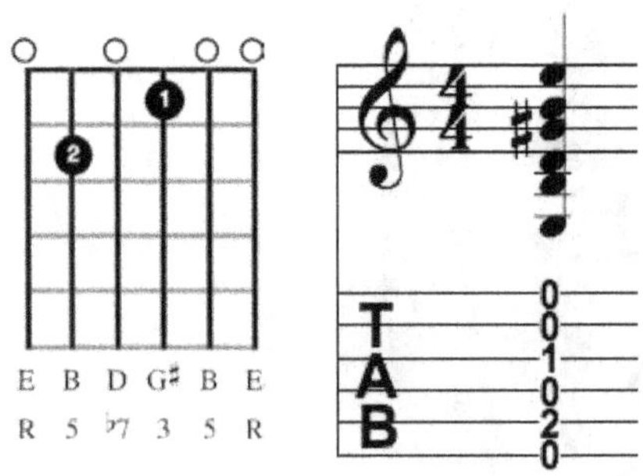

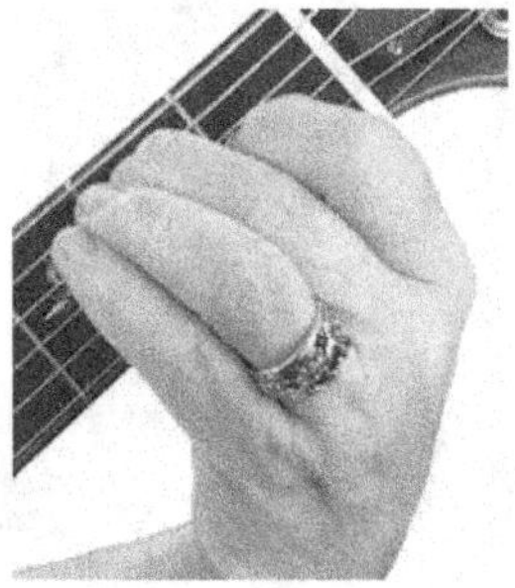

Simplified and Challenge Chords Fingerings

Simplified and challenge chords fingerings for all the chords in this book can be found at *www.bestmusic-publications.com*.

Play & Do... Video examples at *www.bestmusicpublications.com*

- As you play the chord, say its universal name (i.e., when you play an A chord say, "I (one) chord in the key of A").

- Recite the specific names and universal names for the primary chords in the key of A. Say: "The primary chords in the key of A are A—also known as the I chord, D—also known as the IV chord, and E—also known as the V chord."

- Memorize the specific names and universal names for the primary chords in the key of A.

- Fill in the primary chord names for the key of A major in the spaces below:

I = _____   IV = _____   V = _____   V7 = _____

LESSON 2

Transposing "Hot Cross Buns" to the Key of A

> *Lesson Concepts*
> - Transposing: "Hot Cross Buns" – Key of A

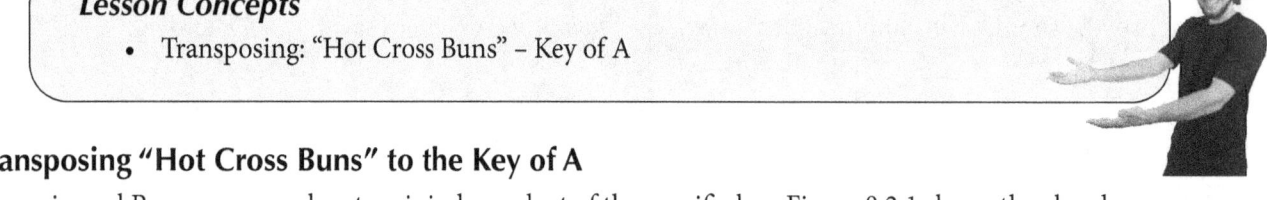

Transposing "Hot Cross Buns" to the Key of A

The universal Roman numeral system is independent of the specific key. Figure 8.2.1 shows the chord progression to "Hot Cross Buns" in Universal Chord notation:

Figure 8.2.1

Figure 8.2.2 shows "Hot Cross Buns" (with melody) in the key of G.

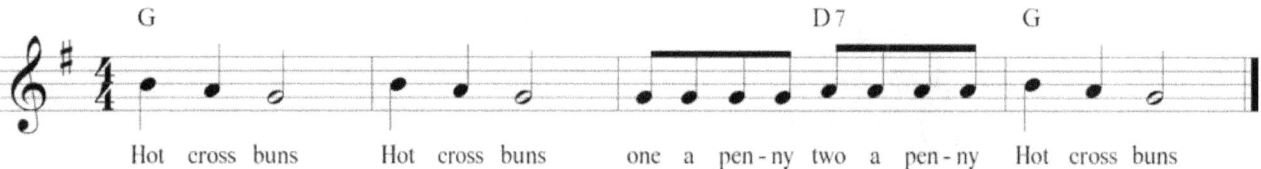

Figure 8.2.2

Figure 8.2.3 shows "Hot Cross Buns" (with melody) in the key of A.

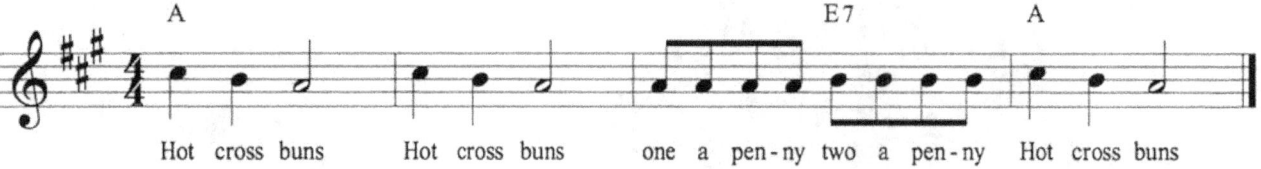

Figure 8.2.3

You can see in the key of G (Figure 8.2.2) and, the key of A (Figure 8.2.3), the chord progressions follow the same universal progression, but the key signatures, chord names, and melody notes are different in each key. When a song is transposed (changed to a different key), it is the same only different!

Play & Do... Video examples at *www.bestmusicpublications.com*

- Play the chords for "Hot Cross Buns" in the key of G with the recording.
- Play the chords for "Hot Cross Buns" in the key of A with the recording.
- Play the melody for "Hot Cross Buns" in the key of G with the recording.
- Play the melody for "Hot Cross Buns" in the key of A with the recording.

LESSON 3

"Janice and Bobby" (Chord Progression)

Lesson Concepts
- "Janice and Bobby" (Chord Progression)

JANICE AND BOBBY *(Chord Progression)*

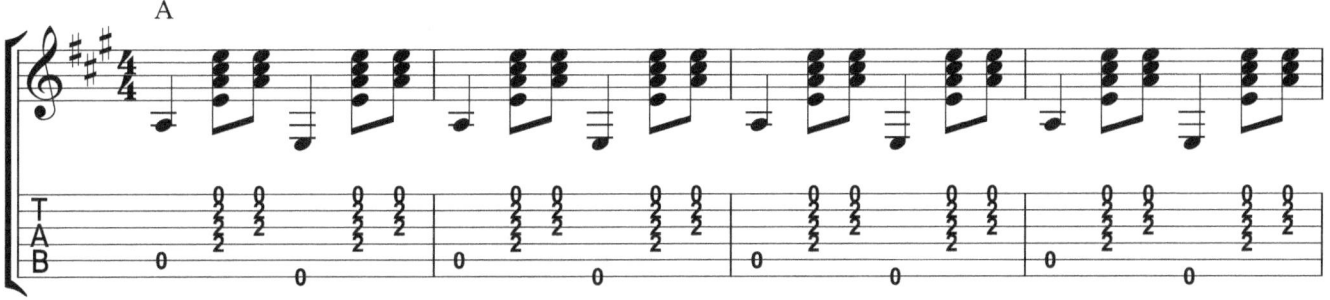

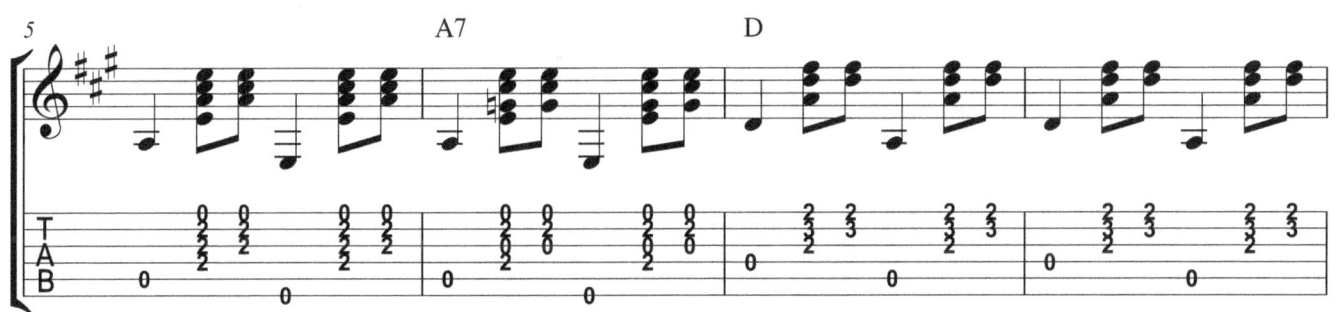

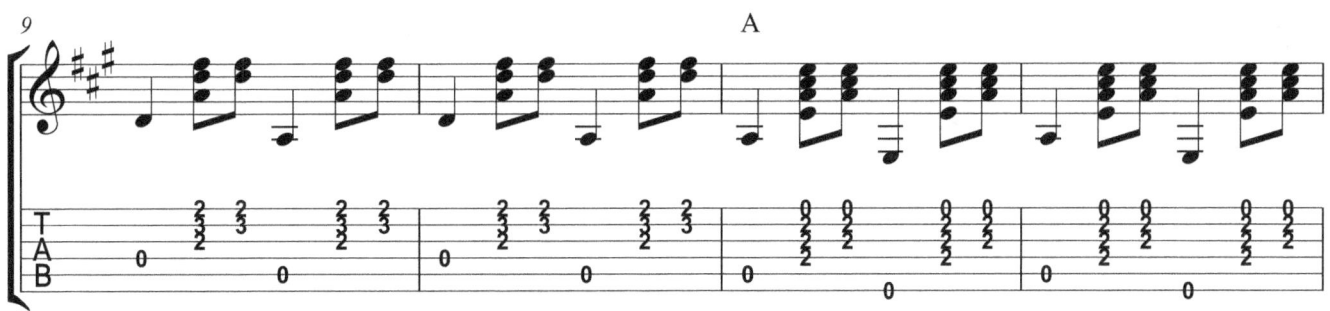

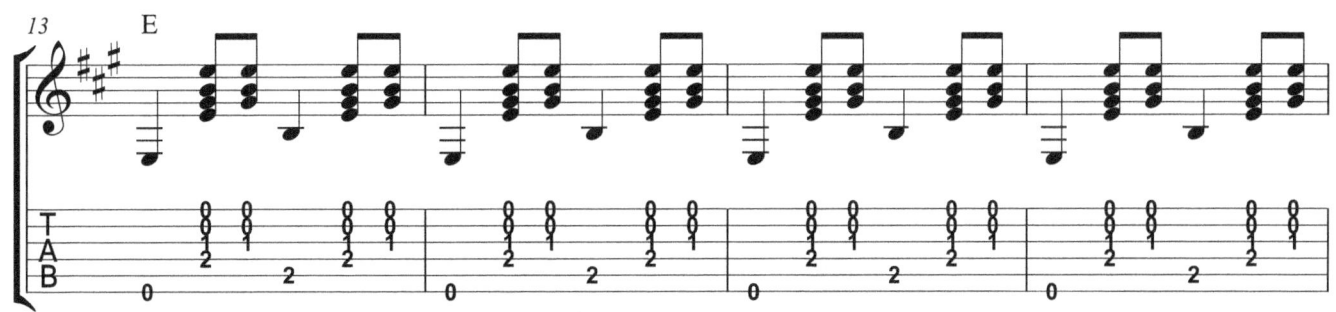

THE BEST GUITAR METHOD

Play & Do... Video examples at www.bestmusicpublications.com

- Practice the alternating bass part for each chord in "Janice and Bobby."
- Practice playing the chord progression "Janice and Bobby."
- Play along with the recording of "Janice and Bobby."
- Repeat the first three steps while playing along with the recorded music.

LESSON 4

Triplets and "Swing" Feel

Lesson Concepts
- Playing Triplets
- Tied Triplets
- Swing Eighth Notes

Playing Triplets

When you play eighth notes, you divide a single beat into two halves. A *triplet* is a way of dividing a single beat into thirds. What can be confusing is that you will still use the eighth note to divide a quarter note—you will just use *three eight notes instead of two*. You place a bracket with a "3" over the eighth notes to indicate the triplet. (Figures 8.4.1 and 8.4.2)

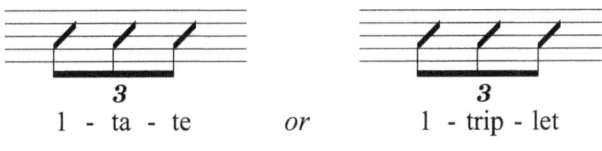

Figure 8.4.1

Figure 8.4.2

You can count these three triplet eighth notes as "1 – ta – te" (Figure 8.4.1) or "1–trip–let" (Figure 8.4.2). These are known as "eighth notes triplets."

Playing triplets can be tricky because you are trying to play three notes by combining down and up motions. Here are some common ways to pick or strum triplets:

DDD DDD DDD DDD (Figure 8.4.3)

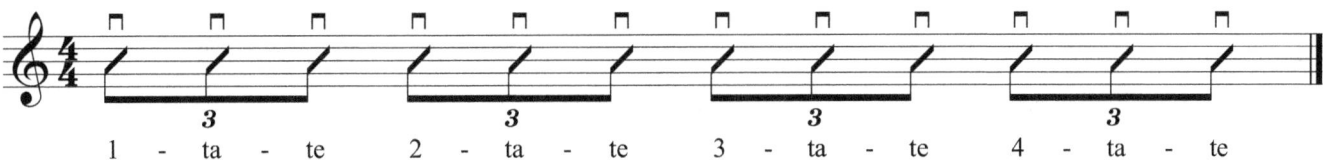

Figure 8.4.3

DUD DUD DUD DUD (Figure 8.4.4)

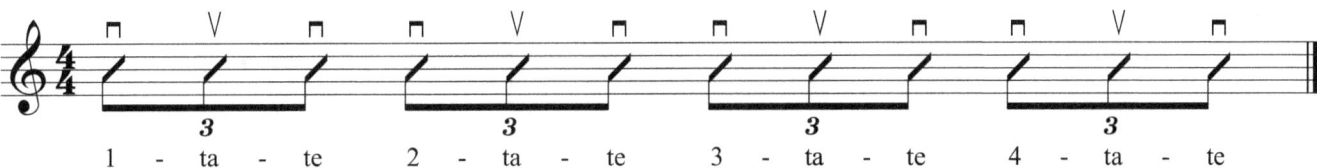

Figure 8.4.4

DUU DUU DUU DUU (Figure 8.4.5)

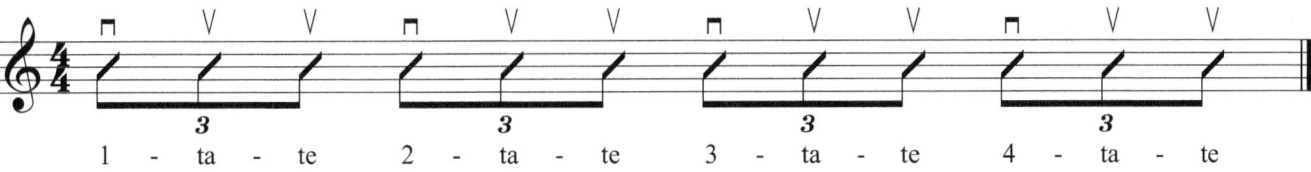

Figure 8.4.5

THE BEST GUITAR METHOD

DUD UDU DUD UDU (Figure 8.4.6)

Figure 8.4.6

 **Play & Do...** Video examples at *www.bestmusicpublications.com*

- Listen to the four recorded versions of the triplets while *counting*, i.e., "1-ta-te, 2-ta-te, 3-ta-te, 4-ta-te." (Example #1) Repeat for examples #2–4.
- Listen to the four recorded versions of the triplets while *saying the picking directions*, i.e., ""down – down – down, down – down – down, down – down – down, down – down – down." (Example #1) Repeat for Examples #2–4.
- Listen to the four recorded versions of the triplets and *count the triplets*, i.e.,"1–ta-te, 2-ta-te, 3-ta-te, 4-ta-te." *Say the picking directions*, i.e., "down – down – down, down – down – down, down – down – down, down – down – down." (Example #1) while *moving your pick in the correct direction without picking the string*. Repeat for examples #2–4.
- Play the triplets while *counting the triplets*, 1-ta-te, 2-ta -te, 3-ta-te, 4-ta-te. Repeat for examples #2–4.
- Play along with the recording while *counting the triplets*, 1-ta-te, 2-ta -te, 3-ta-te, 4-ta-te. Repeat for examples #2–4.

Tied Triplets

You can tie notes in a triplet just like you tied eighth notes in your previous strum patterns.

Here are the above examples with ties between the first and second eighth note of the triplet:

D-D D-D D-D D-D (Figure 8.4.7)

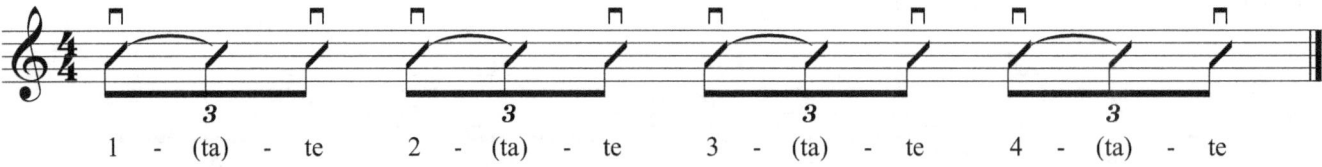

Figure 8.4.7

D-U D-U D-U D-U (Figure 8.4.8)

Figure 8.4.8

D–D U–U D–D U–U (Figure 8.4.9) (This is what DUD UDU DUD UDU [Figure 8.4.6] becomes when ties are added—works well for triplets, feels awkward for tied triplets…)

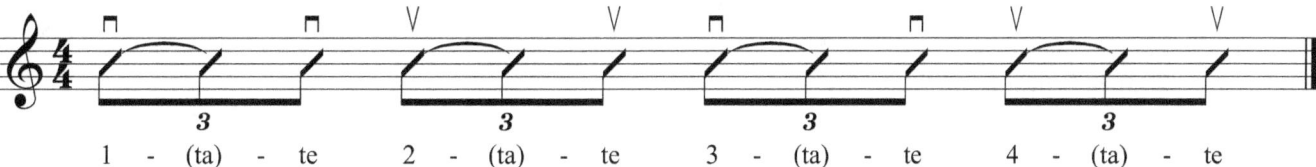

Figure 8.4.9

 **Play & Do…** Video examples at *www.bestmusicpublications.com*

- Listen to the four recorded versions of the tied triplets while *counting*, i.e., "1–te, 2–te, 3 –te, 4 –te." (Example #1) Repeat for examples #2–4.

- Listen to the four recorded versions of the tied triplets while *saying the picking directions*, i.e., "down – down, down – down, down – down, down – down." (Example #1) Repeat for examples #2–4.

- Listen to the four recorded versions of the tied triplets while *counting the tied triplets* and then saying the picking directions i.e.; 1–te, 2–te, 3 –te, 4 –te and then "down – down, down – down, down – down, down – down." (Example #1) while *moving your pick in the correct direction without picking the string*. Repeat for examples #2–4.

- Listen to the four recorded versions of the tied triplets while *counting the tied triplets and then saying the picking directions*, i.e., 1–te, 2–te, 3 –te, 4 –te and then "down – down, down – down, down – down, down – down." (Figure 8.4.7) *while playing the triplets*. Repeat for Figure 8.4.8 and Figure 8.4.9.

Swing Eighth Notes

What it means to "swing" the eighth note is to interpret (play) written eighth notes to sound like the tied triplets you have just learned. *When you see written eighth notes, you will play tied triplets instead.*

You learned eighth note strum patterns in Unit 2 / Lesson 6. When you practiced these strum patterns, you used *straight eighth notes* meaning you divided each beat evenly into two halves. Instead of playing straight eighth notes, you could play the patterns from Unit 2 / Lesson 6 using *swing eighth notes*.

A swing feel is often indicated at the beginning of the music with the word "Swing" or a music notation (Figure 8.4.10).

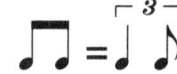

Figure 8.4.10

The concept of "swinging the eighth note" makes notation easier to read. It also allows you to freely interpret the eighth notes as either swing or straight without re-notating the music.

 **Play & Do…** Video examples at *www.bestmusicpublications.com*

- Play the strum patterns from Unit 2 / Lesson 6 with a swing feel.
- Play along with the recordings of the strum patterns from Unit 2 / Lesson 6 with a swing feel.

Lesson 5

2/4 Time — "Itsy Bitsy Spider" (Song)

Lesson Concepts
- 2/4 Time
- "Itsy Bitsy Spider" (Song)

2/4 Time

In 2/4 time there are only two beats in a measure and the quarter note gets the beat. The reason you write in 2/4 instead of 4/4 is to have the strong beat (one accent) occur every two beats instead of every four beats.

Most people know the children's song "The Itsy Bitsy Spider." This song is an example of a song in 2/4 time that is played with a *swing feel*.

ITSY BITSY SPIDER

(Traditional)

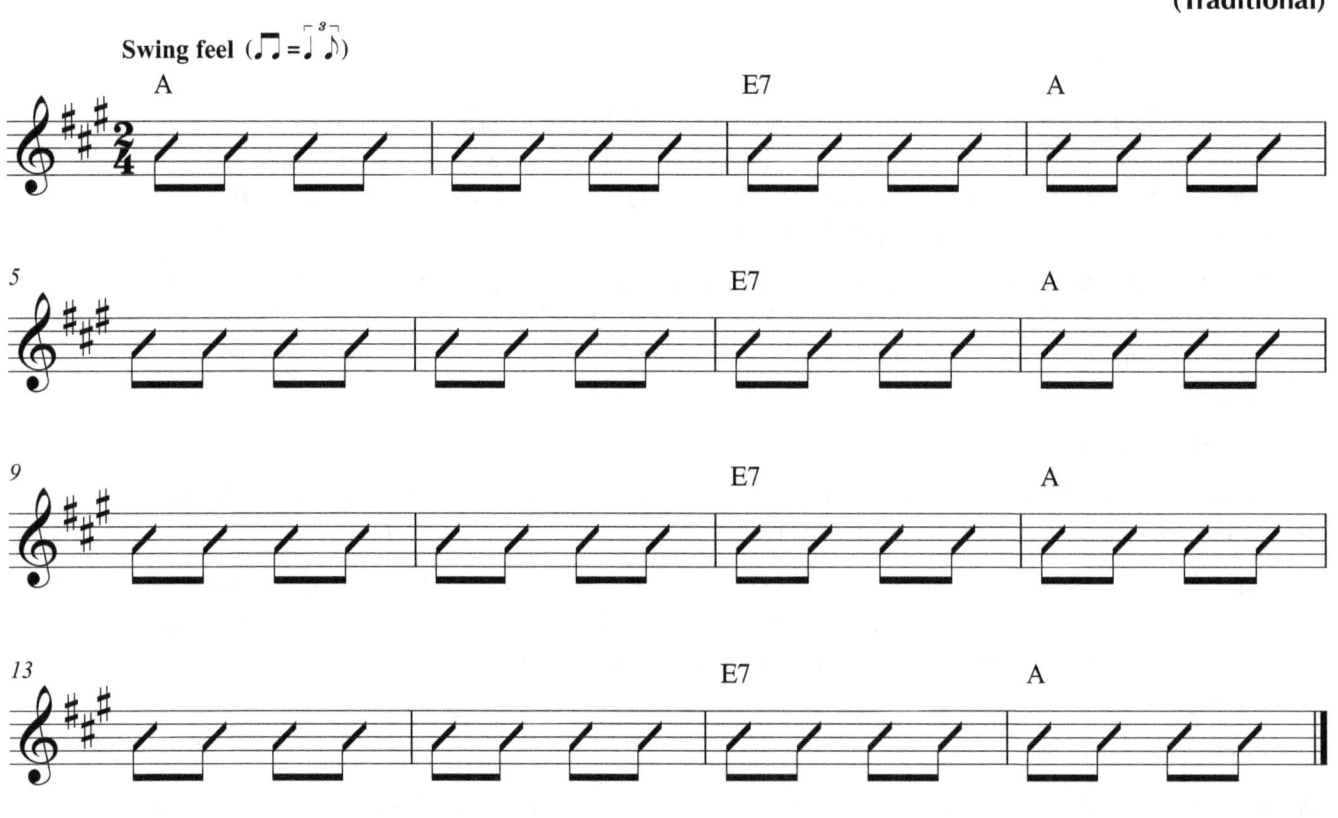

Play & Do… Video examples at www.bestmusicpublications.com

- Listen to the recorded version of "The Itsy Bitsy Spider" while *counting*, i.e., "1 - te, 2 - te, 3 - te, 4 – te."
- Listen to the recorded version of "The Itsy Bitsy Spider" while *saying the picking directions,* i.e., "down – down, down – down, down – down, down – down."
- Play along with the recorded version of "The Itsy Bitsy Spider."

LESSON 6

"12-Bar Blues Shuffle in the Key of A" (Chord Progession)

> **Lesson Concepts**
> - 2-Bar Form
> - 12-Bar Form with Dominant 7th Chords
> - Blues Shuffle Riff
> - "12-Bar Blues Shuffle in the Key of A" (Chord Progesion)

12-Bar Blues Form

Here is a review of the 12-bar blues form in universal notation:

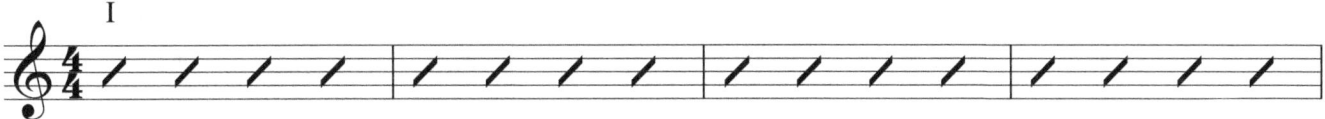

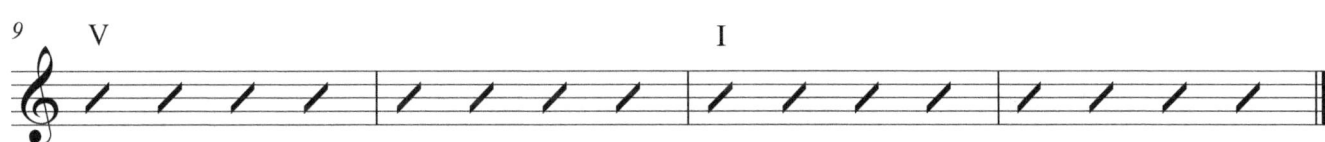

Here is the basic 12-bar blues in the key of A:

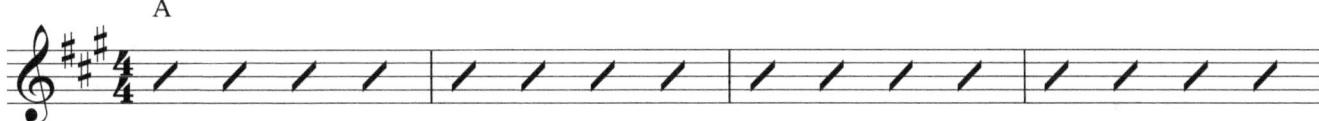

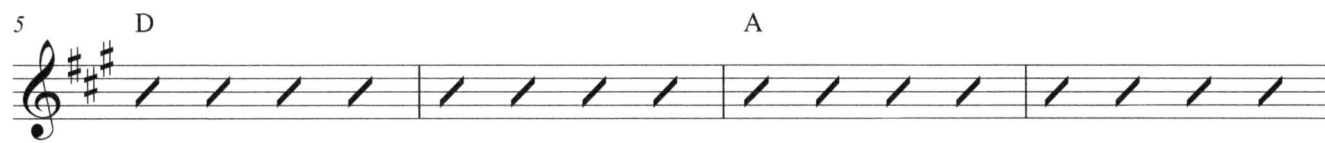

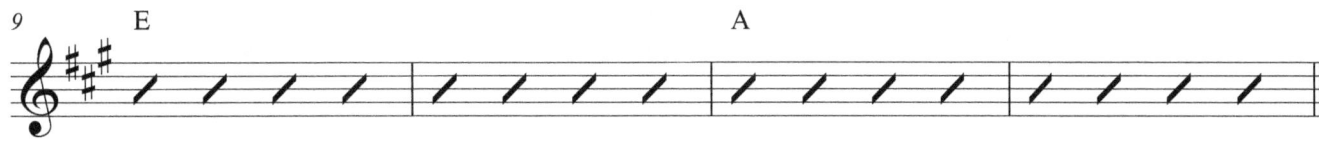

12-Bar Form with Dominant 7th Chords

Here is the more common 12-bar blues in the key of A using all 7th chords:

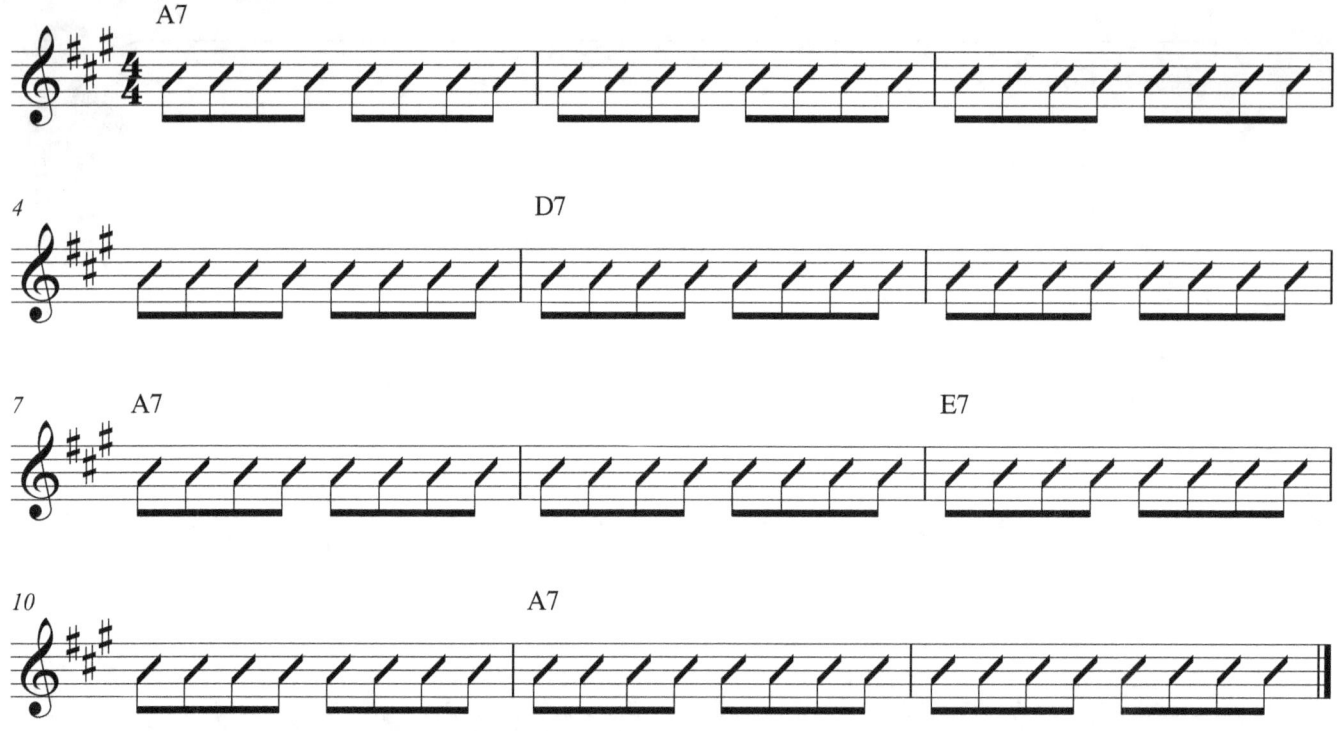

Blues Shuffle Riff

A *riff* is a short repeated melodic or harmonic idea. The next song, "12-Bar Blues Shuffle in the Key of A" is a common variation of the 12-bar blues. This song uses a two-string blues shuffle riff with 7th chords. Play this in the second position, so you are fretting the second fret with your first finger and the fourth fret with your third finger.

12-BAR BLUES SHUFFLE IN THE KEY OF A *(Chord Progression)*

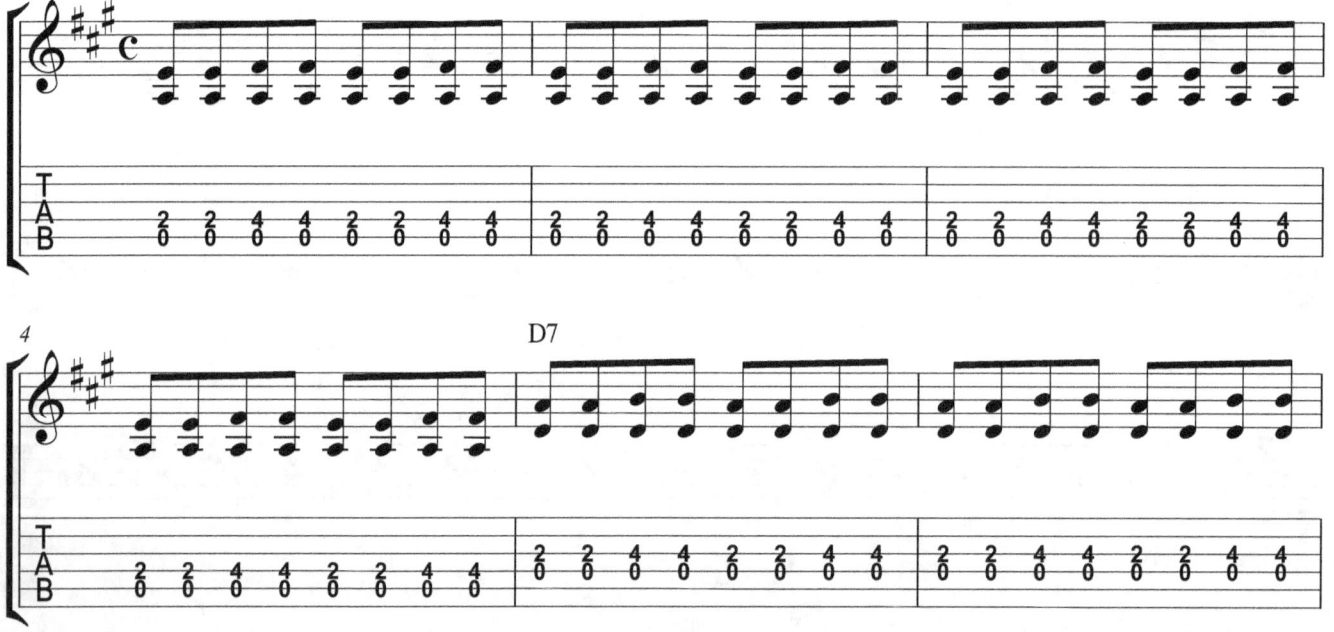

UNIT EIGHT • LESSON 6

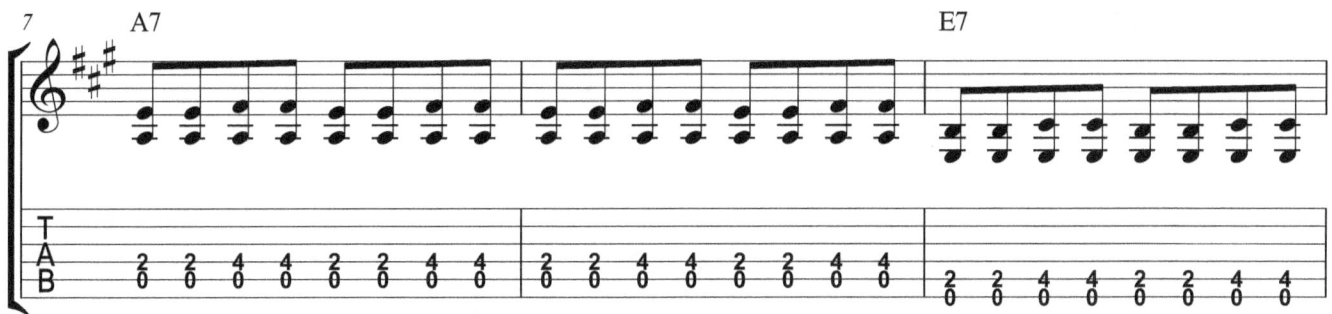

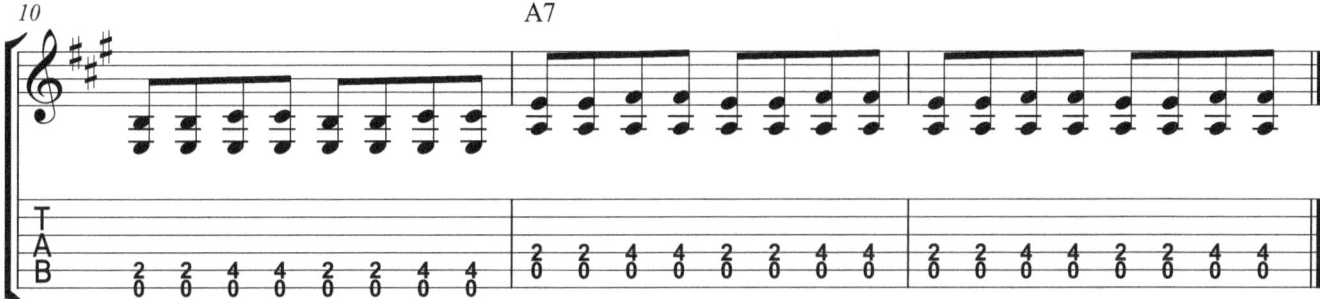

 **Play & Do...** Video examples at *www.bestmusicpublications.com*

- Listen to the recording of the "12-bar Blues Shuffle Riff in the Key of A."
- Play along with the recording of the "12-bar Blues Shuffle Riff in the Key of A."

Lesson 7

Secondary Chords in the Key of A — Bm, C♯m, and F♯m (ii, iii, vi)

> **Lesson Concepts**
> - Secondary Chords in the Key of A — Bm, C♯m, and F♯m (ii, iii, vi)
> - Standard Fingerings for the Secondary Chords in the Key of A — Bm, C♯m, and F♯m (ii, iii, vi)

Secondary Chords in the Key of A — Bm, C♯m, and F♯m (ii, iii, vi)

The secondary chords in any key are minor chords and in the key of A are Bm (ii), C♯m (iii) and F♯m (vi). You already know how to play Bm and F♯m, so the only new chord is C♯m.

Standard Fingerings for the Secondary Chords in the Key of A — Bm, C♯m, and F♯m (ii, iii, vi)

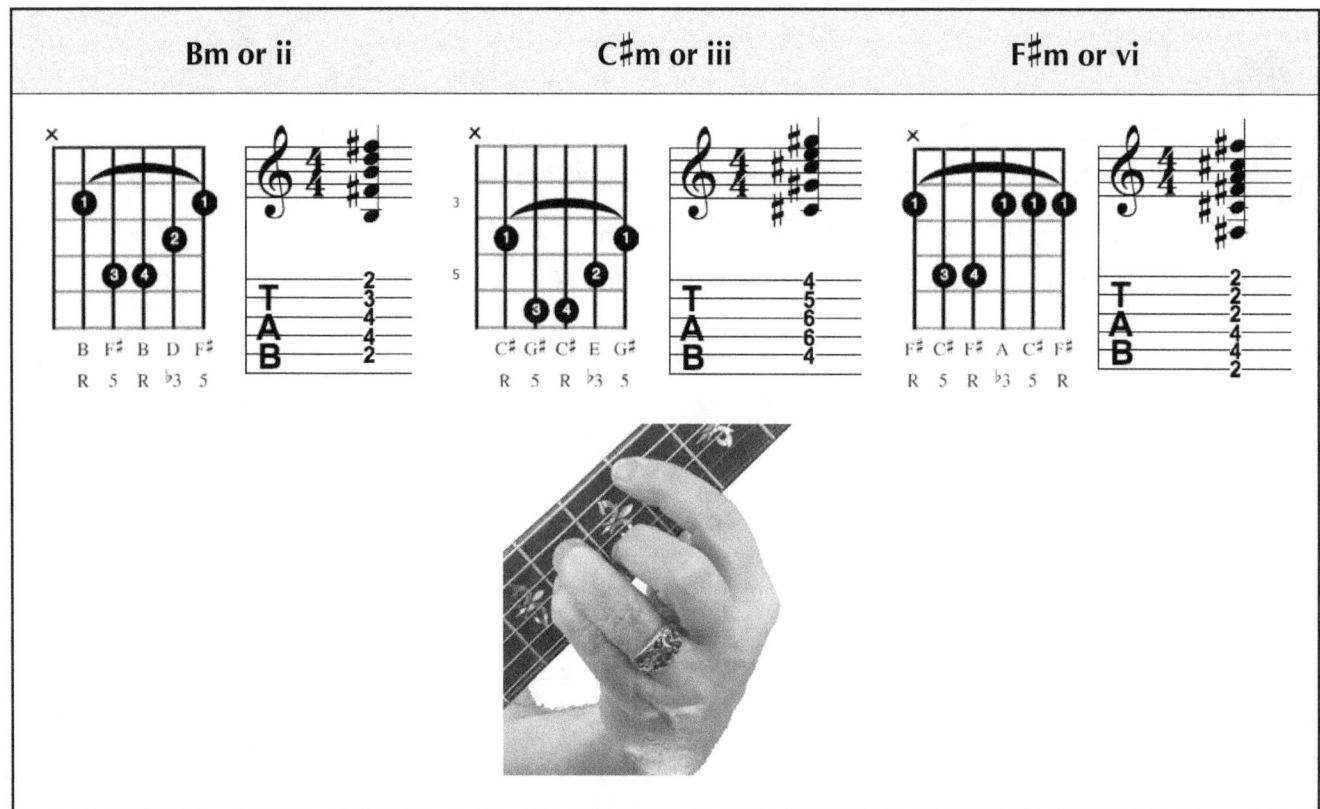

Simplified and Challenge Chords Fingerings

Simplified and challenge chords fingerings for all the chords in this book can be found at *www.bestmusic-publications.com*.

Play & Do... Video examples at *www.bestmusicpublications.com*

- Finger (play) each chord and make sure you are mindful of the three P's of tone production and pick each string of the chord to be sure each string is making a good sound.
- "Catch and release" each chord, strum the chord as you apply pressure, and then check that each string is still sounding good. If it's not, go back and check the three P's of tone production.
- As you play the chord, say the specific names and universal names for the secondary chords in the key of A. Say: "B minor, also known as the ii chord; C♯ minor, also known as the iii chord; and F♯m minor, also known as the vi chord."
- Memorize the specific names and universal names for the secondary chords in the key of A.
- Fill in the chord names for the secondary minor chords in the key of A major in the spaces below:

    ii = _____   iii = _____   vi = _____

- Memorize the specific names and universal names for the secondary chords in the key of A.

LESSON 8

Power Chords —
or, We Interrupt this Unit to Learn a Cool Trick!

Lesson Concepts
- Triad = Complete Chord
- Power Chord = Incomplete Chord
- Power Chord Fingerings Based on Bm, C♯m and F♯m (Or B, C♯ and F♯)
- Root Notes
- Common Usage of Power Chords

Triad = Complete Chord

The simplest complete chords are built from three notes known as a *triad*. The three notes are the root, third and fifth note of a scale. Examples of these chords would be major and minor chords such as a G or Em.

Power Chord = Incomplete Chord

A *power chord* is a guitar-specific term for an incomplete chord. The chord symbol is a root note followed by a "5" similar to seventh chords labeled with the root note followed by the number "7," i.e., D7. A power chord is incomplete because it only has two notes, the root and fifth. "Power chords" can be used in place of either major or minor chords. If you play the lowest three strings of any of the chords from the last lesson, Bm, C♯m, of F♯m, you are playing "power chords."

Power Chord Fingering Based on Bm, C♯m, and F♯m (Or B, C♯ and F♯)

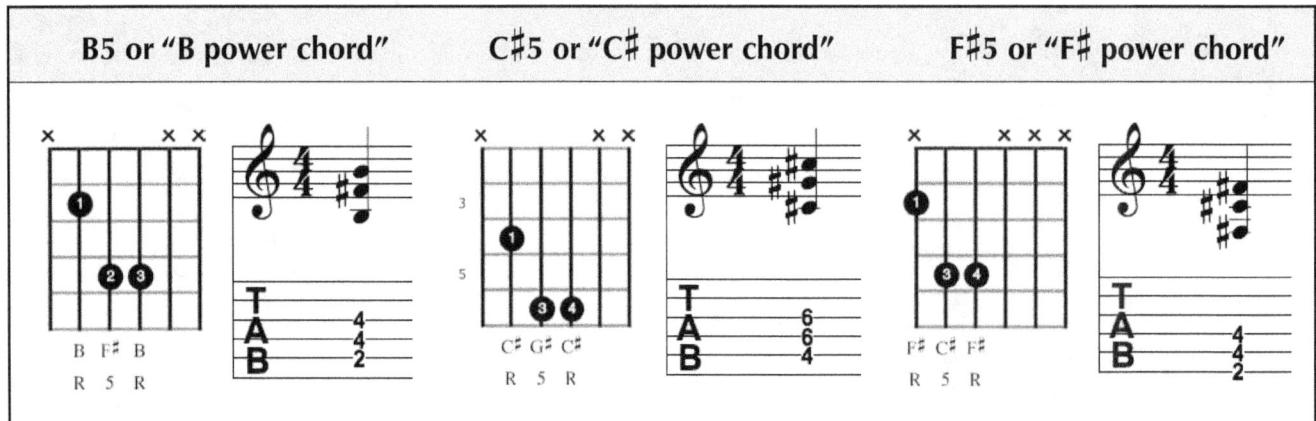

Root Notes

To use power chords, find the root note is on either the Low E or A string (the root note is your first finger). The note names for the E and A strings, along with all the other notes on the guitar can be found in Unit 1, Lesson 7.

Common Usage of Power Chords

Power chords are commonly used in rock and roll, particularly with the electric guitar, but also on acoustic guitar. Power chords sound strong because the harmony is simple and stable. Power chords are practical because they are easier to play than bar chords such as F#, F#m, B or Bm. Virtually any chord can be replaced with a power chord; it just gives a different sound.

Play & Do... Video examples at *www.bestmusicpublications.com*

- Finger (play) each chord and make sure you are mindful of the three P's of tone production.
- Pick each string of the chord to be sure each string is making a good sound.
- "Catch and release" each chord, strum the chord as you apply pressure. and then check that each string is still sounding good. If it's not, go back and check the three P's of tone production.

LESSON 9

Common Variations of the 12-Bar Blues Form

Lesson Concepts
- 12-Bar Form
- The Turnaround
- V–IV Turnaround
- Quick V Turnaround
- Quick IV Chord
- 12-Bar Blues with Variations

12-Bar Blues Form

You have played the 12-bar blues form in various keys and understand the universal progression. The simple 12-bar blues form is the basis for a number of variations. Quite often, the simple chord progression exists inside the variations, i.e., the I chord is always on beat 1 of measure 1, 7, and 11, the IV chord is on beat 1 of measure 5, and the V chord is always on beat 1 of measure 9.

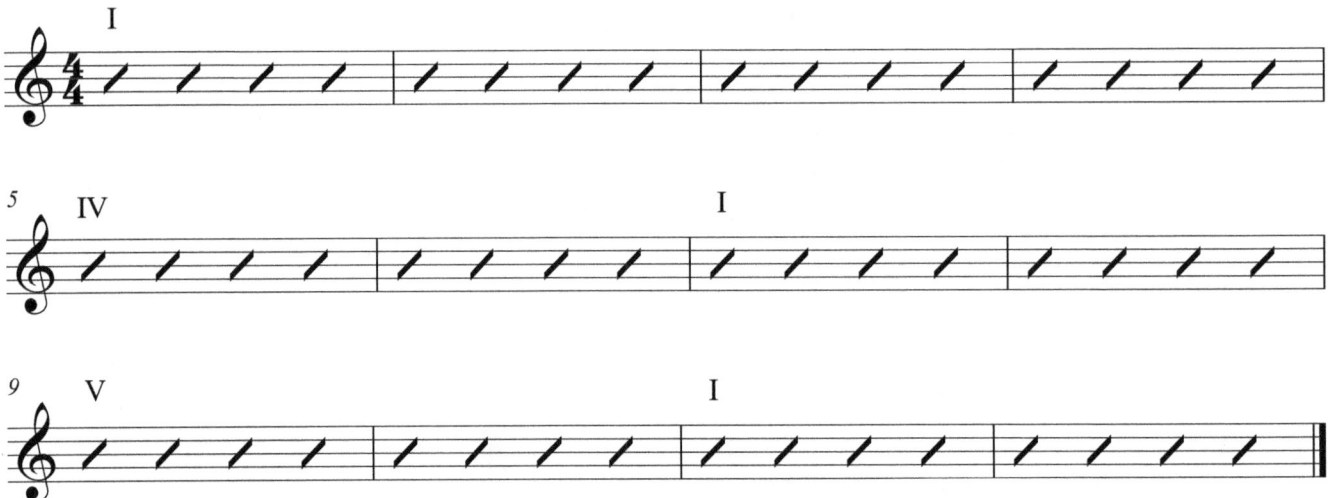

The Turnaround

A turnaround is a section of a chord progression that signals the end of a chord progression or section. Turnarounds usually occur in the last four measures of the chord progression or section. There are thousands of turnarounds, and they often make many 12-bar blues progressions sound cool. You will learn two different turnarounds: an early turnaround at measure 9 and 10 and then a later turnaround on beat 3 of measure 12.

V–IV Turnaround

The V–IV turnaround simply adds a IV chord during measure 10. The turnaround would be considered measures 9 and 10.

Quick V Turnaround

The Quick V turnaround simply adds a V chord on beats 3 and 4 of measure 12. The turnaround would be considered all of measure 12.

UNIT SEVEN • LESSON 9

Quick IV Chord

The quick IV is not a turnaround, but it is a common variation, and it simply adds a IV chord to the simple form for the duration of measure 2.

The next example uses all three of these variations, but they are independent of each other and can be freely combined or used individually to give the simple 12-bar blues some variation.

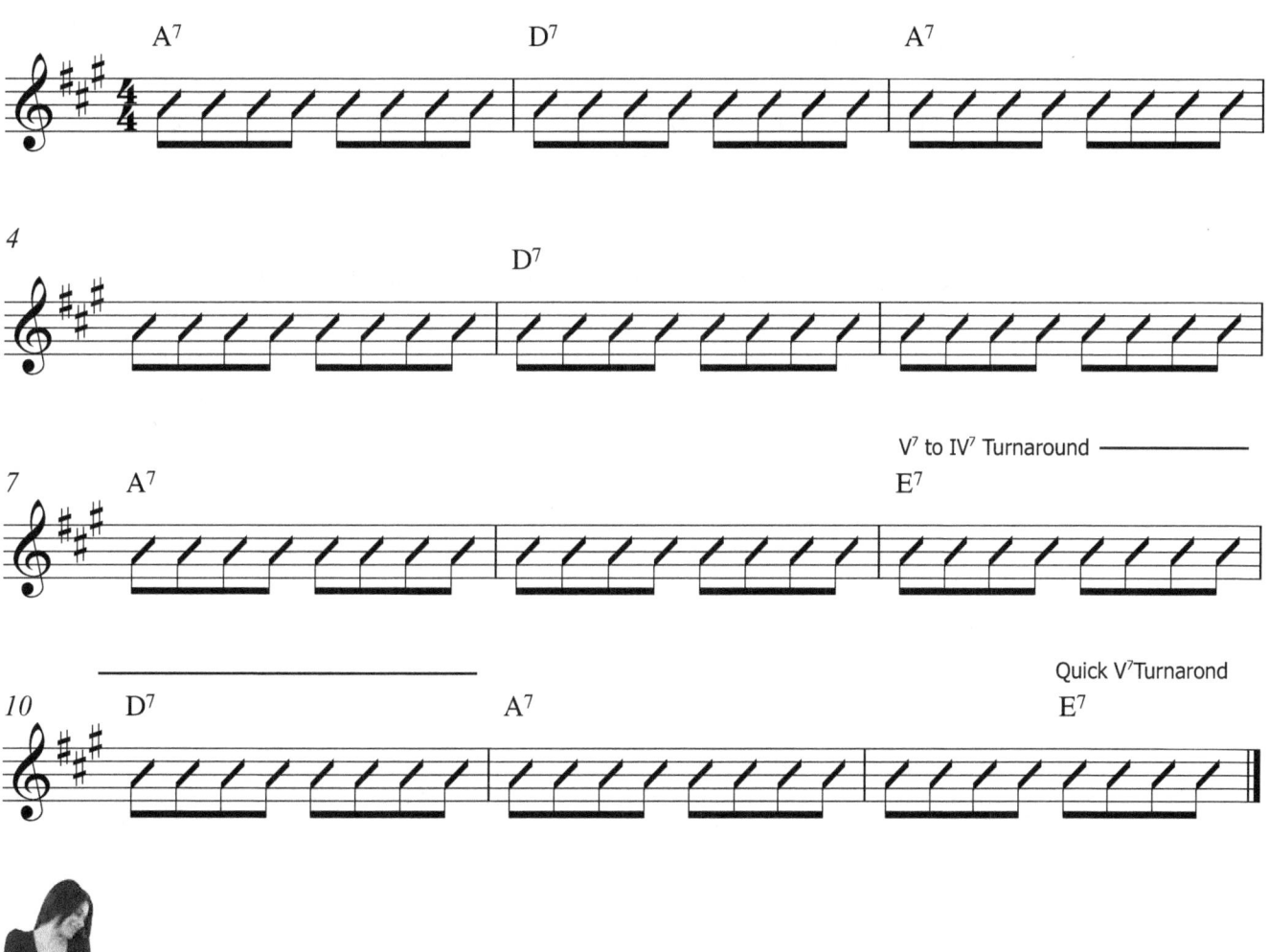

Play & Do... Video examples at *www.bestmusicpublications.com*

- Listen to the recorded version of "12-Bar Blues with Variations in the Key of A." Follow the written music and listen for the variations.
- Play along with the recorded version of "12-Bar Blues with Variations in the Key of A" using all downstrokes and a swing feel.
- Play along with the recorded version of "12-Bar Blues with Variations in the Key of A" using all downstrokes and a swing feel but substitute the blues shuffle riff for the chords.

LESSON 10

"12-Bar Blues Variation with Secondary Minor Chords"

> **Lesson Concept**
> - 12-Bar Blues Form with Variations and Secondary Minor Chords and Variations

12-Bar Blues Form with Secondary Minor Chords

This next 12-bar blues will incorporate secondary minor chords as a way to add variation to the 12-bar form. Adding a secondary minor chord is very common in jazz. You have also added one of the most common jazz rhythms, the "Charleston Rhythm." The Charleston Rhythm is simply playing two strums per measure in a simple syncopated rhythm as shown. Because it is in a jazz style, you should swing the eighth notes.

12-BAR BLUES VARIATION WITH SECONDARY MINOR CHORDS (Chord Progression)

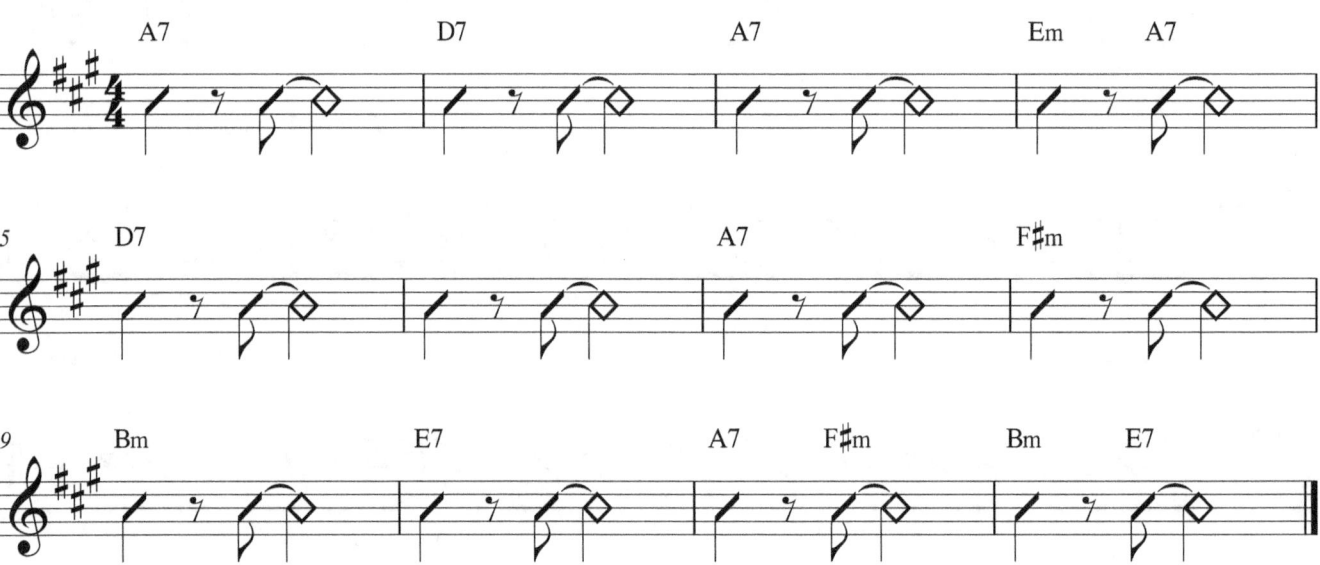

Play & Do... Video examples at *www.bestmusicpublications.com*

- Listen to the recorded version of 12-bar Blues Variations with Secondary Minor Chords in the Key of A. Follow the written music and listen for the variations.
- Play along with the recorded version of 12-bar Blues Variations with Secondary Minor Chords in the Key of A using all downstrokes.
- Play along with the recorded version of 12-bar Blues Variations with Secondary Minor Chords in the Key of A using alternating down/up strokes.

LESSON 11

G♯ Notes

Lesson Concept
- New Note G♯ on the First, Third and Sixth Strings

New Note G♯ on the First, Third and Sixth Strings

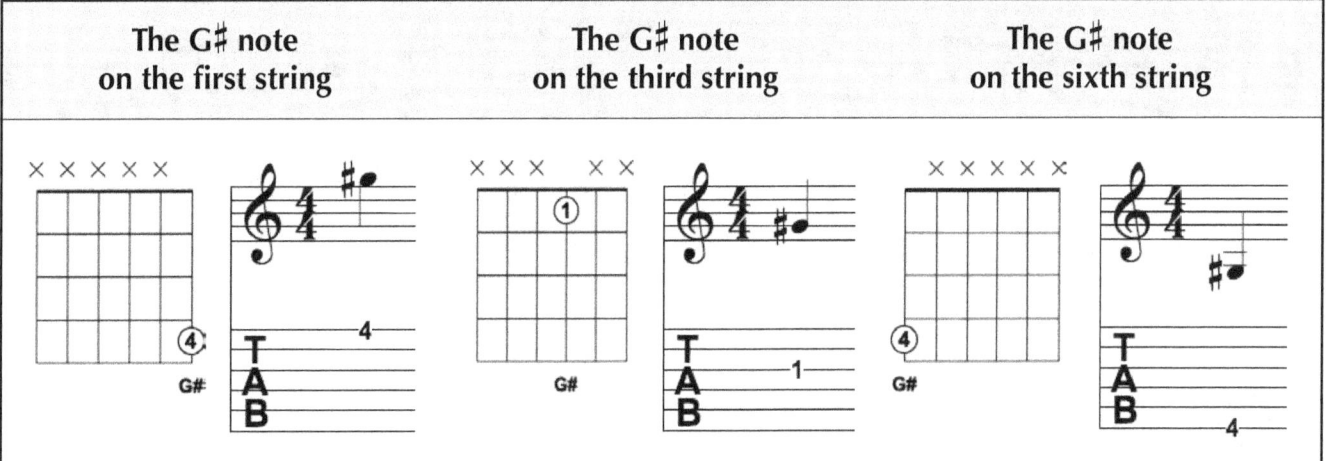

 **Play & Do…** Video examples at *www.bestmusicpublications.com*

- Finger each of the G♯ notes and say the note name while looking at the standard notation.

161

LESSON 12

A Major Scale

> **Lesson Concept**
> - A Major Scale

A Major Scale

 **Play & Do...** Video examples at www.bestmusicpublications.com

- Practice the A major scale with your pick. Use alternate picking.
- Practice the A major scale playing the notes finger style (fifth and fourth string – *p*, third string – *i*, second string – *m*).
- Practice the A major scale playing the notes alternate finger style *(i – m – i – m)*.
- Memorize the A major scale left-hand fingering and note names.

LESSON 13

The Key of A Major — No Training Wheels

Lesson Concept
- The Key of A Major — No Training Wheels (No Tablature)

A MAJOR – NO TRAINING WHEELS

THE BEST GUITAR METHOD

 **Play & Do...** Video examples at *www.bestmusicpublications.com*

- Play A major (no training wheels...) using a variety of right-hand techniques including: pick, standard finger assignment, alternating index and middle fingers, and thumb. Be sure to use the correct fingers for fretted notes!
- Play along with the recording with each picking style.

Lesson 14

"This Beautiful Day" (Song)

Lesson Concept
- "This Beautiful Day" (Song)

THIS BEAUTIFUL DAY

(Brian K. Rivers)

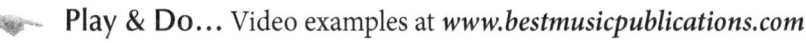

Play & Do... Video examples at *www.bestmusicpublications.com*

- Listen to the recorded version and count along while you follow and point to the music.
- Practice each chord and work on the switching of chords. Remember to anticipate the chord change, so you are always forming the new chord on beat 1.
- Practice playing the chords using this pattern:
- Practice playing the chords with the recorded version.

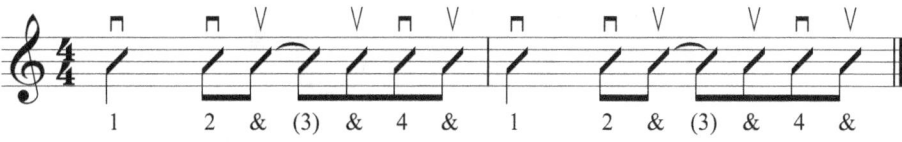

- Practice playing the melody slowly being sure to follow the picking directions.
- Practice playing the melody along with the recorded version being sure to follow the picking directions.

Review and Summary

You should be able to demonstrate and identify the following skills:

- Play and identify the primary and secondary chords in the Key of A
- Play power chords and use power chords
- Play triplets and swing eight notes
- Play a two octave A major scale from memory
- Play a 12-bar Blues with a shuffle riff in the key of A
- Play all songs in Unit 8 with the full speed recordings
- Fill in the primary and secondary chord names for the key of A major in the spaces below:

I = _____ ii = _____ iii = _____ IV = _____ V = _____ V = _____ vi = _____

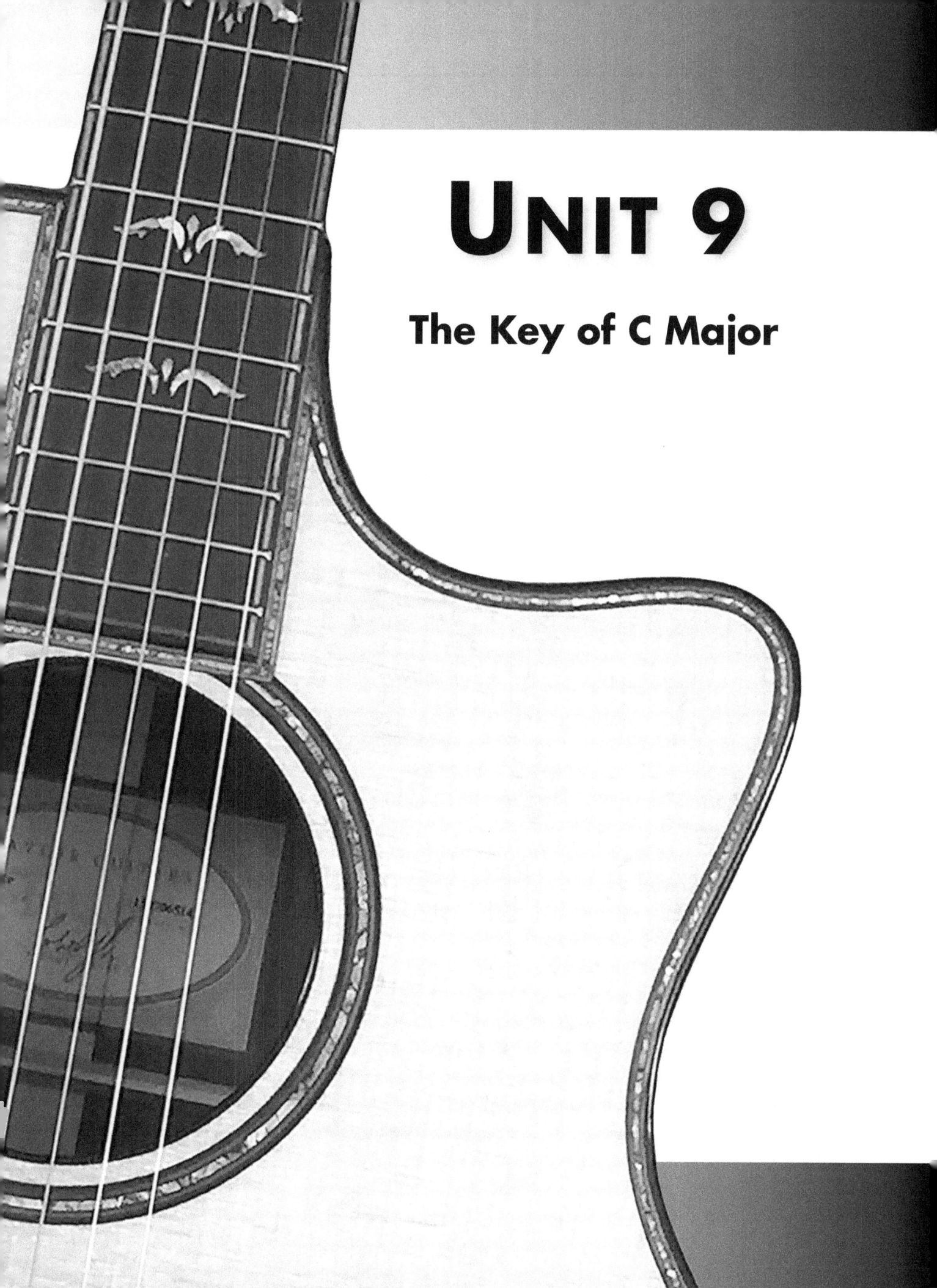

UNIT 9

The Key of C Major

Lesson 1

Primary Chords in the Key of C — C, F, G, G7 (I, IV, V, V7)

> **Lesson Concepts**
> - Primary Chords in the Key of C — C, F, G and G7 (I, IV, V, V7)
> - Standard Fingerings for the Primary Chords in the Key of C — C, F, G and G7 (I, IV, V, V7)
> - Simplified and Challenge Chords Fingerings

Primary Chords in the Key of C — C, F, G and G7 (I, IV, V, V7)

You already know the C and G chord. The new chords are F and G7.

Standard Fingerings for the Primary Chords in the Key of C — C, F, G and G7 (I, IV, V, V7)

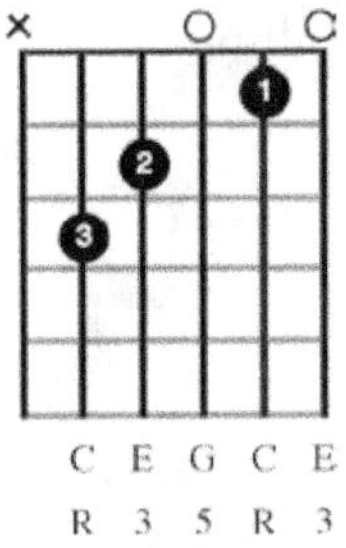

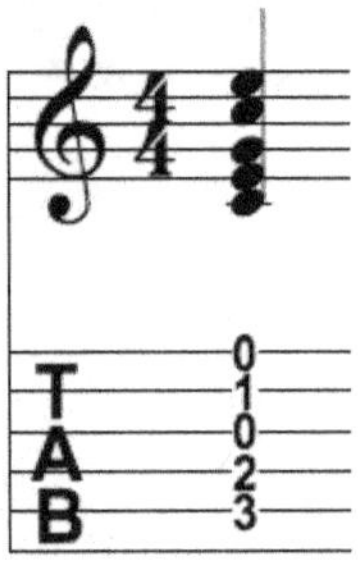

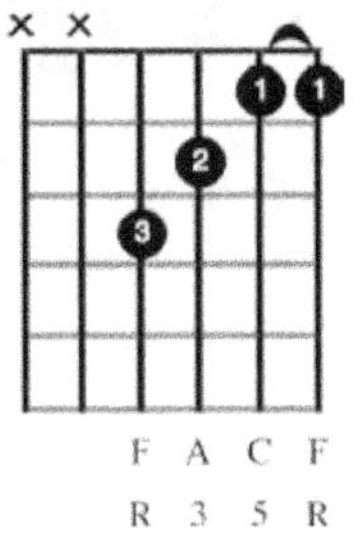

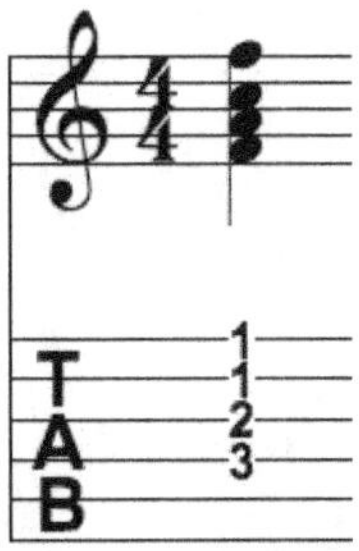

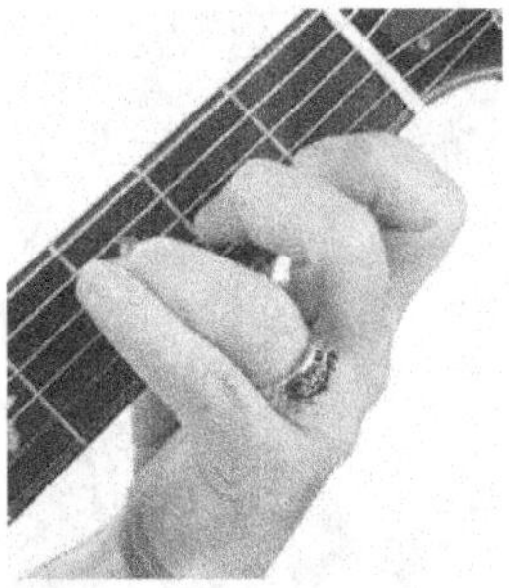

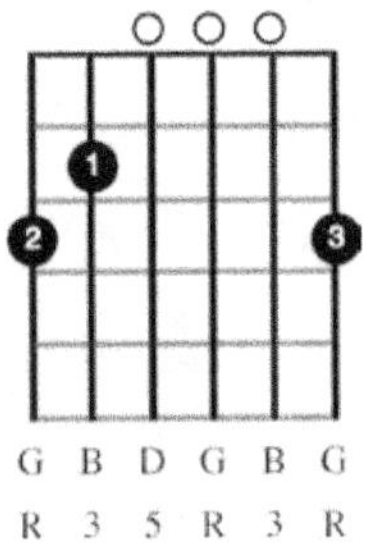

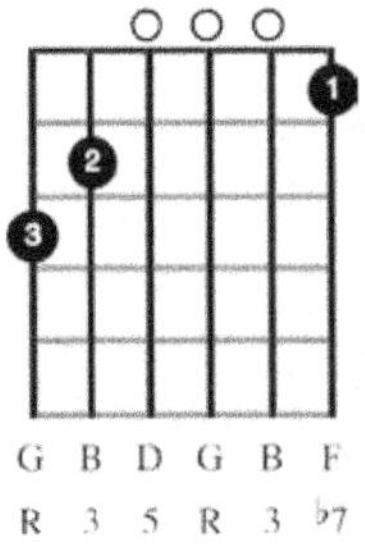

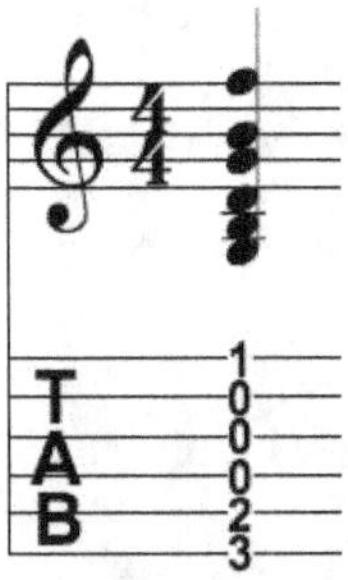

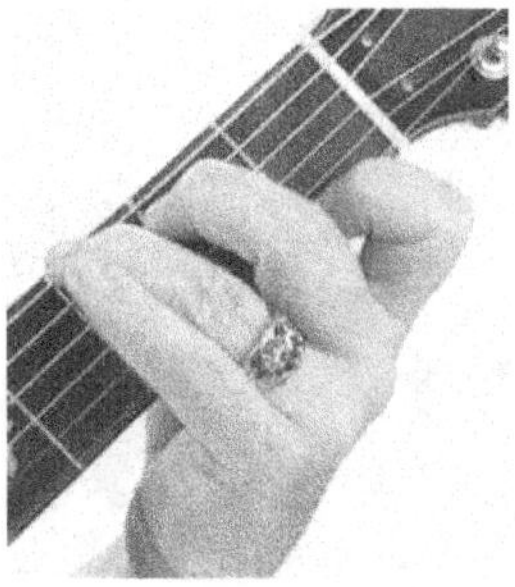

Simplified and Challenge Chords Fingerings

Simplified and challenge chords fingerings for all the chords in this book can be found at *www.bestmusic-publications.com*.

168

UNIT NINE • LESSON 1

Play & Do… Video examples at *www.bestmusicpublications.com*

- Finger (play) each chord and make sure you are mindful of the three P's of tone production and pick each string of the chord to be sure each string is making a good sound.
- "Catch and release" (Unit 2/Lesson 1) each chord, strum the chord as you apply pressure, and then check that each string is still sounding good. If it's not, go back and check the three P's of tone production.
- Play the chords and say the specific names and universal names for the primary chords in the key of C. Say "C, also known as the I chord, F, also known as the IV chord, and G, also known as the V chord."
- Memorize the specific names and universal names for the primary chords in the key of C.
- Fill in the primary chord names for the key of C major in the spaces below:

I = _____   IV = _____   V = _____   V7 = _____

LESSON 2

F Notes and the C Major Scale

> **Lesson Concepts**
> - F Notes on the First, Fourth and Sixth String
> - C Major Scale and Notes in the Key: C, D, E, F, G, A, B
> - Key Signature

F Notes on the First, Fourth and Sixth String

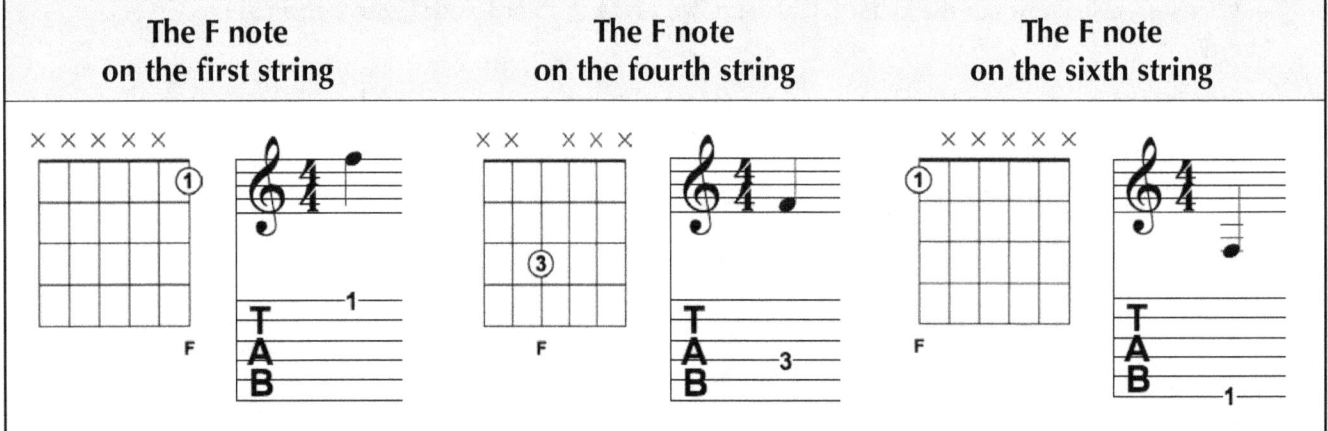

C Major Scale and Notes in the Key: C, D, E, F, G, A, B

Key Signature

It appears as though there is no key signature at the beginning of this piece of music, but there is a key signature. The key signature is blank because the key of C major has no sharps or flats!

Play & Do... Video examples at *www.bestmusicpublications.com*

- Practice the C major scale with your pick. Use alternate picking.
- Practice the C major scale playing the notes finger style (fifth and fourth string – *p*, third string – *i*, second string – *m*).
- Practice the C major scale playing the notes alternate finger style *(i – m – i – m)*.
- Memorize the C major scale left-hand fingering and note names.

LESSON 3

The Key of C — No Training Wheels

Lesson Concept
- C Major — No Training Wheels (No Tablature)

C MAJOR – NO TRAINING WHEELS

THE BEST GUITAR METHOD

 **Play & Do…** Video examples at *www.bestmusicpublications.com*

- Play C major (no training wheels…) using a variety of right-hand techniques including: pick, standard finger assignment, alternating index and middle fingers, and thumb. Be sure to use the correct fingers for fretted notes!
- Play along with the recording with each picking style.

LESSON 4

"Will the Circle Be Unbroken?" (Song)

Lesson Concepts
- "Will the Circle Be Unbroken?" Guitar 1
- "Will the Circle Be Unbroken?" Guitar 2
- "Will the Circle Be Unbroken?" Guitar 3

The song "Will the Circle Be Unbroken?" is a classic folk/gospel song and works well with the alternating bass note technique. The Guitar 3 part uses the alternating bass note technique. The alternate bass notes for the C and G chord should be played by moving the third finger from the root note to the alternate bass note.

WILL THE CIRCLE BE UNBROKEN?

(Charles Gabriel)

Guitar 1

Guitar 2

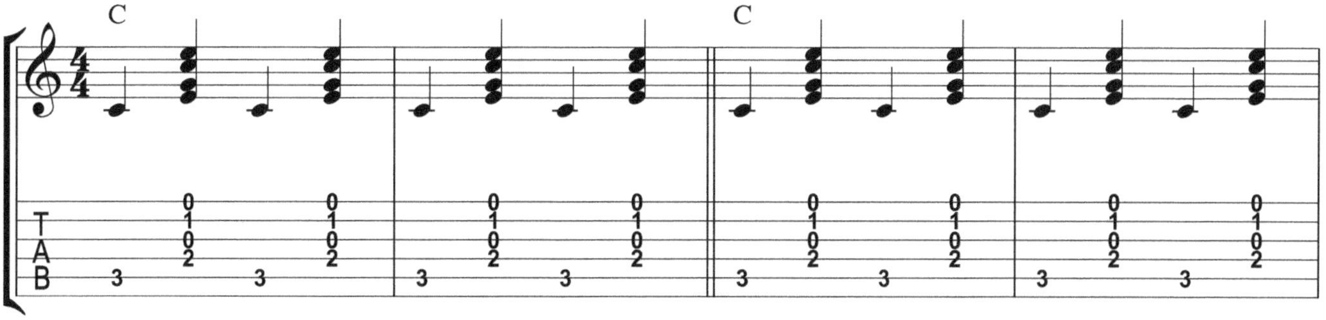

173

THE BEST GUITAR METHOD

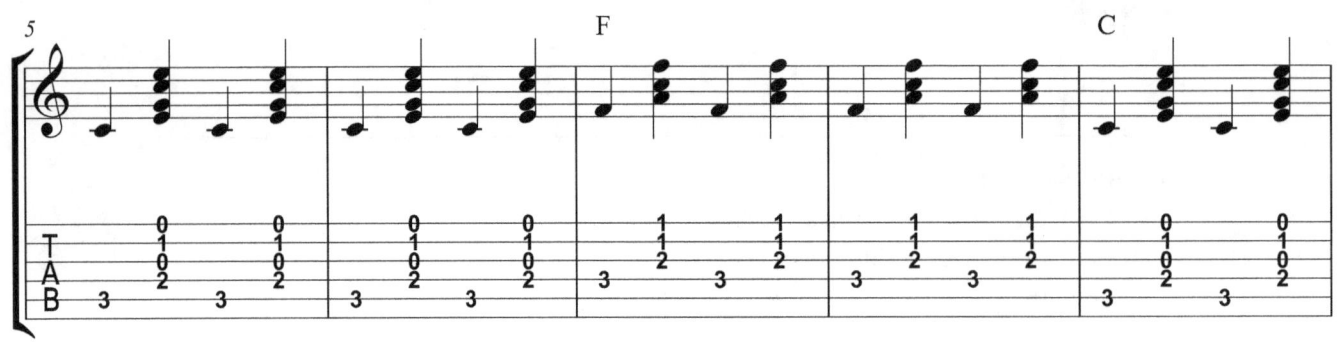

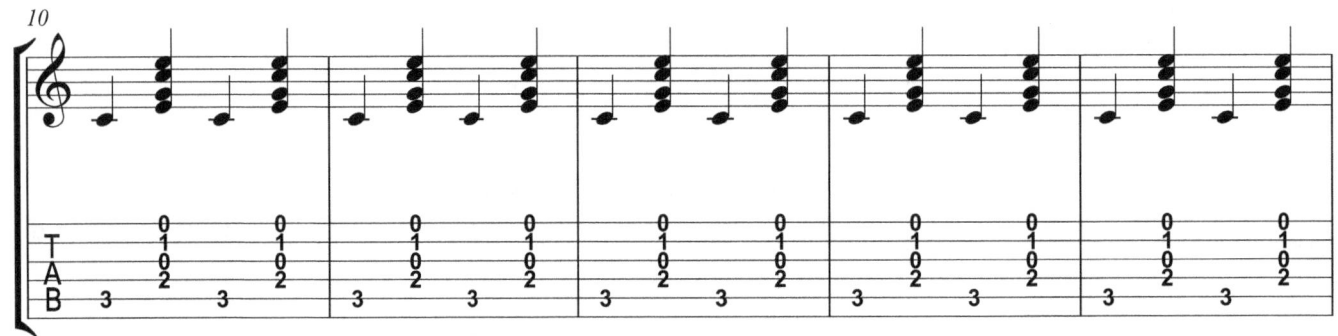

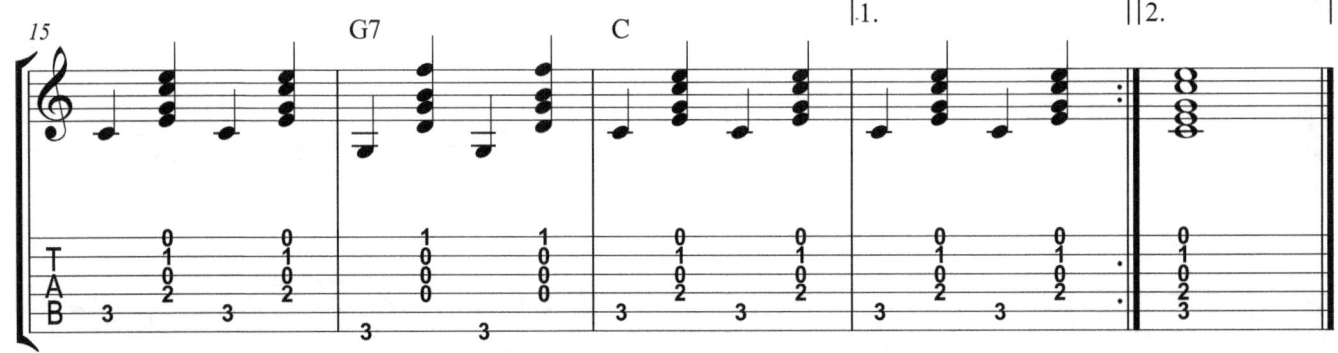

Guitar 3

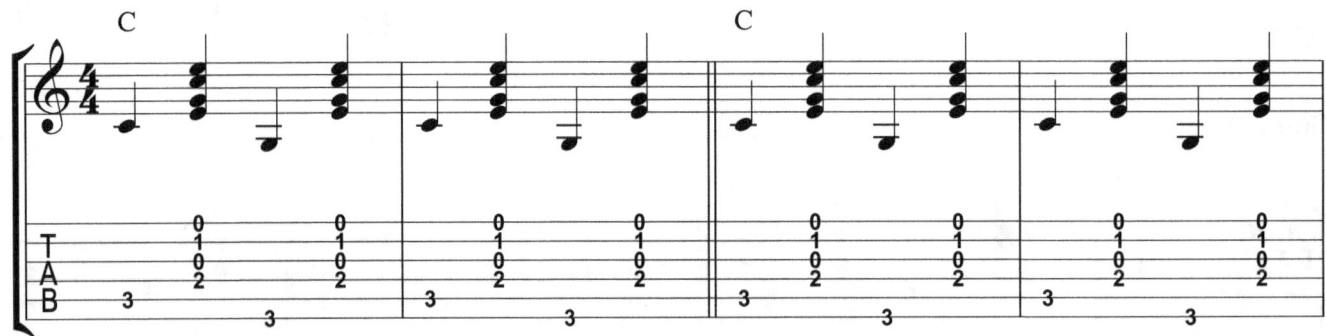

UNIT NINE • LESSON 4

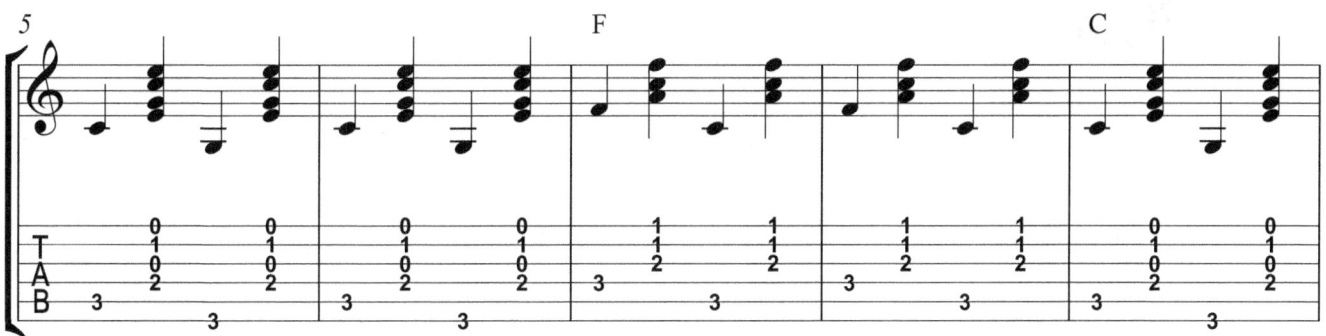

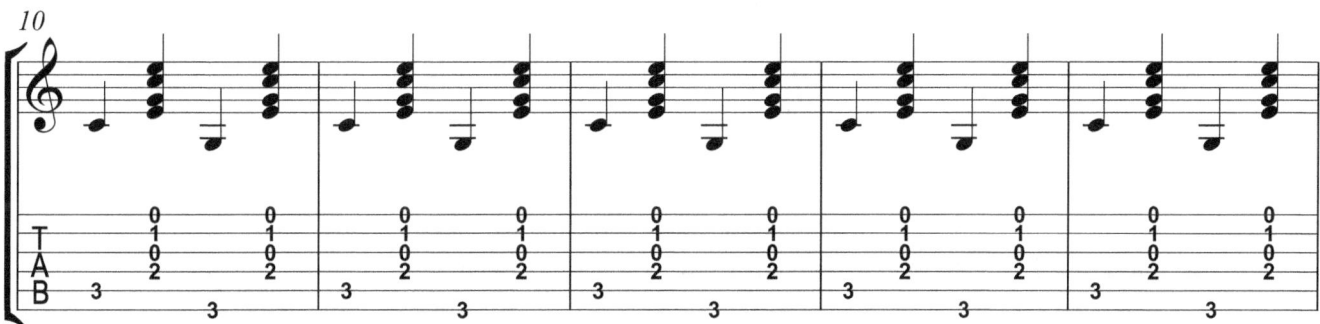

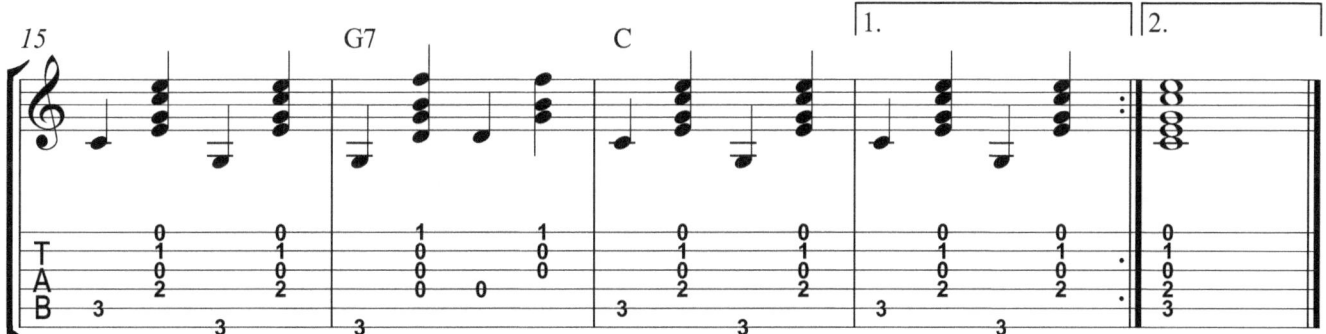

 **Play & Do...** Video examples at *www.bestmusicpublications.com*

- Listen to the recorded version and count along while you follow and point to the music.
- Practice each chord and work on the switching of chords. Remember to anticipate the chord change, so you are always forming the new chord on beat 1.
- Practice playing the chords using the written accompaniment.
- Practice playing the chords with the recorded version using the written accompaniment.
- Practice playing the melody slowly using a variety of right-hand techniques including: pick, standard finger assignment, and alternating index and middle fingers, and thumb.
- Practice playing the melody along with the recorded version.

LESSON 5

Grace Notes

Lesson Concepts
- Target Note
- Grace Note
- Slur

A *grace note* is a very short note preceding a standard note. (Figure 9.5.1)

The grace note is not played as a separate note. The grace note is a way of starting the *target note*. The emphasis should be on the target note, not on the grace note. A grace note is played as a hammer-on since the grace note is a type of *slur*.

The song "Wildwood Flower" brings together many of the concepts and techniques you have learned. The alternate bass notes for the C and G chord should be played by moving the third finger from the root note to the alternate bass note.

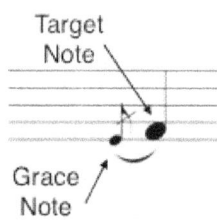

Figure 9.5.1

Play & Do... Video examples at *www.bestmusicpublications.com*

- Locate the grace notes in the next song "Wildwood Flower" and practice playing each *grace note* and *target note*.

LESSON 6

"Wildwood Flower" (Song)

Lesson Concepts
- "Wildwood Flower" Guitar 1
- "Wildwood Flower" Guitar 2
- "Wildwood Flower" Guitar 3

WILDWOOD FLOWER

(Joseph Webster)

Guitar 1

Guitar 2

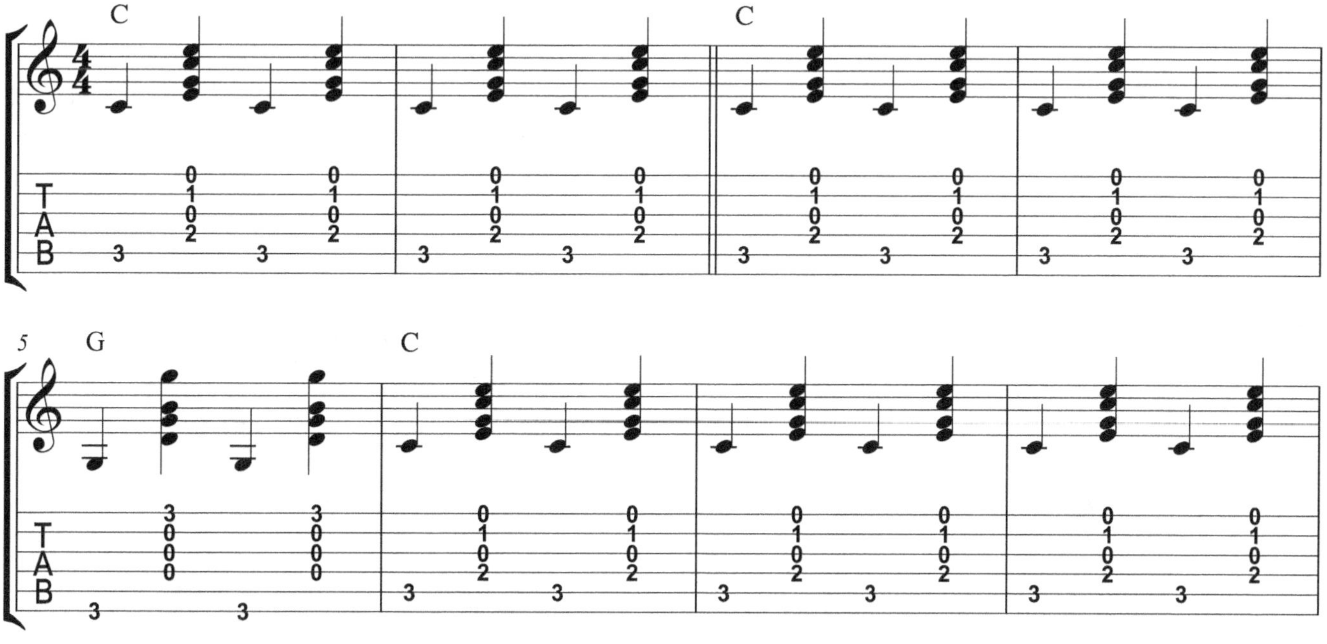

177

THE BEST GUITAR METHOD

Guitar 3

178

UNIT NINE • LESSON 6

Play & Do... Video examples at *www.bestmusicpublications.com*

- Listen to the recorded version and count along while you follow and point to the music.
- Practice each chord and work on the switching of chords. Remember to anticipate the chord change, so you are always forming the new chord on beat 1.
- Practice playing the chords using the written accompaniment.
- Practice playing the chords with the recorded version using the written accompaniment.
- Practice playing the melody slowly with a pick using all downstrokes. Remember the slurs should be played as pull-offs or hammer-ons.
- Practice playing the melody along with the recorded version.

179

LESSON 7

Secondary Chords in the Key of C — Dm, Em, and Am (ii, iii, vi)

> **Lesson Concepts**
> - Secondary Chords in the Key of C — Dm, Em and Am (ii, iii, vi)
> - Standard Fingerings for the Secondary Chords in the Key of C — Dm, Em and Am (ii, iii, vi)
> - Simplified and Challenge Chords Fingerings

Secondary Chords in the Key of C — Dm, Em and Am (ii, iii, vi)

You already know how to play Em and Am. The new chord is Dm.

Standard Fingerings for the Secondary Chords in the Key of C — Dm, Em and Am (ii, iii, vi)

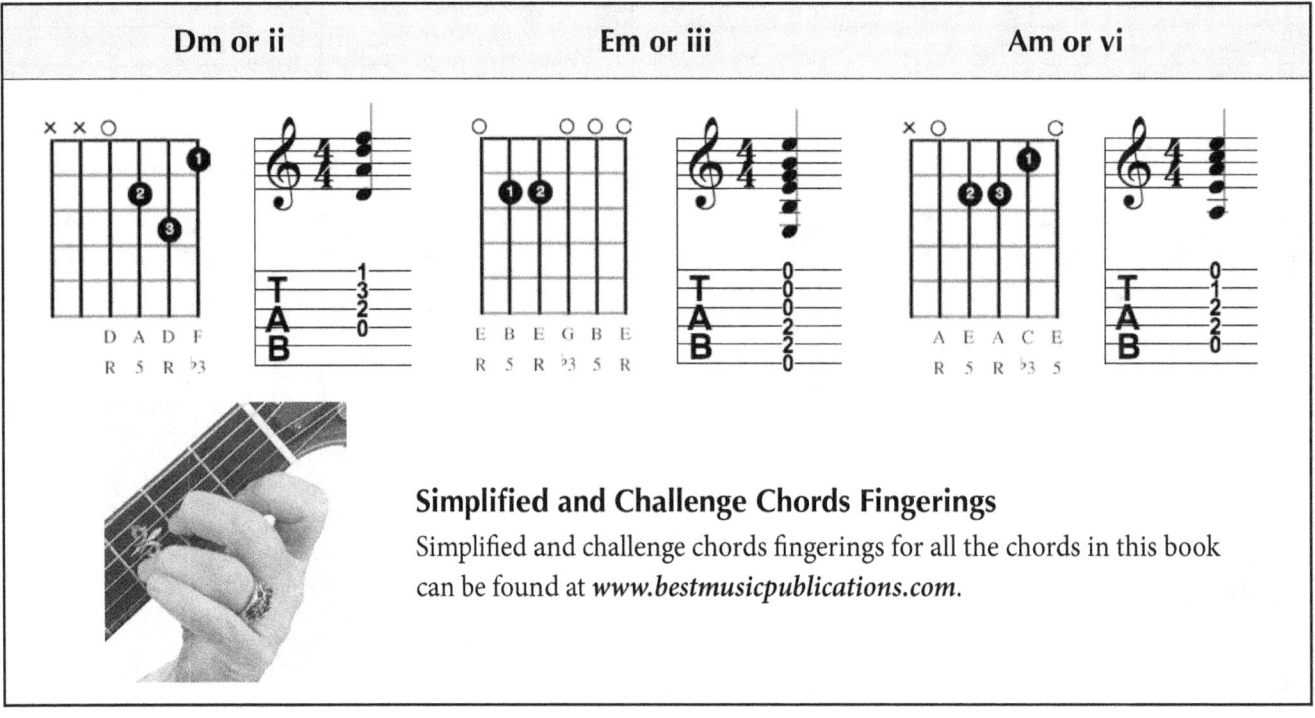

Simplified and Challenge Chords Fingerings

Simplified and challenge chords fingerings for all the chords in this book can be found at *www.bestmusicpublications.com*.

Play & Do... Video examples at *www.bestmusicpublications.com*

- Finger (play) the Dm chord and make sure you are mindful of the three P's of tone production and pick each string of the chord to be sure each string is making a good sound.
- "Catch and release" each chord, strum the chord as you apply pressure, and then check that each string is still sounding good. If it's not, go back and check the three P's of tone production.
- As you play the chords, say the specific names and universal names for the secondary chords in the key of C. Say: "Dm, also known as the ii chord, Em, also known as the iii chord, and Am, also known as the vi chord."
- Memorize the specific names and universal names for the secondary chords in the key of C.
- Fill in the secondary chord names for the key of C major in the spaces below:

    ii = _____   iii = _____   vi = _____

180

Lesson 8

"Aura Lee" (Song)

Lesson Concepts
- Secondary Chords
- Secondary Dominant Chords
- Strum Pattern
- "Aura Lee"

Secondary Chords

"Aura Lee" uses Am which is a secondary minor chord in the key of C.

Secondary Dominant Chords

"Aura Lee" uses A7, D7, and E7. All of these chords are secondary dominant chords. Secondary dominant chords lead to the next chord. The easiest way to think of the secondary dominant chord is that it is the V7 of the chord it proceeds. In this case: D7 is the V7 of G, E7 is the V7 of Am, and A7 is the V7 of D7 (D) (See Unit 10 / Lesson 1 for the E7 chord—it's in the next lesson!)

Strum Pattern

As is often the case for guitar players, in this version of "Aura Lee" there is no strumming pattern provided. When no strumming pattern is provided, you get to choose one! If you need to, refer to Unit 2 and try a few different ones until you find one you like. One little trick to know (especially if you choose a syncopated strum pattern) is to start the strum pattern over on beat three if the chord changes. You play the strumming pattern for beats 1 and 2 on beats 3 and 4 as well.

AURA LEE (Traditional)

Play & Do... Video examples at *www.bestmusicpublications.com*

- Listen to the recorded version and count along while you follow and point to the music.
- Practice each chord and work on the switching of chords. Remember to anticipate the chord change, so you are always forming the new chord on beat 1 or 3.
- Practice playing the chords using the strum pattern you have chosen.
- Practice playing the chords with the recorded version.
- Practice playing the melody using a variety of right-hand techniques including: pick; standard finger assignment; and alternating index and middle fingers and thumb.
- Practice playing the melody along with the recorded version.

Review and Summary

You should be able to demonstrate and identify the following skills:

- Play and identify the primary and secondary chords in the Key of C
- Play grace note hammer-on and pull-offs
- Play a one octave C major scale from memory
- Play all songs in Unit 9 with the full speed recording
- Fill in the primary and secondary chord names for the key of C major in the spaces below:

I = _____   ii = _____   iii = _____   IV = _____   V = _____   V7 = _____   vi = _____

UNIT 10

The Key of A Minor

Lesson 1

Primary Chords in the Key of A Minor — Am, Dm, Em, and E7 (i, iv, v, V7)

Lesson Concepts
- Primary Chords in the Key of A Minor — Am, Dm, Em and E7 (i, iv, v, V7)
- Standard Fingerings for the Primary Chords in the Key of A Minor — Am, Dm, Em and E7 (i, iv, v, V7)
- Simplified and Challenge Chords Fingerings

Primary Chords in the Key of A Minor — Am, Dm, Em and E7 (i, iv, v, V7)

You already know Am, Dm, Em, and E7!

Standard Fingerings for the Primary Chords in the Key of A Minor — Am, Dm, Em and E7 (i, iv, v, V7)

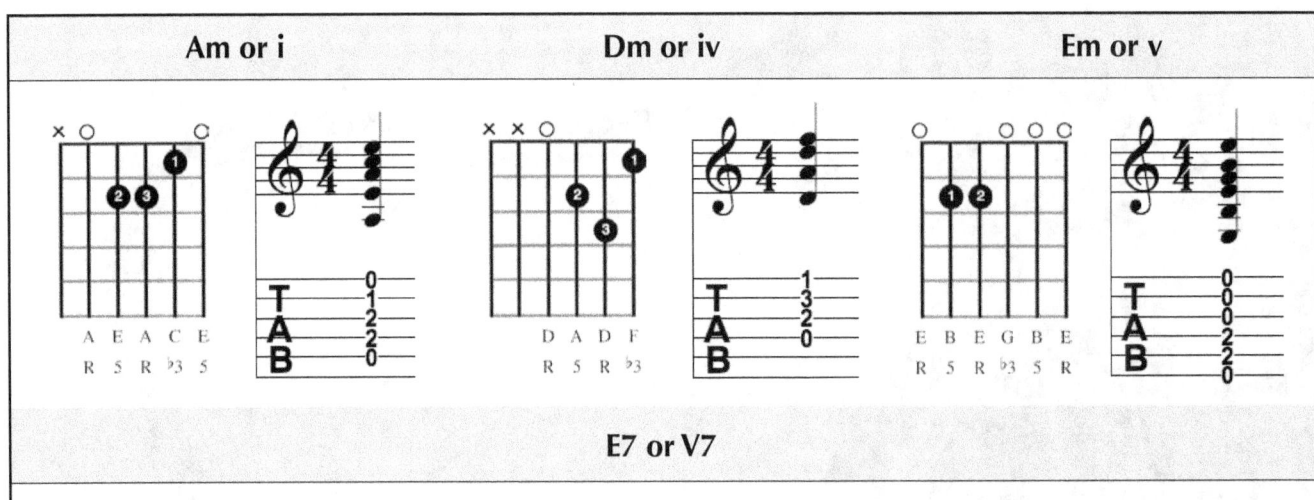

Simplified and Challenge Chords Fingerings

Simplified and challenge chords fingerings for all the chords in this book can be found at www.bestmusicpublications.com.

Play & Do... Video examples at *www.bestmusicpublications.com*

- As you play the chord, say the specific names and universal names for the primary chords in the key of Am. Say: "Am, also known as the i (one) chord, Dm, also known as the iv chord, Em, also known as the v chord and E7 also known as the V7 chord."
- Memorize the specific names and universal names for the primary chords in the key of Am.
- Fill in the primary chord names for the key of A minor in the spaces below:

    i = _____   iv = _____   v = _____   V7 = _____

184

LESSON 2

Secondary Chords in the Key of A Minor — C, F, and G (III, VI, VII)

> **Lesson Concepts**
> - Secondary Chords in the Key of A Minor — C, F, and G (III, VI, VII)
> - Standard Fingerings for the Secondary Chords in the Key of A Minor — C, F, and G (III, VI, VII)
> - Simplified and Challenge Chord Fingerings

Secondary Chords in the Key of A Minor — C, F, and G (III, VI, VII)

You already know C and G! The new chord is F. Some people find it helpful to angle their first finger, so the fingertip is closest to the fret on the second string and angles away from the fret on the first string.

Standard Fingerings for the Secondary Chords in the Key of A Minor — C, F, and G (III, VI, VII)

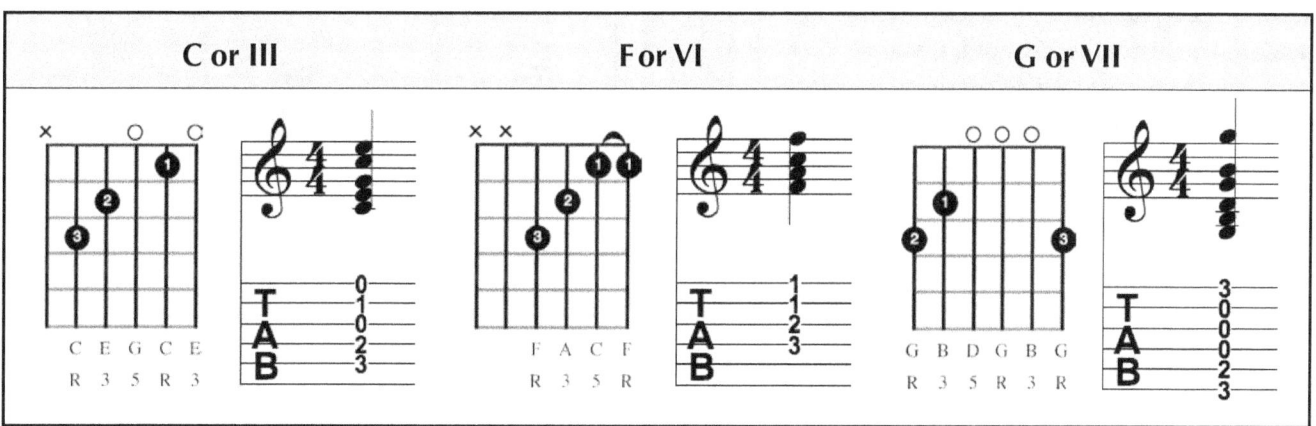

Simplified and Challenge Chords Fingerings

Simplified and challenge chords fingerings for all the chords in this book can be found at *www.bestmusicpublications.com*.

Play & Do... Video examples at *www.bestmusicpublications.com*

- As you play the chords, say the specific names and universal names for the secondary chords in the key of Am. Say: "C, also known as the III chord, F, also known as the VI chord, G, also known as the VII chord."
- Memorize the specific names and universal names for the secondary chords in the key of Am.
- Fill in the secondary chord names for the key of A minor in the spaces below:

   III = _____   VI = _____   VII = _____

185

LESSON 3

Alternate Chord Voicing for E7 — "St. James Infirmary" (Song)

> **Lesson Concepts**
> - Alternate Chord Voicing
> - Catch and Release
> - Transposed to the Key of Am
> - "St. James Infirmary" Guitar 1
> - "St. James Infirmary" Guitar 2

Alternate Chord Voicing

There will be times when you need to use a different *chord voicing*. In the case of "St. James Infirmary," you never pluck the fourth string with the shown picking pattern, which means you would never play the 7th of the chord if you used the standard voicing of the E7 chord. If you use an alternate chord voicing of the E7 (Figure 10.3.1), you will hear the ♭7 of the chord.

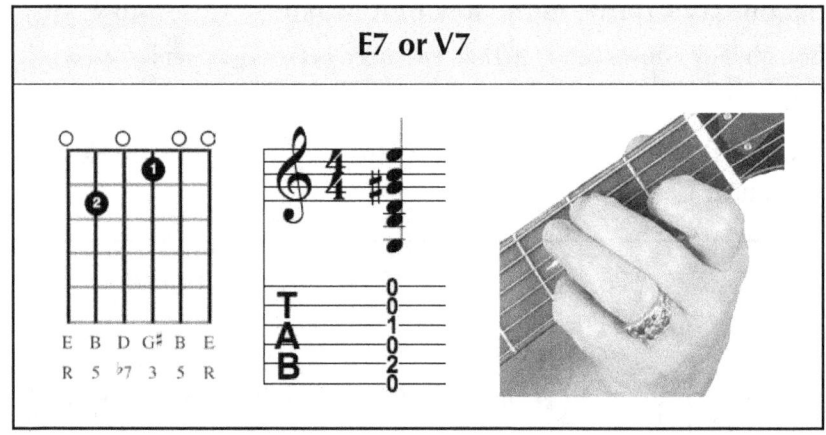

Figure 10.3.1

Catch and Release

Catch and release to be sure you can finger them with all your fingers landing on the strings at the same time. If you can't, then catch and release until you can!

Transposed to the Key of Am

This version of "St. James Infirmary" has been *transposed* to a new key. You originally learned it in the key of Em; now you will learn it in the *key of Am*. In either key, the song uses the same chords. If you think of them in the *universal key system*, they are: i, iv, V7, VI. In the key of E minor the chords are Em, Am, B7 and C. In the Key of A minor the chords are Am, Dm, E7, and F.

ST. JAMES INFIRMARY

(Traditional)

Guitar 1

Guitar 2

<!-- sheet music -->

Play & Do... Video examples at *www.bestmusicpublications.com*

- Listen to the recorded version and count along while you follow and point to the music.
- Practice each chord and work on the switching of chords. Remember to anticipate the chord change, so you are always forming the new chord on beat 1 or 3.
- Practice playing the chords as shown in the accompaniment part using a variety of right-hand techniques including: pick, standard finger assignment, and alternating index and middle fingers, and thumb. Practice playing the melody slowly following the picking directions using a pick.
- Practice playing the melody slowly using a variety of right-hand techniques including: pick, standard finger assignment, and alternating index and middle fingers, and thumb. Practice playing the melody along with the recorded version using a pick.
- Practice playing the melody along with the recorded version using a variety of right-hand techniques including: pick, standard finger assignment, and alternating index and middle fingers, and thumb.

LESSON 4

Relative Minor Key and Minor Scales — Natural, Pentatonic, Harmonic, Dorian and Melodic

> **Lesson Concepts**
> - Relative Major and Minor Keys
> - Minor Scale Types
> - Natural Minor – Same Seven Notes and Key Signature as C major
> - Minor Pentatonic Scale (5 Note Scale) - Skip Second and Sixth Note of Natural Minor
> - Harmonic Minor Scale - Raise (♯) Seventh Note of Natural Minor Scale
> - Dorian Minor Scale - Raise (♯) Sixth Note of Natural Minor Scale
> - Melodic Minor Scale - Raise (♯) Sixth and Seventh Note of Natural Minor Scale

Relative Major and Minor Keys

A minor and C major share the same seven notes: C, D, E, F, G, A, B in the key of C major. and A, B, C, D, E, F, G in the key of A minor. When playing a C major scale, the notes are ordered: C, D, E, F, G, A, B. When playing an *A natural minor scale*, the notes are ordered: A, B, C, D, E, F, G

Minor Scale Types

As you have learned previously, there is more than one type of minor scale. The five most common minor scale types are:

Natural Minor – Same Seven Notes and Key Signature as C major

You will notice that all of these scales are written with the same key signature: the key signature for E minor.

Minor Pentatonic Scale (Five-Note Scale) – Skip Second and Sixth Note of Natural Minor

Pentatonic scales are simply five-note scales, and the *A minor pentatonic scale* is an A natural minor scale missing the second and sixth note. The minor pentatonic is the most common minor scale for improvising and is, therefore, the scale to practice and memorize.

Harmonic Minor Scale– Raise (♯) Seventh Note of Natural Minor Scale

The *harmonic minor* is just like the natural minor scale only the seventh note has been raised a half-step from G to G♯.

Dorian Minor Scale– Raise (♯) Sixth Note of Natural Minor Scale

The *Dorian minor* (also called the *Dorian mode*) is just like the natural minor scale only the sixth note has been raised a half-step from F to F♯.

Melodic Minor Scale – Raise (♯) Sixth and Seventh Note of Natural Minor Scale

The *melodic minor* scale is just like the natural minor scale only the sixth, and seventh notes have been raised a half-step from F to F♯ and G to G♯.

Note: Traditionally this is only an ascending scale when you descend you play natural minor. While this is the traditional definition, modern jazz players regularly use the ascending scale as the descending scale as well.

Here is a two-octave A natural minor scale for reference:

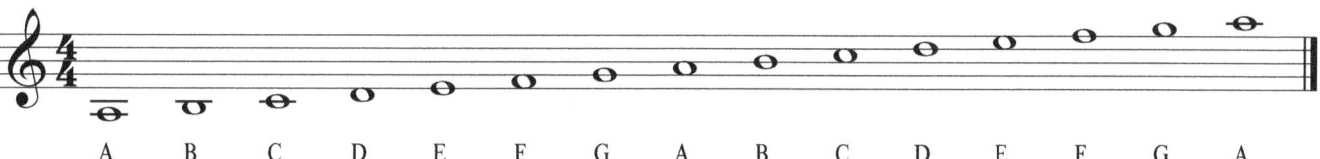

A   B   C   D   E   F   G   A   B   C   D   E   F   G   A

 **Play & Do…** Video examples at *www.bestmusicpublications.com*

- Play the two-octave A natural minor scale as written ascending and descending. Notice how it shares the same notes with the C major scale.
- Memorize the two-octave A natural minor scale as written ascending and descending.
- Play a two-octave A minor pentatonic scale by skipping the (B) and (F) notes of the written A natural minor scale. Play the A minor pentatonic scale ascending and descending ten times.
- Memorize the two-octave A minor pentatonic scale you just practiced.
- Play a two-octave A harmonic minor scale by raising the G note of the written A natural minor scale to a G♯ note. Play the A harmonic minor scale ascending and descending ten times.
- Memorize the two-octave A harmonic minor scale you just practiced.
- Starting on the note A:

  Write the note names for A natural minor scale   ____ ____ ____ ____ ____ ____ ____

  Write the five note names for A minor pentatonic scale   ____ ____ ____ ____ ____

LESSON 5

New Chord — Fmaj7

Lesson Concepts
- Fmaj7
- Fmaj7 — Replaces the F Chord in the Key of C Major or Am Minor
- Simplified and Challenge Chords

Fmaj7 — Replaces the F Chord in the Key of C Major or Am Minor

You can often use a Fmaj7 chord to replace an F chord. Try it, if you like it, then great!

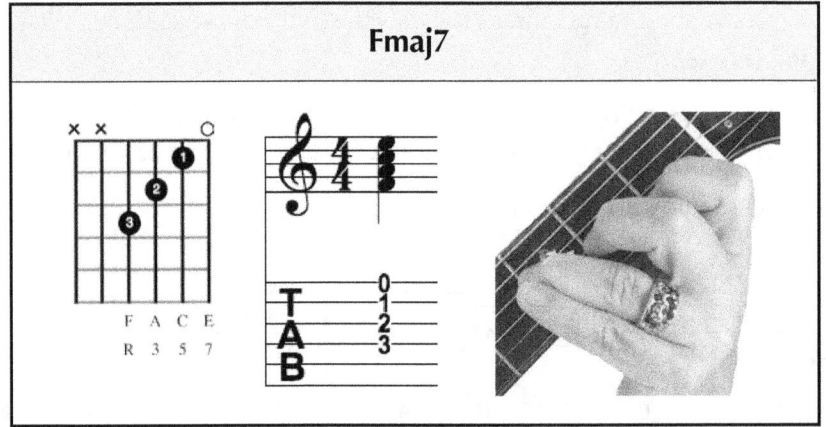

Simplified and Challenge Chords

Simplified and challenge chords fingerings for all the chords in this book can be found at *www.bestmusicpublications.com*.

Play & Do... Video examples at *www.bestmusicpublications.com*

- *Catch and Release* to be sure you can finger them with all your fingers landing on the strings at the same time. If you can't, then catch and release until you can!

LESSON 6

6/8 Time Signature —
"House of the Rising Sun" (Song)

Lesson Concepts
- 6/8 Time
- Compound Meter
- "House of the Rising Sun" Guitar 1
- "House of the Rising Sun" Guitar 2

6/8 Time

In 3/4 time you had three quarter notes in the measure, and every quarter note received one beat. (Figure 10.6.1)

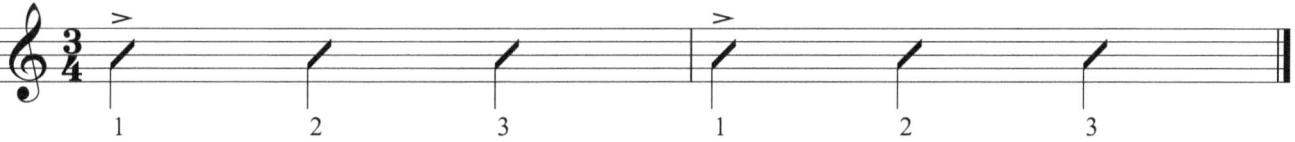

Figure 10.6.1

If you played eighth notes in 3/4 time you would have six eighth notes in a measure grouped in three groups of two. (Figure 10.6.2)

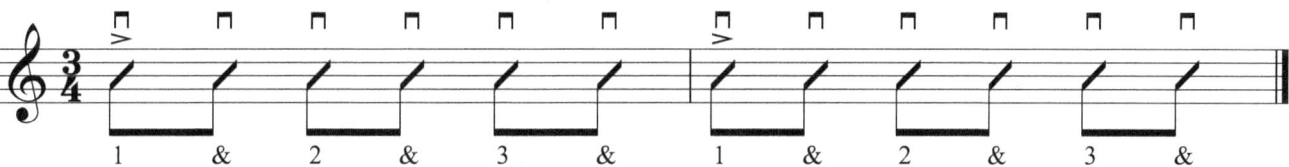

Figure 10.6.2

In 6/8 time you also have six eighth notes, but the eighth note now gets the beat, and the eighth notes are grouped into two groups of three. (Figure 10.6.3)

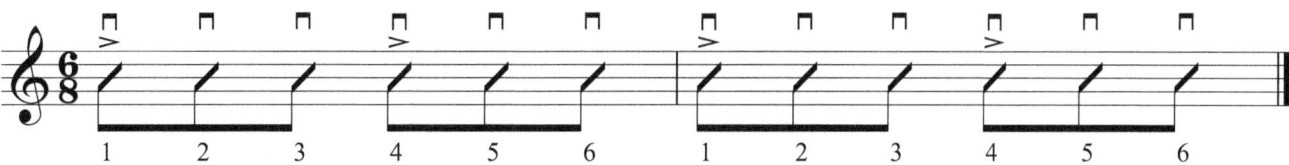

Figure 10.6.3

Compound Meter

Because 6/8 time has both the six pulse (eighth notes) and the two pulse (accents) happening simultaneously, 6/8 time is called a *compound meter*.

This next song is often played in 3/4 time, but the most famous version was played in 6/8 time. It features an arpeggio style accompaniment and a strumming accompaniment par.

191

HOUSE OF THE RISING SUN

(Traditional)

Guitar 1

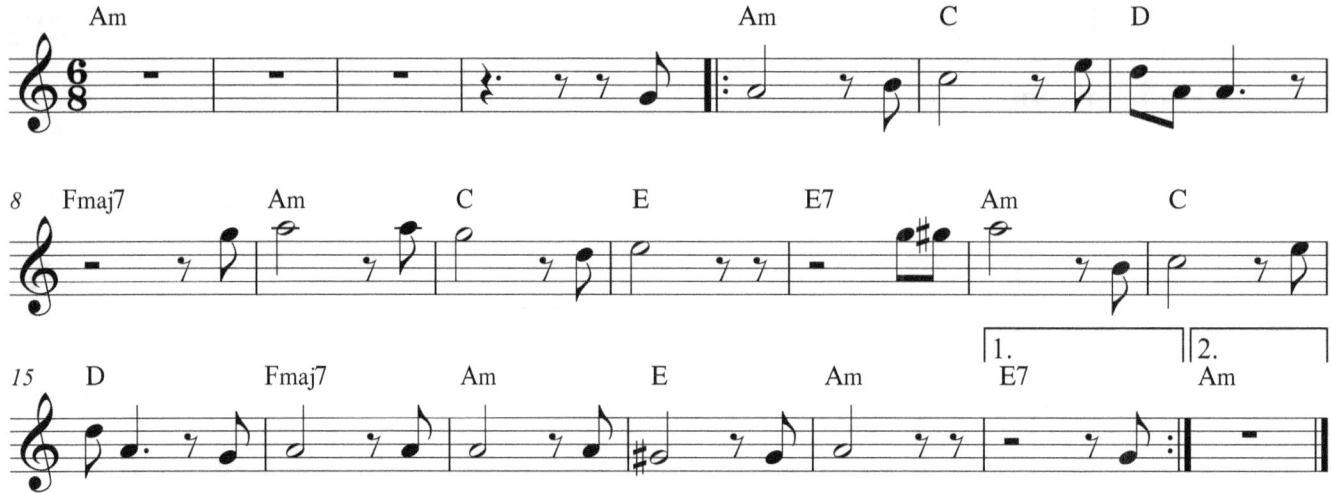

Guitar 2

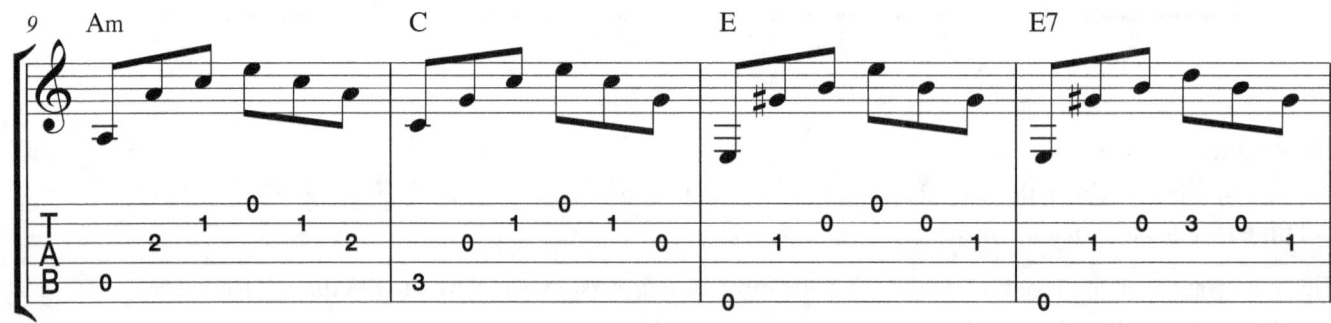

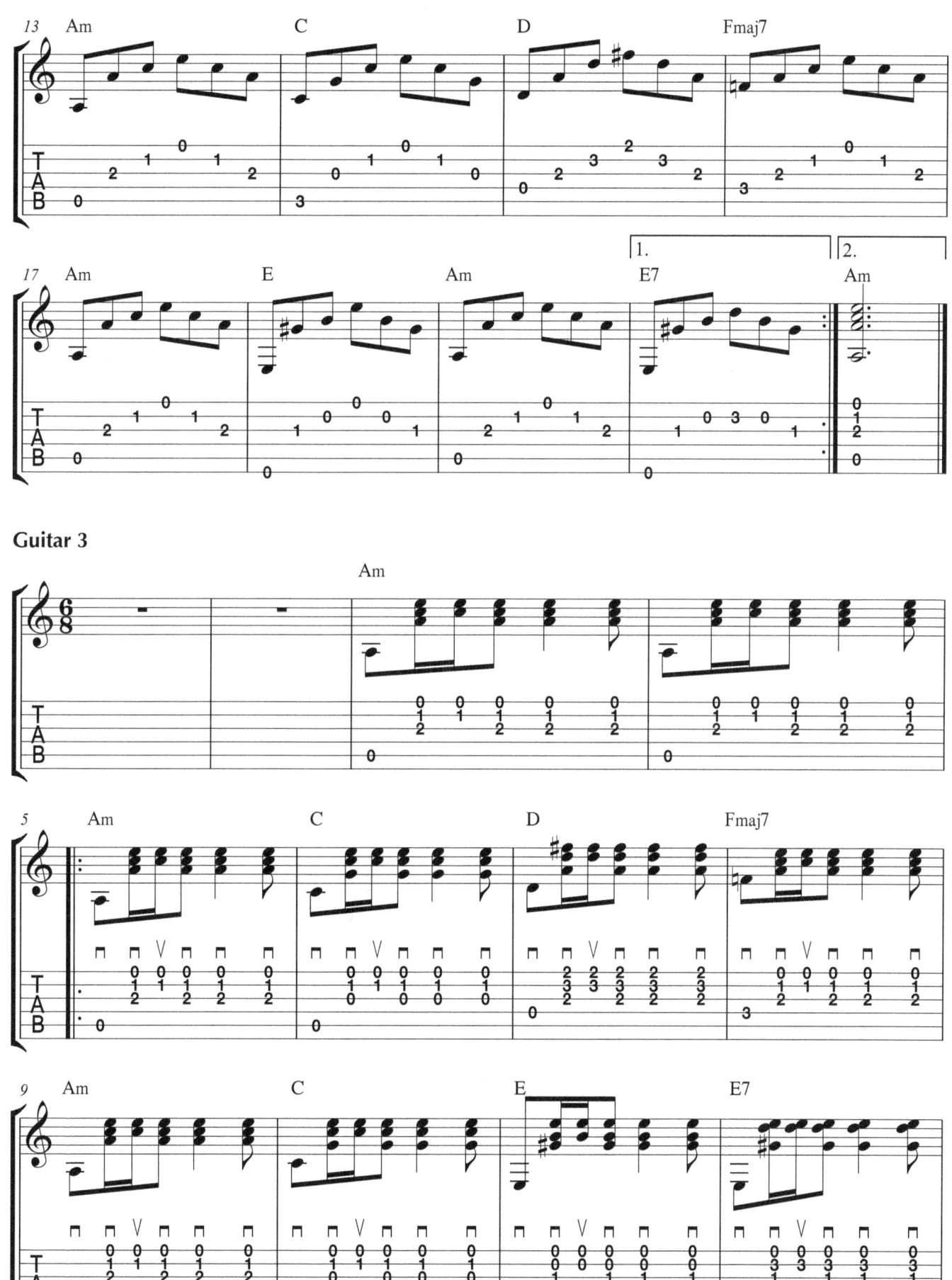

THE BEST GUITAR METHOD

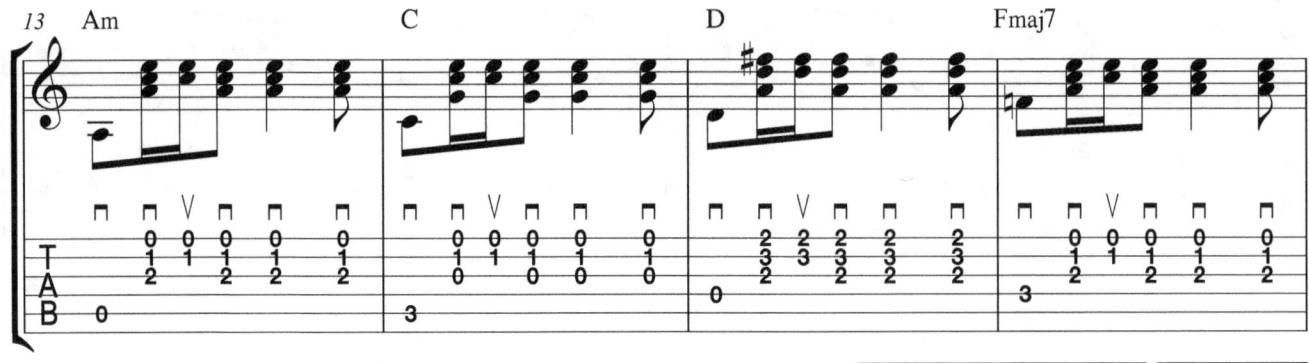

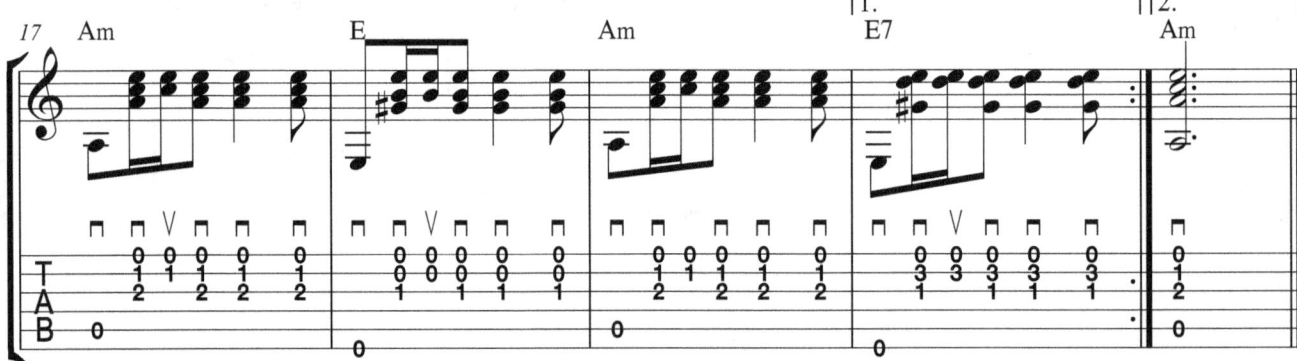

 **Play & Do...** Video examples at *www.bestmusicpublications.com*

- Listen to the recorded version and count along while you follow and point to the music.
- Practice each chord and work on the switching of chords. Remember to anticipate the chord change, so you are always forming the new chord on beat 1.
- Practice playing the chords as shown in the accompaniment part using a variety of right-hand techniques including: pick, standard finger assignment, and thumb.
- Practice playing the melody using a variety of right-hand techniques including: pick, standard finger assignment, alternating index and middle fingers, and thumb. When using a pick, follow the picking directions.
- Practice playing the melody or chords with the recorded version using a variety of right-hand techniques including: pick, standard finger assignment, alternating index and middle fingers, and thumb. Be sure to practice playing both the chords and the melody.

Review and Summary

You should be able to demonstrate and identify the following skills:

- Play and identify the primary and secondary chords in the Key of Am.
- Play in 6/8 time.
- Play a two octave A natural minor scale from memory.
- Play all songs in Unit 10 with the full speed recordings.
- Fill in the primary and secondary chord names for the key of A minor in the spaces below:

  i = _____   III = _____   vi = _____   v = _____   V7 = _____   VI = _____   VII = _____

UNIT 11

The Key of E Major
("E" is for the End!)

LESSON 1

Primary Chords in the Key of E — E, A, B and B7 (I, IV, V, V7)

> **Lesson Concepts**
> - Primary Chords in the Key of E — E, A, B and B7 (I, IV, V, V7)
> - Standard Fingerings for the Primary Chords in the Key of E — E, A, B and B7 (I, IV, V, V7)
> - Simplified and Challenge Chords Fingerings

Primary Chords in the Key of E — E, A, B and B7 (I, IV, V, V7)

You already know E and A, B and B7 chords! The B chord is particularly hard to play. It is very common to use a B7 in place of a B chord when playing a song in the key of E. When playing a B chord you can play the second, third and fourth strings using only your third finger. Using your third finger is an especially a good way to play a B chord if your third finger can bend backward at the knuckle closest to the fingertip.

Standard Fingerings for the Primary Chords in the Key of E — E, A, B and B7 (I, IV, V, V7)

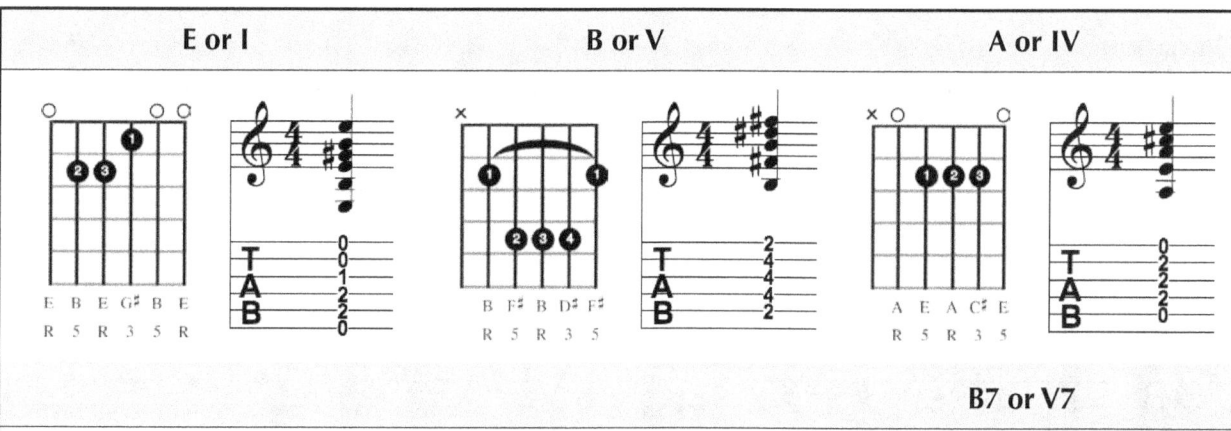

Simplified and Challenge Chords Fingerings

Simplified and challenge chords fingerings for all the chords in this book can be found at www.bestmusicpublications.com.

 **Play & Do…** Video examples at *www.bestmusicpublications.com*

- Finger (play) each chord and make sure you are mindful of the three P's of tone production and pick each string of the chord to be sure each string is making a good sound.
- As you play the chord, say the specific names and universal names for the primary chords in the key of E. Say "E, also known as the I chord, A, also known as the IV chord and B, also known as the V chord."
- Memorize the specific names and universal names for the primary chords in the key of E.
- Fill in the primary chord names for the key of E major in the spaces below:

    I = _____   IV = _____   V = _____   V7 = _____

197

LESSON 2

"Turn Myself Around" — with Lift Chord (Chord Progression)

Lesson Concepts
- Lift Chords
- 12-Bar Variation

Lift Chords

Lift chords are not chords; rather, it's a technique where you will play the last eighth note of beat four as a lift chord meaning you are lifting your fingers off the string and then hammering them down on beat 1. In this song, you are not hammering on because the chord is strummed again on beat 1. If you did not strum the chord on beat one, it would be a hammer-on, but because you are strumming on beat 1 it is not technically a hammer-on. However, the left-hand motion is the same whether you strum or hammer-on.

12-Bar Variation

The next song is a 12-bar blues with a few variations. It uses common variations to the typical 12-bar blues form.

TURN MYSELF AROUND *(Chord Progression)*

198

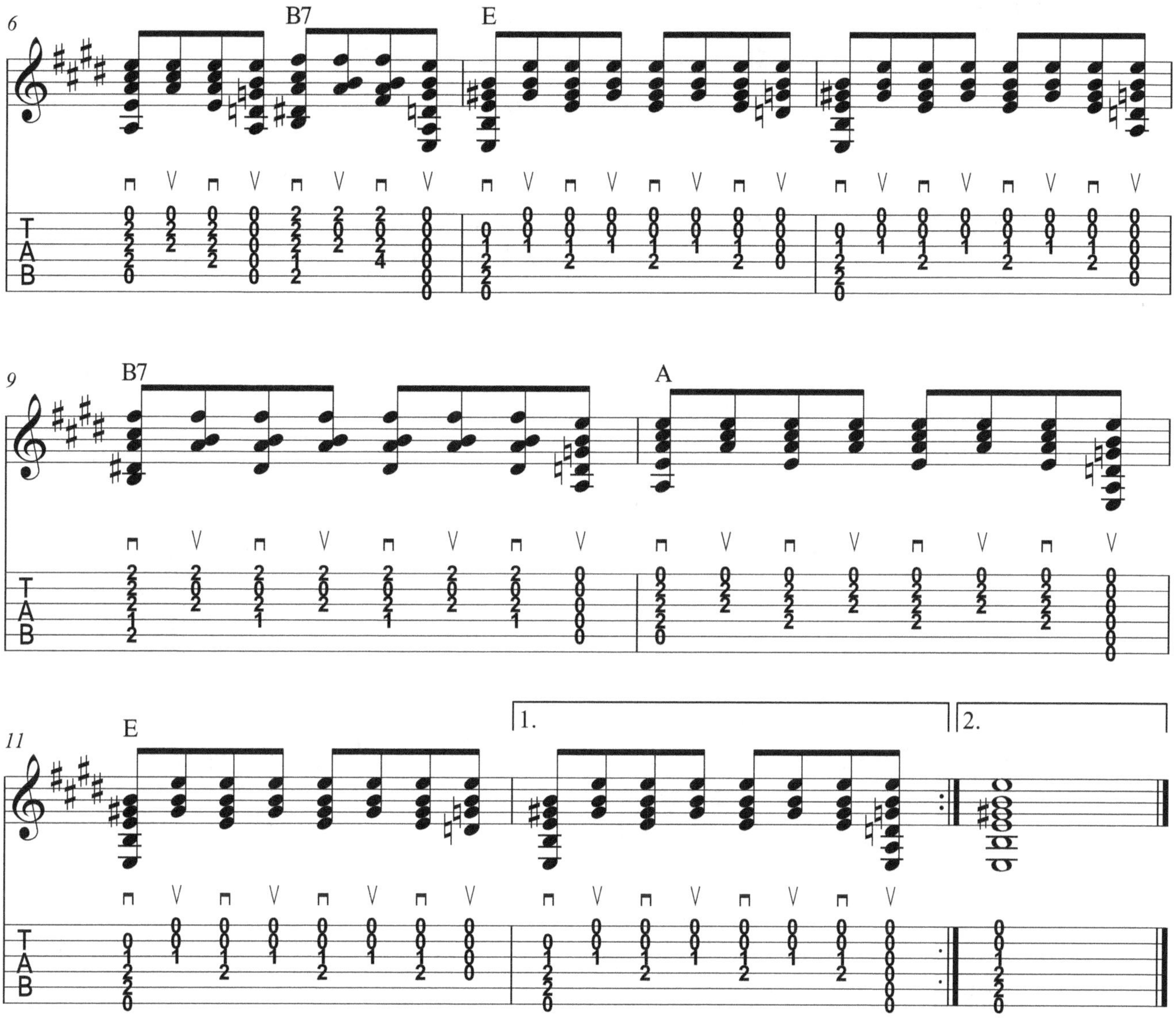

UNIT ELEVEN • LESSON 2

 **Play & Do...** Video examples at *www.bestmusicpublications.com*

- Listen to the recorded version and count along while you follow and point to the music.
- Practice each chord and work on the switching of chords. Remember to anticipate the chord change by lifting your fingers on the last eighth note before a chord change, so you are always forming the new chord on beat 1.
- Practice playing the chords as shown in the accompaniment part using a pick.
- Practice playing the chords as shown in the accompaniment part using a pick with the recorded version.

LESSON 3

Secondary Chords in the Key of E — F♯m, G♯m, and C♯m (ii, iii, vi)

> **Lesson Concepts**
> - Secondary Chords in the Key of E — F♯m, G♯m, and C♯m (ii, iii, vi)
> - Standard Fingerings for the Secondary Chords in the Key of E — F♯m, G♯m, and C♯m (ii, iii, vi)
> - Simplified and Challenge Chords Fingerings

Secondary Chords in the Key of E — F♯m, G♯m, and C♯m (ii, iii, vi)

The secondary chords in any major key are minor chords. In the key of E major, the secondary chords are F♯m (ii), G♯m (iii) and C♯m(vi). You already know how to play C♯m and F♯m, so the only new chord is G♯m.

Standard Fingerings for the Secondary Chords in the Key of E — F♯m, G♯m, and C♯m (ii, iii, vi)

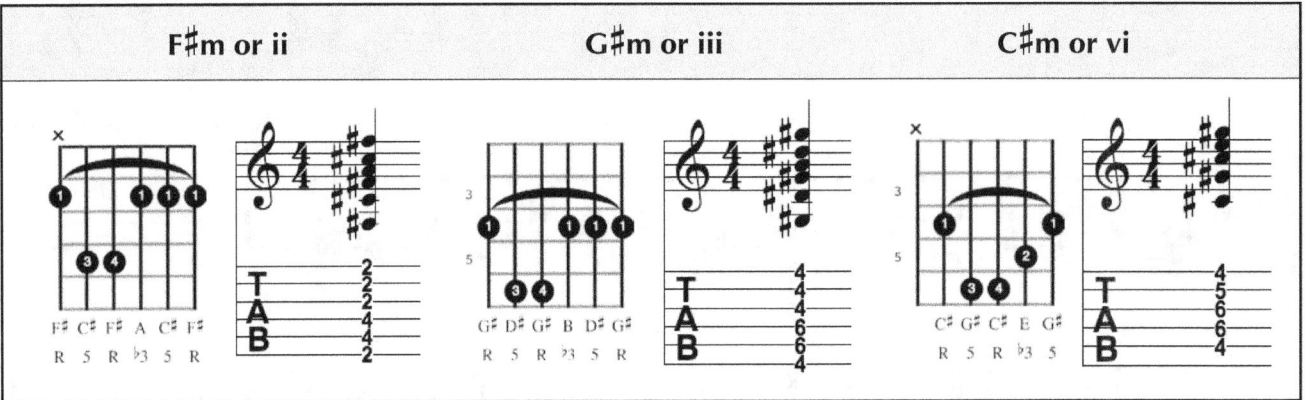

Simplified and Challenge Chords Fingerings

Simplified and challenge chords fingerings for all the chords in this book can be found at *www.bestmusicpublications.com*.

Play & Do... Video examples at *www.bestmusicpublications.com*

- Finger (play) each chord and make sure you are mindful of the three P's of tone production.
- Pick each string of the chord to be sure each string is making a good sound.
- "Catch and release" each chord, strum the chord as you apply pressure, and then check that each string is still sounding good. If it's not, go back and check the three P's of tone production.
- As you play the chord, say the specific and universal names for the secondary chords in the key of A, say: "F♯m, also known as the ii chord, G♯m, also known as the iii chord and C♯m minor, also known as the vi chord."
- Memorize the specific names and universal names for the secondary chords in the key of E.
- Fill in the secondary chord names for the key of E major in the spaces below:

    ii = _____   iii = _____   vi = _____

200

Lesson 4

D# Note Review and the E Major Scale

Lesson Concepts
- D# Notes
- Key Signature
- E Major Scale

D# Notes

You learned D# way back in the key of E minor, but here it is again in case you have forgotten.

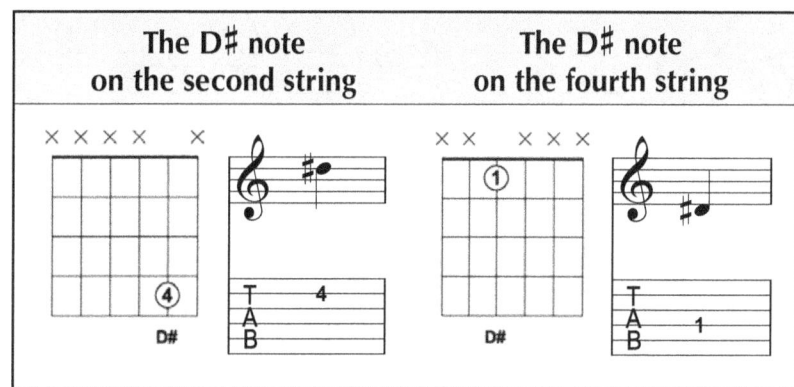

Key Signature

The *key signature* for E major has four sharps, F#, C#, G#, D#

E Major Scale and Notes in the Key: E, F#, G#, A, B, C#, D#

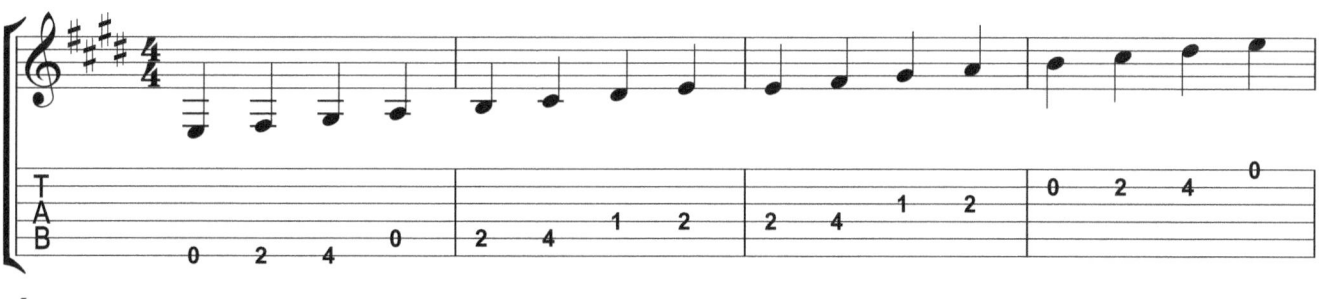

Play & Do... Video examples at *www.bestmusicpublications.com*

- Practice the E major scale using a variety of right-hand techniques including: pick, standard finger assignment, alternating index and middle fingers, and thumb.
- Memorize the E major scale left-hand fingering and note names.

LESSON 5

The Key of E — No Training Wheels

Lesson Concept
- E Major — No Training Wheels (No Tablature)

E MAJOR – NO TRAINING WHEELS

 **Play & Do...** Video examples at *www.bestmusicpublications.com*

- Play E major (no training wheels) using a variety of right-hand techniques including: pick, standard finger assignment, alternating index and middle fingers, and thumb.
- Play along with the recording with each picking style.

LESSON 6

Palm Mute —
"12-Bar Blues Shuffle in the Key of E" (Chord Progression)

> **Lesson Concepts**
> - Palm Mute
> - 12-Bar Blues Shuffle in the Key of E

Palm Mute

The *palm mute* is a *right-hand downstroke technique* that allows us to change the sound of the guitar by slightly *muting the strings*. Usually, the palm mute is only used on the lower strings.

Here is a picture (Figure 11.6.1) of the right-hand doing a palm mute:

Figure 11.6.1

Play & Do… Video examples at *www.bestmusicpublications.com*

- Place your right-hand close to the bridge and allow the fleshy part of the palm at the base of the little finger to gently rest across the lower strings right at the *very end of the string* close to the bridge.
- After positioning your palm, strum downward on the lowest four strings. You will need to experiment with placement and pressure to get the correct sound. When done properly, the string will sound muted but resonant.
- Listen to the audio examples or watch the video example to hear how a palm mute should sound.

UNIT ELEVEN • LESSON 6

12-BAR BLUES SHUFFLE IN THE KEY OF E *(Chord Progression)*

(When you play the 12-bar blues in E with palm mute you should use a palm mute the whole time.)

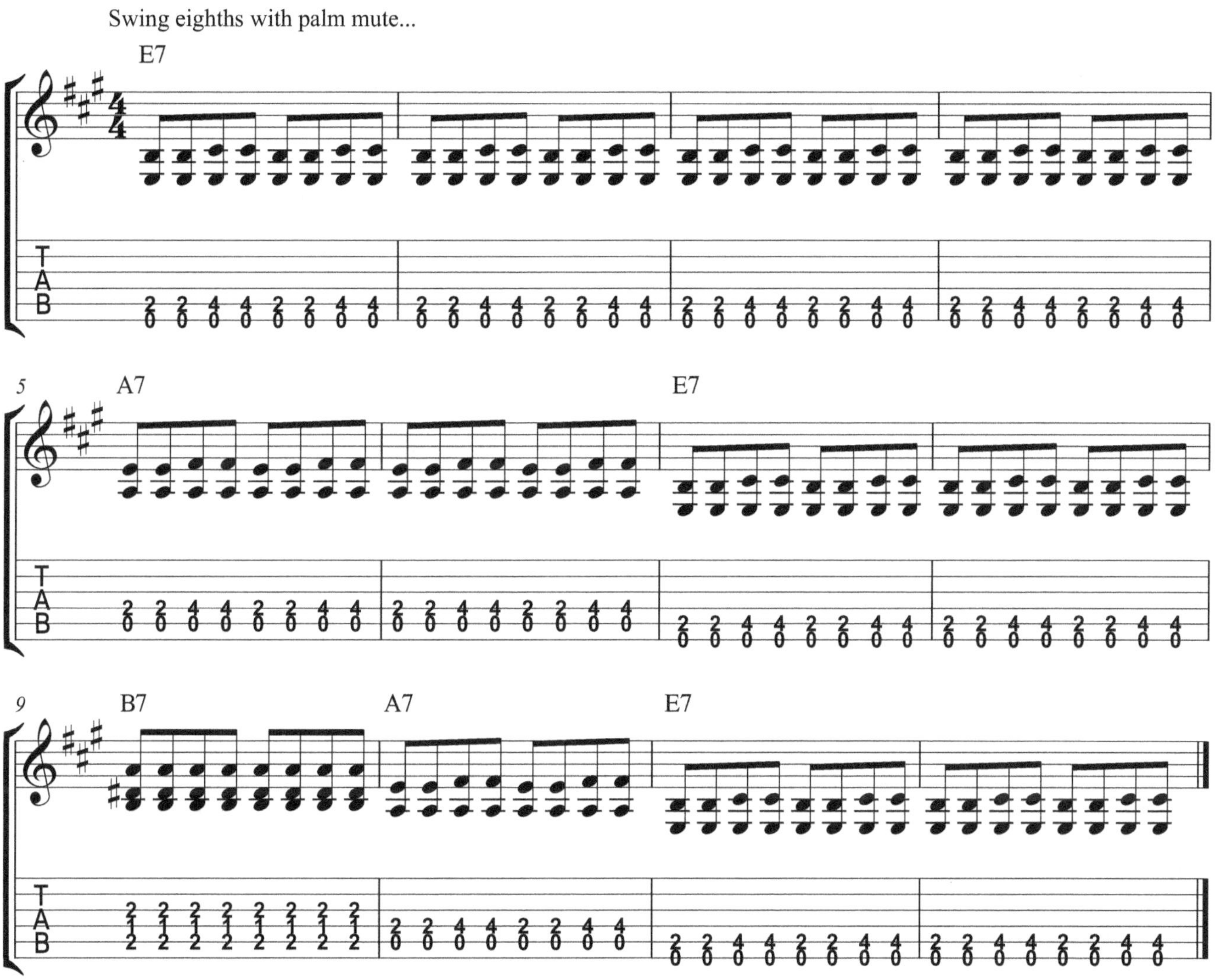

Swing eighths with palm mute...

Play & Do... Video examples at *www.bestmusicpublications.com*

- Listen to the recorded version and count along while you follow and point to the music.
- Practice each chord and work on the switching of chords. Remember to anticipate the chord change, so you are always forming the new chord on beat 1.
- Practice playing the shuffle riff or chords as shown using a pick and palm mute.
- Practice playing the shuffle riff or chords as shown using a pick and palm mute with the recorded example.

205

LESSON 7

Accented Syncopated Eighth Note Rhythms

Lesson Concepts
- Accented Eighth Note Groupings
- Two Measure Variations
- Bo Diddley Rhythm/3-2 Clave Rhythm/Son Clave

Accented Eighth Note Groupings

It is common to *accent eighth notes* to create *accented eighth note groupings*. In this example, you have two sets of three eighth notes followed by one set of two eighth notes to create a *syncopated rhythm*. (Figure 11.7.1)

Figure 11.7.1

It is also common to only play only the accented notes. (Figure 11.7.2)

Figure 11.7.2

Two Measure Variations

You can carry the three-note groupings over the bar line to create a two-measure long strumming pattern. (Figure 11.7.3)

Figure 11.7.3

It is also common to only play only the accented notes in the two-measure strumming pattern. (Figure 11.7.4)

Figure 11.7.4

This two-measure syncopated accent rhythm is very common many styles of music. In popular music, it is often called the *Bo Diddley rhythm*, because many of Bo Diddley's songs used this rhythm. It is also the most common rhythm pattern for the clave in Latin music. In Latin music, it is often called the *3-2 Clave rhythm* or *Son Clave rhythm*.

Play & Do... Video examples at *www.bestmusicpublications.com*

- Play each rhythmic example using an E chord while counting out loud.
- Play each rhythmic example using an E chord while counting silently inside your head.
- Play each rhythmic example using an E chord by "feel" instead of counting silently inside your head.
- Play along with each recorded example using the E chord.

Lesson 8

"Bo's Blues" (Song)

Lesson Concepts
- Syncopated "Bo Diddley" Rhythm
- Refingered A Chord (Bar)
- "Bo's Blues"

Syncopated "Bo Diddley" Rhythm

This next song uses the *syncopated Bo Diddley rhythm* within a *12-bar blues*. The quick A chords that fall on beat 2 can be played by using your third finger of your left-hand to *bar* across the fourth, third and second strings at the second fret so you can quickly return to the E chord on beat 3.

Refingered A Chord:

BO'S BLUES

(Brian K. Rivers)

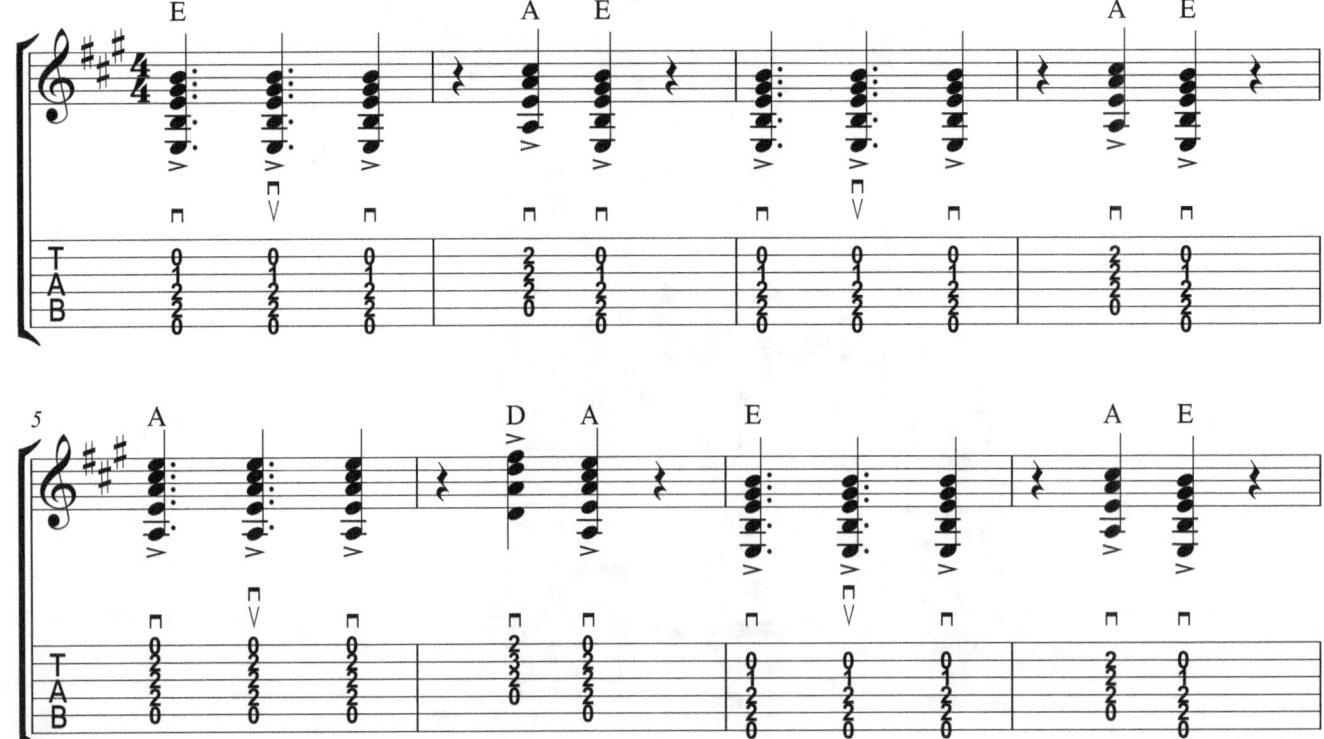

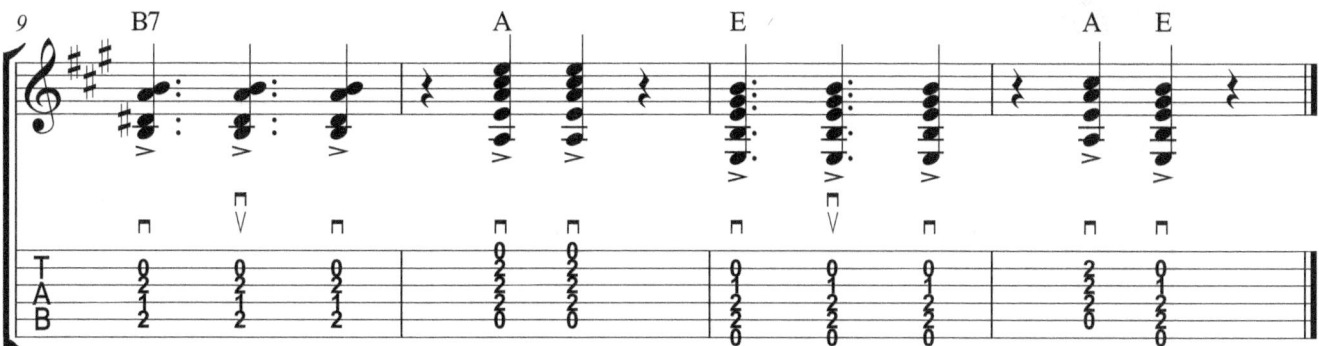

 **Play & Do...** Video examples at *www.bestmusicpublications.com*

- Listen to the recorded version and count along while you follow and point to the music.
- Practice each chord and work on the switching of chords. Remember to anticipate the chord change, so you are always forming the new chord on beat 1.
- Practice playing the chords as shown in the accompaniment part using a pick.
- Practice playing the chords as shown in the accompaniment part using a pick with the recorded version.

LESSON 9

"Grand Final-E" (Song)

Lesson Concepts
- Common Tones
- E (Alternate Fingering), F#m11/C#, G#m(b6)/D#, Aadd9/E, Badd11/F# and C#m/G# Chords
- Slash Chords
- Harmonics
- D.S., al Coda, and the Coda
- "The Grand Final-E" (Song)

Common Tones

Common tones are notes that stay the same when you change chords. In the song "The Grand Final-E" you will use common-tone chord voicings by letting the first and second strings ring open as you move between chords.

E (alternate fingering), F#m11/C#, G#m(b6)/D#, Aadd9/E, Badd11/F# and C#m/G# Chords:

Playing the chords is much easier than the names! The ridiculous chord names are a result of the common tones adding additional notes to the simple chords.

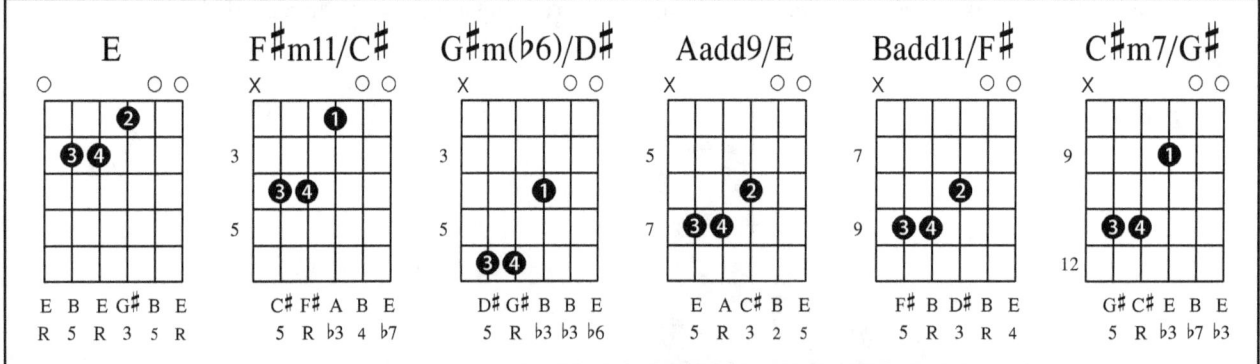

Slash Chords

Many of the chords have a bass note other than the root note of the chord and use a slash chord to show the bass note. An example is F#m11/C#. The F#m11 is the chord is shown to the left of the slash, and the C# is the bass note is shown on the right side of the slash.

Harmonics

Here are the steps to play an octave harmonic:

1. Gently contact a single string *directly* over the 12th fret with a left-hand fingertip, but do not push the string down to the fret!
2. While continuing to lightly touch the string with your left hand, pick it with the right hand.
3. Remove your left-hand finger from the string shortly after picking it. The note should still ring when you are no longer touching it.

A 12th fret harmonic is indicated in standard notation as a small circle over the note head. In TAB a harmonic is indicated with "harm." placed under the tab notation. The next song, "Grand Final-E" has octave harmonics indicated in the Guitar 1 part at measures 3, 22, 46 and 59-63.

210

D.S., al Coda, and the Coda

Composers use *D.S., al Coda* and *Coda* as ways to direct the player to a section of the music.

D.S. is an abbreviation for "Dal Segno" which is Italian for "from the sign." In music, the "sign" looks like this: 𝄋 When a D.S. appears in the music, it is telling the player to "go back to the sign" and play from there.

D.S. al Coda means to go back to the sign and then go to the Coda when directed. You will know where to skip to the Coda because there will be a place in the music that says, *"To Coda."* The Coda is the final section of the music. The Coda section has a Coda symbol at the beginning to identify the Coda section of the music. A Coda symbol looks like this: ⊕

In the next song, "Grand Final-E," the "sign" appears at the beginning of measure 5 and the "To Coda" directive appears at the beginning of measure 19 and indicates you should skip to The Coda section that starts at measure 48.

"Grand Final-E"

There is one new rhythm that first appears in measure 6 and then reoccurs throughout the song. Be sure to listen to the audio recording or watch the video to get an idea of how it should sound. It is a very even rhythm that starts on an upbeat. If you follow the picking directions and listen to the song, most students can play this rhythm even though it looks complicated.

THE BEST GUITAR METHOD

UNIT ELEVEN • LESSON 9

Guitar 2

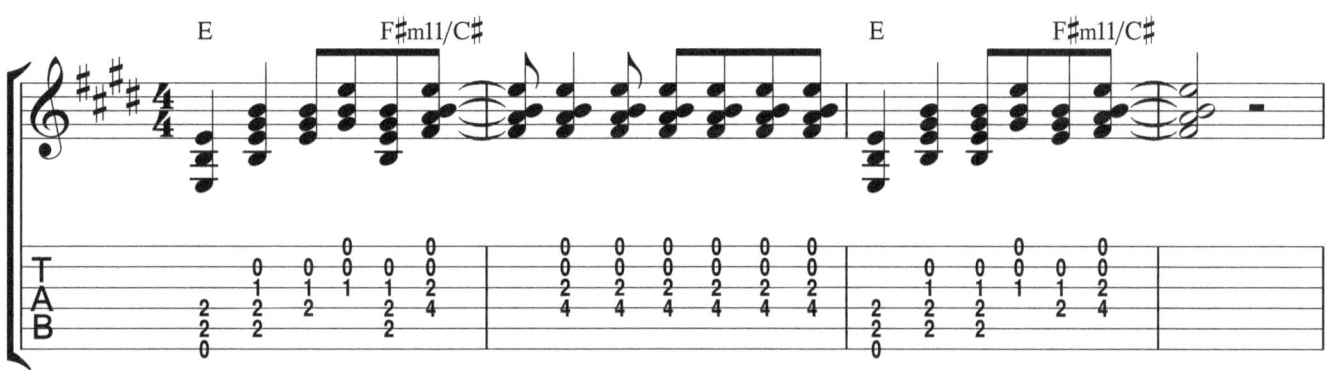

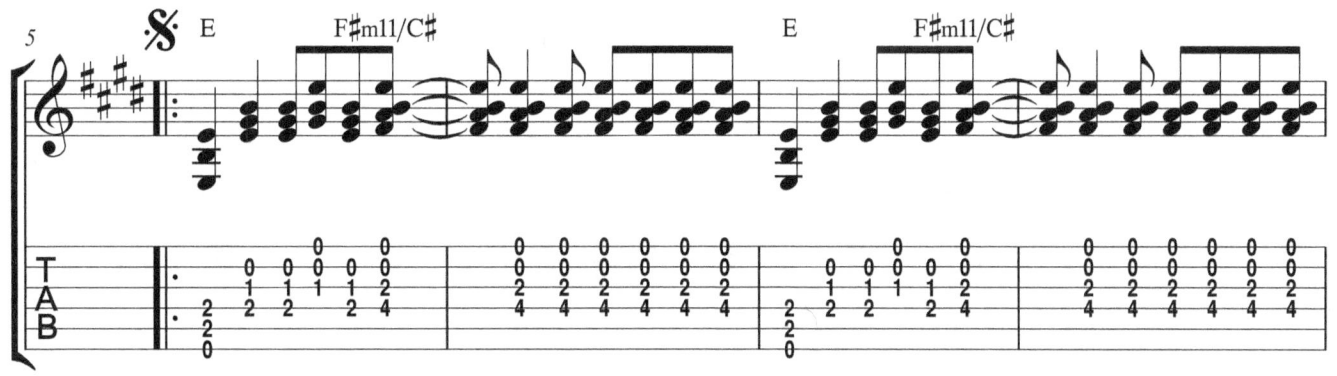

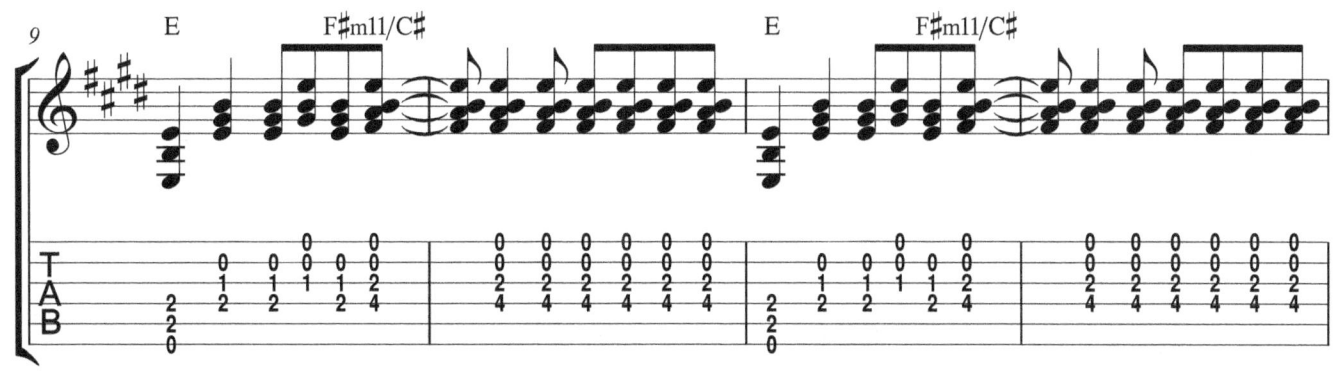

213

UNIT ELEVEN • LESSON 9

215

THE BEST GUITAR METHOD

UNIT ELEVEN • LESSON 9

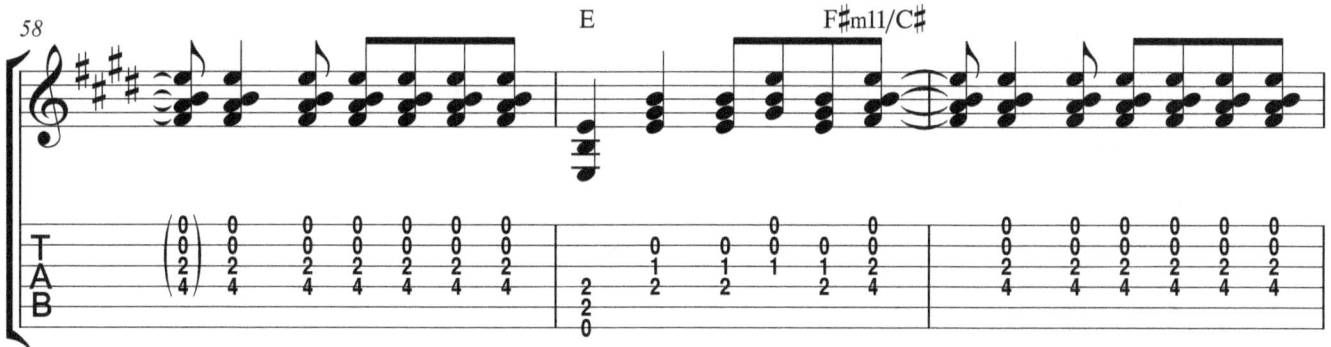

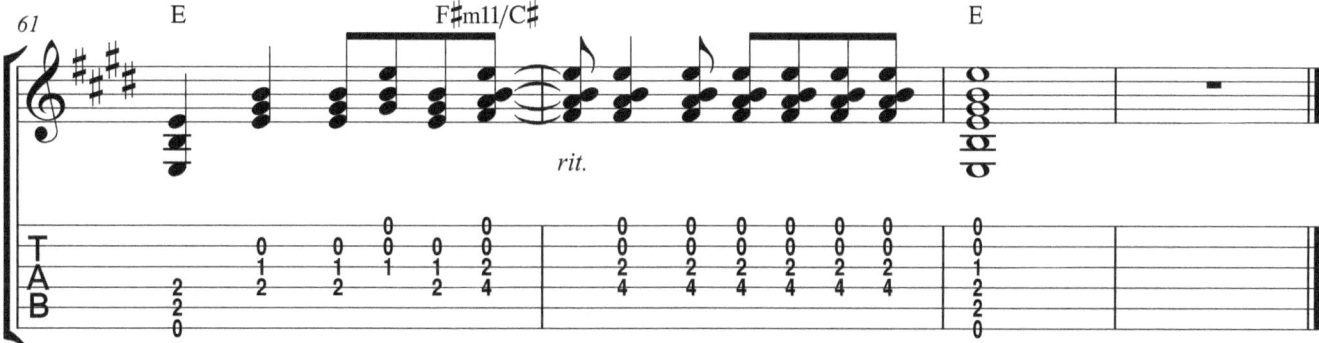

 **Play & Do...** Video examples at *www.bestmusicpublications.com*

- Listen to the recorded version and count along while you follow and point to the music in either Guitar 1 or 2.
- Practice each chord and work on the switching of chords. Remember to anticipate the chord change.
- Practice playing the chords as shown in the Guitar 2 part using a pick.
- Practice playing the chords as shown in the Guitar 2 part using a pick with the recorded version.
- Practice playing the melody as shown in the Guitar 1 part using a pick.
- Practice playing the melody as shown in the Guitar 1 part using a pick with the recorded version.

THE BEST GUITAR METHOD

Review and Summary

You should be able to demonstrate and identify the following skills:

- Play and identify the primary and secondary chords in the Key of E
- Play "lift chords"
- Play accented syncopated rhythms (Bo Diddley Rhythm)
- Play all songs in Unit 11 with the full speed recording
- Fill in the primary and secondary chord names for the key of E major in the spaces below:

I = _____   ii = _____   iii = _____   IV = _____   V = _____   V7 = _____   vi = _____

Congratulations!

You have completed Book 1 of *The Best Guitar Method*!

You now have a fantastic start to your guitar playing.

Keep on practicing and be sure to check out the other books offered by Best Music Publications!

www.bestmusicpublications.com

www.ingramcontent.com/pod-product-compliance
Lightning Source LLC
Chambersburg PA
CBHW082036300426
44117CB00015B/2501